Indians in Prison

Indians in

University of Nebraska Press
Lincoln and London

Prison

Incarcerated Native Americans in Nebraska

Elizabeth S. Grobsmith

© 1994 by the University of Nebraska Press
All rights reserved
Manufactured in the United States of America

The paper in this book meets the minimum requirements of American National Standard for Information Sciences—Permanence of Paper for Printed Library Materials, ANSI Z39.48–1984.

Library of Congress Cataloging-in-Publication Data
Grobsmith, Elizabeth S.
Indians in prison: incarcerated Native Americans / Elizabeth S. Grobsmith.
    p.   cm.
Includes bibliographical references (p.   ) and index.
ISBN 0-8032-2137-1
1. Indians of North America—Nebraska—Crime.   2. Prisoners—Nebraska.
3. Indians of North America—Nebraska—Social conditions.   I. Title.
E78.N3G76   1994
365′.6′08997—dc 20   93-5381   CIP

for my husband and children

James A. Gibson
Miriam Grobsmith
Jeremy Grobsmith
Sarah Gibson

for special friends

Perry Wounded Shield
Leo Blue Thunder

and for all incarcerated Native Americans

Contents

Illustrations

Plates

Following page 92

The NASCA drum

The Black Road mural, painted by Indian inmates

A partial view of the Lincoln Correctional Center

The LCC visiting room

Items used in a Hand Game during a NASCA activity

NASCA club members around the drum

Figure

Tables

Acknowledgments

It is difficult to imagine, at the beginning of a project of this sort, how many people one will come to depend on for their assistance. Because of the complex nature of this book, help was obtained from all reaches of the community. So as not to overlook any individuals, I would like to mention them by their agency or affiliation.

Foremost are those offices and agencies on the University of Nebraska–Lincoln campus that provided financial and other support for this project. For three years, the Center for Great Plains Studies awarded me Summer Faculty Fellowships, which enabled me to conduct research on incarcerated Native Americans and alcoholism. The Research Council provided two grants-in-aid that funded material, equipment, and supplies for research. Their funding also enabled me to hire Jennifer Dam, then an undergraduate in the Department of Anthropology, who assisted me during the summer of 1988 by evaluating alcohol treatment centers throughout the state that were utilized by Indian ex-offenders. Her invaluable assistance is deeply appreciated, and she is owed the credit for much of the information on alcohol treatment programs presented in chapter 5. Appreciation is also owed Jeanine Stamp, who tabulated the prison survey data summarized in chapter 7.

The Department of Anthropology and College of Arts and Sciences provided financial support that enabled me to purchase laptop computer equipment needed to conduct intensive interviews in the varying correctional facilities. Dorothy McEwen, secretary of the Department of Anthropology, provided countless services and performed endless tasks that aided in the production of this manuscript, and I am in her debt. Claire Bohn, secretary and loyal friend, also provided essential clerical support. Stanley Parks, Gene Wiggins, and Bob Duros all assisted, at various times, with production of the tables. Sue Drammeh produced all the tables in their final form and assisted with the revisions and production of the final manuscript. Thanks are owed Dr. James Gibson, Associate Professor of Anthropology, for his assistance with correct orthographic style of all the Lakhóta terms.

Jerry Flute, Assistant Director for Community Development of the Association on American Indian Affairs in New York, deserves special thanks, for it was he who brought me into the area of Native American juvenile justice concerns, and it was his suggestion that I learn more about the special problems of Native American youth by going to talk to the men "behind the walls." I wish also to thank my longtime friend and colleague Dr. Murray Wax, whose insights concerning the ethical matters involved in writing this book were extremely helpful and have been incorporated into the final manuscript.

Within the Nebraska Department of Correctional Services, my deepest gratitude is extended to Dr. John Shaw, Associate Warden of the Nebraska State Penitentiary, whose personal and professional encouragement and support enabled me to continue, especially during difficult phases of the research. Dr. Shaw expedited all inmate interviews at the Nebraska State Penitentiary and additionally permitted me access to plaintiffs in prison lawsuits so that I could more effectively prepare testimony for use in court. When many doubted the worth of this project Dr. Shaw was unrelenting in his encouragement, for his belief is that information such as this was critical to the correctional system's ability to respond to Native American needs and rights. His broadsightedness will never be forgotten. Dr. Shaw's secretary, Karen Michaelson, was extremely helpful in setting up interviews, visits, and special meetings with inmates.

I wish to express my appreciation to Winfield Barber, who assisted me with historical information about the correctional system. In the Central Office of the Department of Correctional Services were a number of individuals who consistently offered their assistance in a variety of ways: Steve King, in charge of research; Judy Egger, computer programmer for DCS, who provided prison data and assisted in my tracking parolees over a three-year period; Jim McKenzie of Parole Administration, who assisted me in tracking inmates returning for parole violations; Jeanine Douglass, who explained the complexities of "good time" and prison sentencing to me; and Ed Slips of the Parole Administration, who also assisted me in tracking the forty-five offenders whom I interviewed. Sincere appreciation is owed Mike Kenney, former Superintendent of the Hastings Correctional Center, who familiarized me with the Hastings prison; Max Gumm, Chaplain for the Omaha Correctional Center, who facilitated my contact with Indian prisoners in that facility for several years; Mary Bartels of the education program; Danny Siebold, head of case management, and Mike Last, psychologist, both at the Evaluation Unit of the Lincoln Correctional Center; and especially Jim Steere, case manager, who spent a lot of time and energy educating me and answering questions about the inmate intake process.

I'd like to thank many alcohol treatment program personnel for discussing their programs with my research assistant and me and for sharing their perspectives on substance abuse treatment for Native American ex-offenders in general. They include the staffs at the Lincoln Indian Center, the NOVA Program in Omaha, the Santee Sioux Alcoholism Program, the Alcoholism Treatment Unit of the Hastings Regional Center, the Winnebago Indian Health Service Hospital, Medicine Wheel, Valley Hope, the Independence Center at Lincoln General Hospital, the Veterans Administration Hospital in Lincoln, the Lincoln Correctional Center inpatient treatment program, the Intertribal Treatment Center of Nebraska (formerly Four Winds), and the Macy Alcoholism Center.

In the legal arena, Kathy Jaudzemis, a federal magistrate and former member of the law firm Cline, Williams, Johnson, Wright, and Oldfather, provided ongoing legal information and expertise pertaining not only to litigation by Native American plaintiffs but also to general matters of sentencing and incarceration. Her time, patience in reviewing legal components of this book for accuracy, and perspective are deeply valued and acknowledged. Other attorneys I wish to thank are those who are involved in representing Indian plaintiffs in the lawsuits discussed in this book, and who spent considerable amounts of time sharing their views on these legal difficulties: Dana Baker, Mike Higgins, Charles Humble, Steve Speicher, Thomas Maul, John Hendry, and Jefferson Downing. I am deeply indebted to Judge Warren K. Urbom, Chief Judge of the U.S. District Court of Nebraska, for providing personal insights and clarifications concerning litigation brought by Indian inmates, and for his time in reviewing the manuscript for legal accuracy. I admire his reluctance to alter the "sense" of my interpretive statements concerning litigation, for he did not wish to alter my personal analysis of the events in question.

My greatest debt and gratitude is to the Indian inmates and ex-offenders in the Nebraska penal system, many of whom have invested years in my clear understanding of the phenomenon of Indian incarceration and the political struggles therein. I would especially like to recognize Perry Wounded Shield, whose friendship, support, wisdom, and experiences contributed significantly to my own understanding, not only of incarceration but of its unique impact on Native American culture and spirituality. Others I wish to thank include Tony Laravie, Gideon Bison, Rupert Dick, Cornelius Black Bonnett, Richard Walker, Tatanka SapaNajin, and all the Indian brothers and sisters in the varying facilities of the Department of Correctional Services who shared their lives, histories and thoughts with me. I would especially like to remember two Native Americans who died during the period of study—Duane Jones and Albert BirdHead.

Little Rock Reed, an Indian inmate from the Southern Ohio Correctional Facility, shared a great deal of information concerning his personal efforts to gain access to traditional religious practices in prison, and I wish to express my gratitude to him. His work on Indian prisoners will also document national efforts of Indian inmates to practice their religion in prison.

The Nebraska Board of Parole deserves special thanks for their willingness to be studied, their openness in discussing parole issues with me, and above all their willingness to show flexibility in accommodating Native American cultural and religious beliefs. Former board members Mary Wieseman and Carlos Alvarez are owed particular recognition for the effort they expended in reaching out to the Indian prison population by going out to the prisons and meeting with the Native American offenders to discuss their concerns on their own turf. Their extra efforts have also been recognized, acknowledged, and appreciated by the Native American prison population.

Leslie Boellstorff, formerly of the *Lincoln Journal* and presently of the *Omaha World-Herald*, shared many resources, references, and news clippings that assisted my efforts at reconstruction of inmate historical events.

Many colleagues and friends read drafts of this manuscript for accuracy, and I am very grateful to them for their editorial assistance: John Shaw, Jim Steere, Mike Kenney, Kathy Jaudzemis, Richard Walker, Ralph Thomas, Jerry Fallis, Wesley Buchanan, Claire Bohn, and Judge Warren K. Urbom.

Finally, living with me for the last several years has not been easy, and it is my husband, James A. Gibson, and our children, Miriam and Jeremy Grobsmith, to whom I owe my final thanks. My preoccupation, my involvement in prison activities during the evenings and weekends, my time spent in court and preparing for testimony, my travel and financial burdens, and most of all my psyche as I became more and more involved in this project—all must have compromised my ability to be a reasonable person in a family. Their flexibility, patience, and tolerance are things for which I will always be indebted.

Indians in Prison

Introduction

Some inmates say the Nebraska prison system is a paradise, a "Holiday Inn." Others characterize prison as a holding tank, a degrading, dehumanizing, institutionalizing social system, an explosion waiting to happen. Regardless of the prisoner's attitude, entering prison is embarking on a new life, being socialized into a system whose structure, values, and regulations will dominate every event for the next block of time, be it six months, five years, or a lifetime. With the termination of one's status as a free individual and completion of the rite of passage that makes one an "inmate," a transformation process occurs that, with little question, will render the individual changed for life. Whether punished or rehabilitated, whether adjusted or embittered, whether accepting or rebellious, a prisoner becomes enculturated to a system whose procedures and patterns must become his or her own. For the one hundred or so Native Americans imprisoned by the Nebraska Department of Correctional Services, adjustment to prison life involves more than acceptance of incarceration. It involves a process of reconciliation whereby each individual must decide how to merge being Indian with being a prisoner, must determine where sacrifices in maintaining one's heritage and identity can be made, and where they cannot.

For Indian inmates in Nebraska, the last eighteen years have been an evolution in decision-making concerning individual and collective identification with Native American heritage in prison. The Native Americans have not been the only ones to modify their culture and behavior as a result of incarceration; the process of culture contact—as with cultural change anywhere—has simultaneously resulted in an adjustment for the "dominant society," in this case, the institutions where they reside. The prison experience is definitely different as a consequence of the administration's accommodations to Native American concerns (although such changes probably would not have occurred without the court's intervention). The prisoners themselves have changed as a result of the struggles and political decisions they have had to make concerning the preservation of their right to remain Native American despite their incarceration.

This book is about Indians in prison—or Indians and prison, and the coexistence and mutual adjustment they have achieved. The correctional system, in its efforts to comply with court orders and decrees, has had to respond to legal mandates that accommodate Indian religion and culture as well as procedural matters that enable inmates to express their Native American heritage and unique legal status. The purpose of this book is not only to review the history of this symbiotic evolution but also to analyze the dynamics of such a process. Nebraska Indian inmates have, after all, been exemplary in the United States in instigating such an adjustment on the part of the correctional system. They did not do it by going through proper prison administrative channels. They did it in the courts. Their suits have been predicated on their special legal status as Native Americans. But what makes the Nebraska situation so interesting is that resolution was reached by the federal courts for the Nebraska prisons four years prior to the passage of the 1978 American Indian Religious Freedom Act, which ultimately required accommodation to Indian religion under federal mandate. What made the Nebraska Indian inmates so precocious in their litigious pursuits? What factors precipitated this early crisis in American Indian prison identity?

In an attempt to describe the symbiotic and dynamic relationship between prison and Native American prisoner, I have adopted an anthropological approach, hoping to view the entire system as a culture—ever evolving and changing and consisting of subcultures, particularly the Indian population and the institutional culture of the prison administration. Each certainly has its own values, mores, attitudes, beliefs, and policies. As they merge, each becomes altered. Due to the specific focus of this study no attempt has been made to offer a comprehensive analysis of other analogous prison subcultures (e.g. Hispanics, African-Americans, or white groups). Additionally, I have hoped that in my adoption of an ethnographic approach I could more accurately depict prison life and its routines and conflicts, from the perspective of those incarcerated. Toward that end I have relied on the anthropological method of participant-observation where possible.

Of course, participating in life in prison is an impossibility for an outsider; but to the extent I could, I observed prison routines and special events and tried to imagine what it would be like to go through them. I visited all the facilities, interviewed inmates in all of them, and became familiar with prison administrative functions. For example, I attended "court," where an institutional disciplinary committee deals with offenders' conduct violations. I observed intake interviews as inmates were being processed into the system. I sat in on custody classification hearings and observed interaction between psychologist, case manager, and inmate. I went through prisoner orientation to see exactly what coming into a facility is like. I attended parole hearings and revocations for four years to try to understand what that experience is like, both for inmates and for the parole board.

Often it became impossible simply to observe and I switched into the role of participant, sometimes testifying in favor of an inmate's parole or bringing to light mitigating circumstances that I hoped the board would consider before revoking an offender's parole. Sometimes I attended a parole or revocation hearing of an inmate I was tracking and, perhaps as a consequence of my frequent presence at hearings, ended up being asked by the parole board if I wanted to make any comments on behalf of an inmate.

In a study on alcohol and crime conducted in 1986 and 1987, I analyzed the correctional records of 106 Indian inmates, gathering vast amounts of data on their backgrounds, criminal histories, and offenses. I spent ninety hours formally interviewing inmates about the impact alcohol and drugs had on their criminal activity, and during that time I was able to evaluate the degree to which correctional assessments of them were accurate or were unrealistic reflections of their real involvement in criminal activity (Grobsmith 1989a). They talked of their alcohol recovery plans, their problems with the parole system, the reasons for their reluctance to participate in the prison's mental health programs.

I attended meetings and functions of the Native American Cultural and Spiritual Awareness (NASCA) groups in all of the prison facilities, observing, participating, and supporting. Often, I was a guest or keynote speaker at the group's annual symposia and powwows. I attended or served as expert witness in most of the trials in which Indian inmates have brought suit against the Department of Correctional Services. For years, my involvement with Indian prisoners had brought me to appreciate their integrity and vitality as a culture and to observe the process of change and growth they have undergone. Finally, I have tried to assume the proactive role of the advocate anthropologist in using my knowledge to facilitate their efforts, whether in the capacity of liaison, intermediary to prison authorities or the parole board, or simply as a friend.

It would be unrealistic to assert that, during the years in which materials were being gathered for this book, my life did not become inextricably bound up with those of many Native American prisoners. Assuming a role that varied from investigator to advocate brought me into considerable personal contact with many inmates, and that contact had to be re-evaluated upon their release from prison. The involvement of anthropologists in the personal lives of their clients or consultants has long been known; but how do anthropologists—and female ones at that—interact with male offenders? When do professional relationships turn into friendships, and when does advocacy stop and personal struggle on behalf of a particular inmate begin? Many of the struggles of inmates became my own, and there have been periods of involvement provoking such despondence that I had difficulty carrying on my professional life. Inmates with whom I worked sometimes became regular callers at work—and collect callers at home. Anticipating release from prison, sometimes one would ask me to dinner or a trip to the park. Could I be certain of my safety in a nonprison environment? Did my role as researcher/advocate necessarily transfer into that of friend?

Inmates with whom I worked sometimes appeared at my office or home upon release from prison—some by invitation, others not. A not uncommon event was the arrival of an ex-offender accompanied by his or her friends, drinking and in need of money, frequently for travel. (In fact, such visits still occur.) Should I support drinking and driving? Should I risk refusing a drunk and make him or her angry? These episodes frightened me and threatened my personal sense of security as well as the privacy and safety of my family and colleagues at work. One inmate, whom I had known for years, arrived at my home drunk and later admitted to stealing from me. Does one press charges against a client, friend, consultant? Do I even have the right of confrontation? Inmates sometimes assumed that my interviewing them left me obliged to return a favor, and favors were requested for a wide variety of needs—from the purchase of cigarettes for friends to checking in on loved ones, to wiring flowers to funerals, to providing bail after a post–prison release drinking spree. One inmate even requested that I assist him in disposing of the stolen goods for which he was doing time.

But financial obligations became the least of my concerns. Interviewing inmates posed a special challenge. While for the most part I felt comfortable and safe, with correctional authorities not far away, I worried when an inmate seemed especially distant or remote. In some cases, I knew the inmate was high on drugs. One event truly horrified me and left me in a terrible ethical dilemma. As an interview began to come to a close, the inmate began to masturbate under the table at which we were seated. I had no idea what to do. I sat there, watching him, afraid to call the guard lest I bring harm to an inmate whose rights to privacy I had promised to protect. On the other hand, was I about to be a victim of sexual assault? I persisted in talking (way too much, I'm sure) and saving my interview data on the diskette of my little portable external floppy drive, and quickly packed up and left. When I went home, I couldn't stop crying: I felt violated, humiliated. I felt the victim, if not in person, in fantasy. I was disgusted and sickened. My family was sure I'd been physically harmed. But I hadn't. The harm that had been done was to my spirit.

Often the tasks of translating inmates' needs to correctional authorities or parole board members necessitated my personal commitment to assume physical responsibility for a parolee as a legal sponsor or even a guardian or custodian if we were leaving the prison premises. For example, I took an inmate to an alcohol treatment program a hundred miles away from the prison, and weeks later my family and I picked him up and took him to the Sun Dance in South Dakota, where we camped for a week, and later returned him to treatment. Upon completion of that program, we returned him to Lincoln. All of this "sponsorship" requires the approval of both the correctional authorities and the board of parole, which must approve all out-of-state travel. What if an inmate in my custody took off? Was I responsible for the escape? How could I guarantee that this would not occur? In some instances, relationships between my family and some offenders became deeply personal. One very difficult component of this personal involvement was the effort I felt I had to make on behalf of inmates' requests for furloughs, to travel to Sun Dances, permission to travel to funerals, or other personal desires. Their goals became mine. Sometimes I felt that I could and wanted to completely support their efforts, and, being convinced of their sincerity, undertook an aggressive struggle for them to achieve their goals. Other times, I felt torn about endorsing an inmate's request and was reluctant to support it lest the prison authorities regard me as undiscriminating. Would the authorities take my requests more seriously if I endorsed fewer of them? How well *did* I know an inmate and how sure was I that I could trust him? Knowledge of an inmate during her incarceration might have little to do with her behavior on the outside, and unless I knew the offender was a good risk, was it appropriate for me to promise my support? How upset would an inmate be who had agreed to be a subject in my research, but later wanted a letter of support for parole that I did not feel I could provide? How much wrath could I endure? What kinds of risks would I be subjecting my family to if I refused to "return the favor"? Should I compromise my integrity for a reduction in vulnerability? These became a few of the dilemmas I faced over the years.

Probably the deepest worry I had was over the welfare of Indian prisoners upon their release from prison. How would they fare? Would they return to the activities that led to their incarceration? Could I assist them in preparing for a life of sobriety upon release? Was it even my place to do so, or was that overstepping the bounds of advocacy? Often—in fact, the majority of the time—an ex-offender returned to drinking and encountered, once again, contact with the criminal justice system. My reaction, without fail, was disappointment, frustration, sometimes rage. With some inmates, these were sentiments I never felt comfortable expressing. With others, my friendship with the individual was strong enough to warrant my crossing the cultural barrier and behaving in the familial role of critic, parent, angry friend. I never dreamed I would tell the parole board (much less the offender) of my disappointment in an offender whose parole was revoked because of inappropriate or illegal behavior; I never dreamed I would tell an ex-offender who went to county jail over the weekend that I would never bail him out again because I was so disappointed—infuriated—by his return to drinking. But, in actuality, my personal involvement frequently became so great that I could only behave in a manner that reflected my being true to myself as well as to that individual. And I never saw an instance in which the individual did not respect my candor and even my right to comment.

Even more traumatic for me were the failures of some inmates to stay sober upon release from prison—which I tried not to take personally but of course did—and my personal disappointment and confusion at what sometimes seemed their total inability to reverse the course of their lives. These personal emotional setbacks were among the most maddening experiences I have ever faced; and yet they were the very same ones that continued to drive me to serve as advocate and contribute, if I could, to the hope of a different lifestyle for these Native Americans. In the majority of cases, there were no major changes in lifestyle nor abandonment of youthful self-destructive behavior. As will be seen in the chapters that follow, the return to drinking, the revocation of parole status, and the return to incarceration were depressing realities for which I had no rational answer or explanation.

Chapter 1 provides a historic framework for incarceration in Nebraska and outlines the indoctrination procedures for becoming an inmate. Chapter 2 focuses on the political identity of the Native American prison population and details some of the cultural activities in which they are engaged. Chapter 3 presents a review and analysis of the litigation Native American prisoners in Nebraska have pursued, and the impact such litigation has had on the expression of religion in prison. In chapter 4, the impact drugs and alcohol have had on inmates' lives is considered, along with a discussion of their familial and personal histories. Chapter 5 considers the alcohol and drug treatment avenues available to Native American prisoners, and how and why the approaches have failed for this population. In chapter 6, the parole process is detailed; the parole successes and failures of Nebraska inmates are discussed. Chapter 7 offers the results of a nationwide survey of Native American activities in state and federal penal facilities. Chapter 8 offers some concluding remarks and recommendations as to how all the parties involved—inmates, correctional and parole authorities, and the courts—might develop some more effective strategies for addressing the broad problem of Native American incarceration.

If the publication of this book could have one major effect, my hope would be that the information presented here could shed light on the concerns, perceptions, and needs of Indian inmates, and, even more importantly, that such knowledge could inform the correctional policies and programs that are designed to serve their needs. Clearly, prison rehabilitation is not occurring. Increasing incarceration and alcoholism rates, disruption of Indian families, and great increases in crime all point to the failure of the many sorts of programs developed to serve the Indian clientele.

This, then, is the story of Indians in prison—their lives, their struggles, and, most of all, their accomplishments. It is my hope that knowledge of their existence and vitality will bring insight, informed policy, enlightenment, and a clearer vision for both Native American prisoners and the correctional systems throughout the country in which they are incarcerated.

1

Life in Prison

The location of the Nebraska prisons—in the central plains—and the unique political climate of Indian militancy in the late 1960s and early 1970s had a great deal to do with setting the stage for the historical events that will unfold here. The growing intolerance of and dissatisfaction with social, political, and economic conditions on plains reservations, especially those in South Dakota, had contributed significantly to the development of the American Indian Movement (AIM), an urban militant organization founded in Minneapolis in 1968. The occupation by Native Americans of symbolic sites, including Alcatraz Island in 1969, the Bureau of Indian Affairs in Washington, D.C., in 1972, and the ten-week takeover of Wounded Knee, South Dakota, in 1973, were demands that the federal government recognize the state of crisis that characterized most Indian communities, particularly those in the plains.

The heavy drug use so common throughout the country during the counterculture period also had an impact on the Indian population in the plains. It is no coincidence that these events of the late 1960s and early 1970s occurred simultaneously with the rumblings going on in the Nebraska penal system. Many of the individuals who were active in AIM during this period resided either on the reservations of Nebraska and South Dakota or in the northwest Nebraska towns directly south of the large Sioux reservations of Rosebud and Pine Ridge. Those Indians who became involved in criminal activity often served time in the Nebraska penal system. Frequently their attitude was neither acquiescent nor subdued. They were not of the opinion that surrendering their freedom meant an abandonment of their cultural heritage and identity, nor did they believe that incarceration carried with it a requirement to abandon their religious practices. They wore their hair long, with headbands, or in Indian hairstyles such as a Mohawk. They demanded their right to participate in sweat lodge ceremonies, and to use the Sacred Pipe and its required tobaccos. They demanded their right to participate in the Sun Dance, and to hold Native American Church ceremonies (see chapter 2 for a discussion of these ceremonies). Never before had a correctional system been bombarded by a group of culturally distinct individuals whose First Amendment rights required that the correctional system modify its structure, procedures, and tolerance for cultural differences.

The battle that ensued between Indian inmates and the correctional system began in the early 1970s, and it continues today. In the 1990s, however, the Indian prison reform movement is no longer local but nationwide—actually international—and highly organized, complete with research and advocacy organizations such as the Native American Prisoners Rehabilitation Research Project, newsletters such as the Iron House Drum, and now a scholarly periodical entitled *Journal of Prisoners on Prisons,* published at the University of Ottawa. The struggle has resulted in considerable adjustment on the part of prisons to Indian religious and cultural mandates, not only in physical facilities and privileges, but in the conceptual realm as well. The correctional system has been forced to accommodate Native American beliefs and precepts, to learn their cosmologies and view of the universe, to appreciate their rituals and approaches to rehabilitation, to adjust to their view of kinship and family, and to undertake the awakening of correctional employees to these issues.

Nebraska Indian inmates have been national trendsetters in their efforts to achieve recognition for their right to a unique and distinct cultural identity behind the walls. Nebraska's correctional system was the first in the United States to obtain a court order permitting prisoners to practice the sweat lodge. The Nebraska Consent Decree—the legal document that provided the framework in 1974 for the state's policy regarding treatment of Indian inmates—has been distributed all over the United States and serves as an example of the settlements Indians and prison administrators can achieve. Inmates in other states are entering into class action suits based on the legal precedents set in Nebraska. The historical import of this unique group's activities will reverberate throughout America's prisons throughout the next century, influencing correctional policy, programming, and process in an irreversible fashion.

The Nebraska prisons

In 1856, a board of commissioners was established, authorizing Nebraska's first penal institution, a territorial prison housed in an old barn. Legislative appropriations funded prison development through the 1860s, but it was not until 1870—three years after statehood—that a bill to construct a state penitentiary in Lincoln was passed. The first prisoner arrived in 1871, and records indicate that Indian inmates followed in this early facility. The penitentiary had a contract with the United States government to house federal as well as state prisoners. In fact, agreements permitted the confinement of any criminal convicted by any court in the Nebraska system, and the prison population even included some state prisoners from Colorado and Wyoming. The Nebraska prison system is still authorized to accept federal inmates on an emergency basis or for safekeeping (temporary housing during transfer), and it is audited by federal as well as state inspectors to insure proper accommodations for federal prisoners.

Various administrative units have handled the correctional system since its inception. The Nebraska prisons were under the Nebraska Department of Public Institutions (DPI), founded in 1962, until 1973, when, as a result of Nebraska statute 83–171, the Department of Correctional Services (DCS) became a separate state institution. The main administrative center, the Central Office, took over the functions of accounting, budgeting, engineering, and research from the DPI. Today, the Central Office and two large male facilities are located in Lincoln, Nebraska, with a women's prison and two minimum-security institutions located to the east and west within a 100-mile radius of Lincoln.

Nebraska, like many other states, has separate correctional facilities to house different types of inmates according to gender, severity of offense, security concerns, and rehabilitative needs. As of August 1992, six adult and two juvenile facilities constituted the Nebraska Department of Correctional Services (see Table 1 for a breakdown of the adult prison population by facility, custody level, and race). The two juvenile facilities, which are not dealt with in this study, are the Youth Development Center for males at Kearney, and a similar center for females in Geneva. The majority of adult institutions are located in Lincoln, and the others in the nearby towns of Omaha, to the east, and Hastings and York to the west.

Despite the expansion and construction of facilities throughout the

Table 1

Nebraska Inmate Population by Facility, Custody Level, and Race as of August 31, 1992

Facility / Custody Level	African American no. of inmates	African American % of population	American Indian no. of inmates	American Indian % of population	Hispanic no. of inmates	Hispanic % of population	White no. of inmates	White % of population	Other no. of inmates	Other % of population	Facility Totals
Lincoln Correctional Center	286	34.2	27	3.2	29	3.4	493	60.0	1	0	836
Evaluation	91	35.3	8	3.1	10	3.8	149	57.7	0	0	258
Administrative Unit*	171	33.9	14	2.7	15	2.9	304	60.1	1	0	505
Minimum	18	30.0	4	6.6	3	5.0	35	58.3	0	0	60
Community Custody	6	46.2	8	7.6	1	7.6	5	38.4	1	0	13
Nebraska State Penitentiary	286	36.9	34	4.3	43	5.5	411	53.0	1	0	775
Maximum	174	42.9	23	5.6	18	4.4	190	46.9	0	0	405
Medium	112	30.2	11	2.9	25	6.7	221	59.7	1	0	370
Omaha Correctional Center	158	37.6	12	2.8	29	6.9	221	52.6	0	0.0	420
Medium	1	50.0	0	0.0	0	0.0	1	50.0	0	0.0	2
Minimum	157	37.8	12	2.8	29	6.9	217	52.2	0	0.0	415
Community Custody	0	0.0	0	0.0	0	0.0	3	100.0	0	0.0	3
Community Corrections (Lincoln and Omaha)	89	31.6	7	2.4	20	7.1	165	58.7	0	0	281
Hastings Correctional Center	27	18.1	8	5.3	18	12.0	96	64.4	0	0.0	149
Minimum	27	18.4	8	5.4	17	11.6	94	64.3	0	0.0	146
Community Custody	0	0.0	0	0.0	1	33.3	2	66.6	0	0.0	3
Nebraska Center for Women (York) Minimum	57	42.8	6	4.5	4	3.0	64	48.1	2	1.5	133
Inmate Totals	903	34.8	94	3.6	143	5.5	1,450	55.8	4	0	2,594

*The Administrative Unit of the Lincoln Correctional Center houses primarily maximum- and medium-custody inmates.

state in the last decade, Nebraska prisons are overcrowded—overall the facilities are 54 percent over design capacity (*Lincoln Star*, Sept. 17, 1992)—as well as underfunded and lacking many of the programs and employment opportunities desired to effect inmate rehabilitation. Consistent with other prisons throughout the country, which overall showed a 6.1 percent increase in inmate population from 1987 to 1988 and an 8.1 percent increase from 1988 to 1989, growth in the Nebraska prison population has been dramatic: from 1988 to 1989, 1989 to 1990, 1990 to 1991, and 1991 to 1992, the increases have been 5.9 percent, 9.9 percent, 4.5 percent, and 4.6 percent respectively (Camp and Camp 1989, 1990, 1990; Department of Correctional Services Annual Statistical Report for Fiscal Year 1992). Significant increases in drug trafficking convictions have forced most Nebraska facilities to operate beyond their capacities, and are responsible for continuing requests to the state legislature to fund expansion. Even with the addition in the summer of 1993 of a community custody facility, intended to house 200 inmates (44 of them female) adjacent to the Lincoln Correctional Center, the prison population is projected to be 40 percent over capacity (*Lincoln Star*, Sept. 17, 1992).

Although the Lincoln Correctional Center is technically the largest prison in the state, the prison proper has fewer inmates than the Nebraska State Penitentiary in Lincoln, "the Pen," which housed 775 medium- and maximum-custody male inmates in 1992. The original penitentiary, the territorial prison, built in 1869, has been torn down and repeatedly renovated and enlarged. With the most recent major reconstruction, in 1981, the expected capacity of the Pen was 320. Originally, the old facility had two cell houses, the west, built in 1876, which had single-occupancy cells, and the east, built in the 1890s, which housed one to four inmates in a cell. When plans for expansion were initiated, the correctional system requested that funds be appropriated to build seven housing units and convert the old trusty dormitory into a school and service center. Funds were appropriated for only four housing units. As a result, crowding is considerable—ever since the new facilities opened, inmates have been doubled up. By 1992 the Pen was operating at approximately 158.8 percent over capacity, housing 554 rather than 320 in the maximum-custody area and 221 in the Medium Security Unit (MSU) in the old trusty dormitory (Department of Correctional Services, Monthly Statistical Report, Aug. 31, 1992). Recent requests to the state legislature for additional funds have not met with success. The overcrowded conditions have resulted in pressure on the board of parole to release inmates at the earliest possible opportunity to alleviate crowded conditions. However, crimes committed by several parolees in 1991–1992 resulted in a public outcry for stricter standards for granting parole. A crime committed by one parolee during this period resulted in a demand that the governor call for the resignation of the parole board members responsible for the inmate's release.

At the Pen, inmates are divided into maximum- and medium-custody groups. The prison generally houses older offenders, and technically there should be no minimum-custody inmates there, but overcrowding has landed some there anyway. Those minimum-custody inmates must be treated as medium-custody inmates—that is, the controls on them cannot be lessened since that would pose a security risk for higher-custody prisoners. Maximum-custody inmates are housed in one of the four housing units and, except for jobs and programs, they are segregated from the medium-custody offenders. The medium-custody offenders live behind another security fence in the old trusty dormitory, now called MSU, which was supposed to house 150 prisoners—50 to a "bay" or dormitory (barracks-style living quarters). These inmates have separate recreation, sports, hobby, store, library, barber, and dining areas, and only cross the yard with a pass and en route to their jobs, the majority of which are located on the main prison grounds. A recently constructed library and a barber shop in the main prison yard serve inmates from MSU as well as from the main housing areas. Maximum-custody inmates cannot go into MSU, except with a special pass for school.

In the maximum-custody area at the Pen, the four housing units contain four galleries each. Housing Unit #4 resembles the others except that it is designed for special security. Death row inmates are housed there, and one gallery accommodates the overflow of inmates from Control Unit #5, the Adjustment Center (i.e., protective custody). Presently, death row is filled to capacity. Condemned inmates are "locked down" all day, except for meals and an hour in the yard; they are never permitted to mix with the other inmates. Although Nebraska's laws permit capital punishment, there has not been an execution in the state since Starkweather was executed in 1959.

The Lincoln Correctional Center (LCC), also for male medium- and maximum-custody inmates, was erected in 1979 and replaced the Nebraska State Reformatory in Lincoln. The reformatory had opened in 1921 on the site of a former boys' school. Today, LCC comprises two separate facilities, the prison, or Administrative Unit, which housed 531 in

1992, and the Evaluation Unit, which housed 305. The Evaluation Unit used to be a separate facility, the Diagnostic and Evaluation Center (referred to as "D & E" by inmates), performing evaluations of all incoming male inmates in the system. Budgetary constraints placed the unit under the administrative arm of LCC, but it still is the intake processing center for all male inmates in the state (intake for women prisoners is done at the Nebraska Center for Women in York). The Evaluation Unit also houses protective custody inmates for the entire Department of Correctional Services, that is, for male inmates at all levels who require special protection for their own safety or for others'.

Although the Penitentiary and Lincoln Correctional Center appear to duplicate each other's functions by housing the same custody level of male prisoner, the Pen generally houses multiple offenders and recidivists who have been accustomed to prison life and would better survive the rigors of intense or long-term incarceration. Young offenders whose records do not suggest long histories of criminal involvement may be sent to the Lincoln Correctional Center as a way of diverting them from contact with the more hard core offenders who are serving longer sentences at the Pen.

Two facilities in the state house minimum-custody male inmates: the Omaha Correctional Center, in Omaha, and the Hastings Correctional Center in Hastings. The Omaha Correctional Center opened in 1984 and presently houses 420 inmates. The Hastings Correctional Center opened in 1987, occupying a renovated building of the Hastings Regional Center campus. Today, Hastings houses 149 male minimum-custody inmates. Like the penitentiary, these prisons are operating beyond capacity. The two minimum-custody institutions are geared toward readying the prisoners for release into the community, and at both the Hastings and Omaha facilities, remunerative employment in telephone sales is available to assist inmates in establishing a successful work record. All of the Nebraska penal facilities are fully accredited by the American Correctional Association.

When women were initially incarcerated in Nebraska, in the 1920s, they were housed on the third floor of the men's penitentiary and supervised by a matron who was the warden's wife. Today, women of all custody levels are housed at the Nebraska Center for Women in York, which opened in 1920. Female inmates who are eligible for either work release or education release as a final preparation for their return to society are housed at Community Correction centers in Omaha or in Lincoln.

The Community Corrections Administration, established in 1967, governs the work release and education release programs, which allow a select group of inmates to be employed in the community but be institutionally housed during nonworking hours. Since 1971 inmates have been able to work or attend school through participation in this program. Other "postcare" centers were established in Norfolk, Sidney, and Omaha, but only the Lincoln and Omaha centers remain, housing 277 inmates (236 males and 41 females). In order to be assigned to a Community Correction Center, inmates must have attained the level of community custody.

All the facilities in the state (with the exception of the Evaluation Unit of the Lincoln Correctional Center) have their own chief executive officers—wardens or superintendents—all of whom are under the director of the entire correctional system. Although administrative regulations are the same for all institutions, policies and procedures vary significantly because of the relative autonomy of each facility. For example, visitors are thoroughly searched before they may enter the Pen but are not searched at all at the Lincoln Correctional Center, despite the fact that both house medium- and maximum-custody inmates. Similarly, visiting regulations, club functions and scheduling, and flexibility of the administration in accommodating Native American practices are variable. Problems sometimes result when inmates at one institution find themselves denied permission to participate in certain activities to which they had become accustomed when housed at a different facility.

The Central Office in Lincoln encompasses the entire correction department's computer tracking system, the parole administration, and all inmates' records, and it serves other functions such as regulating research on prisoners. The parole administration, unlike the Nebraska Board of Parole, which is autonomous and reports to the governor of the state, is part of the correctional system and regulates the return of inmates to state custody, including their re-evaluation and parole revocation.

Inmate intake

When an inmate is first brought to the Evaluation Center by the county sheriff, having just received a court sentence, the period of processing and adjustment begins. After receiving an identification number that will appear on all clothes, on all correspondence within the administration, and on all mail leaving the system, inmates are required to strip, shower with antiseptic soap for crab lice, and undergo a cursory body search (no body cavity other than the mouth is examined). Fingerprints and photographs are taken. Uniforms are issued, and the inmate's own clothes can either be shipped home at the inmate's expense or donated to a charitable organization. An initial interview ascertains the individual's history—where he or she came from (whether from another penal institution), any previous criminal history, a review of health, medical and/or dental needs, prior drug or alcohol treatment—and assesses the person's needs and desires, particularly with regard to drug and alcohol therapy. This interview phase is critical for the staff to determine whether an inmate is troubled, has suicidal tendencies, or requires immediate referral to a mental health professional. When it is deemed necessary, a mental health counselor will perform an emergency psychiatric evaluation to assess the likelihood that an inmate will inflict self-harm. A stripped cell may be required to temporarily house someone who might pose a danger to him- or herself—for example, sheets that could be used for committing suicide will be removed. Indian inmates, and probably most others, are generally fairly passive or intimidated during the intake process. They just listen and hope to end the interview as quickly as possible, eager to get it over with and get settled in.

Inmates are invited to request visits with an alcohol or drug counselor and are asked to consider whether they would like to involve themselves in such programming when they are assigned to a more permanent facility to begin serving their sentence. With the exception of emergency counseling, regular mental health services are not available at the Evaluation Center, but must be delayed until inmates have been transferred to a regular facility. For the month or two that the prisoners are housed at the Evaluation Unit, they learn the institutional policies, programs, and rules and begin the slow process of adjustment to and acceptance of their current fate. Placement at a facility will depend on when a bed is available and upon the determination of a custody hearing (since all women, regardless of custody, go to York, no determination needs to be made about location).

Establishing whether an inmate has enemies is an important consideration prior to assignment to an institution, and even at the Evaluation Unit inmates with concerns for their security—or those threatening the safety of others—will be segregated if necessary. When the staff is assured that the inmates' basic needs have been met—they understand the system of sending memos, or "kites," to their supervisors, they feel they can get along with their roommates, and they have been given a few stamps, paper, and pencil—they are ready to begin the more intensive phase of intake processing: assignment to one of five case managers, administration of psychological tests such as the Minnesota Multiphasic Personality Inventory (MMPI), custody classification, and assignment to a prison facility. Once inmates are assigned to a case manager, they are interviewed in greater depth and apprised of the fact that their total evaluation will take at least a month.

The case managers are responsible for responding to the needs of the individuals in their caseload; they perform a detailed evaluation of each inmate, either for the prison or for the court to complete its sentencing; they inform the inmate about custody classification procedures and carry out the custody hearing; they tell the client about the different institutions in the system and the programming available at each, and expedite the transfer of the client to the appropriate facility. Interviews with one of the two psychologists on the staff provide a profile on each inmate, to be used in conjunction with personality inventories in assessing each offender's case history and psychological needs.

Time passes slowly for inmates at the Evaluation Unit, as there is little to do. While there may be in excess of 300 inmates there at any given time, only forty jobs are available; there is no real programming. Yard time (time spent in recreation outdoors) and other freedoms are considerably more curtailed than in the long-term facilities. Inmates look forward to ultimate placement at a regular facility because it will get them away from D & E (the old name for the Evaluation Unit is still preferred by inmates), allow them to establish a regular and more frequent schedule of visits from family and friends, and allow them to attend school, seek employment, and get on with their regular routines.

During their stay at the Evaluation Unit, visits with approved individuals are permitted, but only once a week. Contact with ex-offenders or those on probation or parole is expressly forbidden. Regulations concerning proper behavior and attire must be followed by visitors or visits will be terminated by the staff. Correctional officers tolerate a certain amount of kissing, but if a couple's passion appears to be getting away from them, the couple is usually warned. Not all officers at all facilities are equally vigilant about physical contact between inmates and their girlfriends or wives—some guards admit to occasionally turning their backs when they see a couple engaging in sex in a corner of the visiting room.

Either in Evaluation or a regular facility, there is a definite prison protocol about conduct and attire for visitors. Generally, female guests cannot wear shorts to the prison unless they are children. Women are frisked by female guards: sleeves, underarms, and legs are checked for objects, and women's bras are felt for possible hidden items. Insides of shoes are scanned to see if the lining has ever been removed, hair is felt, especially behind the ears and around the nape of the neck, and if a woman is wearing a dress, she must raise her skirt to reveal that she is wearing panties and a slip. No see-through blouses or bralessness is permitted. A stamp placed on the inside of the left wrist indicates clearance, and this stamp is always viewed under a special light before prison guards will allow a visitor to leave.

The Evaluation Unit of the Lincoln Correctional Center houses a variety of types of inmates. First are all incoming offenders, both new and returning, and prisoners requiring protective custody, who are housed separately. An incoming inmate requesting protective custody may or may not be granted such protection; granting such a request would depend on the outcome of an investigation to establish risk. Next are the ninety-day evaluators, males who have been convicted of a felony offense and are sent to be evaluated prior to being sentenced to probation or incarceration. This evaluation by case managers and psychologists enables the court to better consider all the factors involved in the person's offense and criminal history before sentencing. With younger first-time offenders, this period of evaluation is especially useful in that it provides the sentencing judge with better information on which to make a decision about what to do with the beginning offender. Finally there are "safekeepers," males who for some reason (being known troublemakers, for example, or having given testimony against a drug dealer), must be held somewhere other than the county or city jail. The majority of safekeepers are county prisoners, although some are state or federal detainees and others are parole violators or returnees from the Community Correction (work release) Center.

There are ten units in the Evaluation Center. Each houses thirty-two men, with the exception of the segregation unit, which houses sixteen, and the protective custody unit, which houses forty-eight. The hospital unit can accommodate sixteen men, eight beds being reserved for inmates with medical problems and eight for individuals with border or limbo status, meaning they are not really behavior problems requiring segregation, nor are they mental health patients, yet there are some concerns about their behavior. These men associate only with others in their unit for the duration of their stay at the Evaluation Unit, even during meals and recreation periods in the yard. Such separation reduces mingling and potential for trouble and prevents older, rougher returning inmates ("wolves") from preying on younger inmates. This is especially important in avoiding homosexual encounters or unbalanced relationships involving newer, more naive inmates. New first offenders are generally isolated from others.

Probably the event with the greatest significance during a prisoner's stay at the Evaluation Unit is the custody classification hearing. Assignment to a facility is contingent upon the case manager's assessment of a number of variables, the most important of which is his potential for violent behavior or escape. Prison regulations require that an inmate be notified forty-eight hours prior to the classification hearing. However, because having the hearing expedites assignment to a facility and getting on with life in prison, most inmates waive the forty-eight hour notice and have their classification hearings at the staff's earliest convenience.

A person's custody level, and consequently the facility he will be assigned to, reflects many varied aspects of the individual's case history: the results of the pre-sentence investigation and the offender's psychological evaluation, reports from social service agencies, and prior criminal history. Using a rating instrument based on points, hearing officers score categories of activity numerically. For example, if an offender has an outstanding sentence for which he is responsible elsewhere (a "detainer"), or he has been imprisoned before, his score reflects the severity of that consideration. Each of the six major categories is rated from 1 to 10 on a scale of increasing severity: *current detainer* (outstanding sentence elsewhere), *current offense* (the most serious offense for which the inmate is currently sentenced), *prior commitment* (the most serious offense for which the inmate has at another time been incarcerated), *escape or attempted escape* (from supervision, such as parole, probation, or furlough, or attempting an escape from an institution), *past violence* (use of weapons or causing harm to others), and *projected length of incarceration* (the amount of time the inmate is expected to serve before his release).

A score of 0 to 7 points results in assignment of community custody status, and the inmate will be sent to either the Lincoln or the Omaha Community Correction Center. Community custody is further divided into two levels: A, the most restrictive, is for inmates assigned to community residential work under intermittent supervision; B-level inmates may participate in either the work release or the education release program, requiring only intermittent supervision or none at all. Inmates are usually assigned to an on-the-grounds work detail when they first arrive at a community custody facility, and later may obtain employment or go to school.

To be eligible for community custody, inmates must be within one year of their tentative release date or scheduled for a parole hearing, and must be emotionally and physically able to participate in work or school activities. Furthermore, they must have served a sufficient amount of their sentence that return to a more secure adult institution would not be necessary.

A score of 8 to 15 points results in assignment to minimum custody (also divided into A, the most restrictive, and B). Minimum A inmates may be allowed to participate in activities outside the prison's security perimeter, as long as there is direct and constant supervision by correctional authorities. Minimum B inmates are also eligible to work outside the security perimeter, and because they are considered more trustworthy, they may have only intermittent supervision. Minimum A and B inmates go to the Omaha Correctional Center or the Hastings Correctional Center.

If an inmate scores between 16 and 23 points, he is classified as medium custody and is housed either at the Medium Security Unit of the Nebraska State Penitentiary or at the Lincoln Correctional Center. Finally, 24 points or more means classification as maximum custody, and, once again, inmates go either to the Pen or to LCC. There are some instances where custody classification grades may be increased or decreased because of special needs, such as those of the handicapped, or security concerns, or assignment to inpatient treatment. Changes in assignment to a particular institution may also be made if an inmate has a problem getting along with another and either would be in potential danger if they were housed together.

Female prisoners undergo an analogous evaluation at the women's facility in York and are classified according to the same principles. They remain at York until they are eligible for community custody.

Although the purpose of a custody classification hearing is ultimately to decide the location of each inmate, the in-depth interview of the inmate yields important information for addressing his or her needs. Attitudes about offenses, family problems, difficulties in care of children, marital conflicts, and substance abuse are all issues that require analysis and consideration by the staff. Since normally both a case manager and a psychologist are present at each hearing, the staff together can assess the individual's psychological state and make recommendations accordingly. Mild confrontation techniques and getting the offender to talk about the nature of his or her crime gives the staff insight into the individual's perceptions of the reasons for incarceration. Some inmates may be in a state of total denial or refusal to acknowledge complicity in their acts; such behavior would give the staff some guidelines about the person's potential for inclusion in inpatient treatment or intense mental health counseling. A sentence of first degree sexual assault or sexual assault of a minor child, for example, might bring a recommendation that the inmate participate in the inpatient sex offender program at the Lincoln Correctional Center. However, the inmate's refusal to accept responsibility for the offense would enable the staff to assess his receptivity to such programming. The hearing—which is really a very personal interview—provides much of the basis for the staff's understanding of the inmate's case history, life, crime, and attitude, and they use it to offer advice on how the inmate can resolve some of the unsettled issues that affected his life up until the time he was incarcerated. Such concerns range from child custody conflicts to rationalization for offense commission to conflicts in personal relationships—problems that tend to be more the norm for incoming offenders than the exception.

In the intake interviews I observed, inmates guardedly discussed their offenses or the circumstances that led to incarceration. Each one knows, after all, that the counselor has his "jacket" and full criminal history right before him. Most prisoners deliberately do not open up, striving to keep the case manager as distant as possible from their personal life. Of course, the case managers are accustomed to being frozen out, and make note if the inmate is unwilling to own responsibility for criminal actions. These comments now become part of the jacket as well.

After custody level has been established and an inmate is housed at the appropriate institution, he or she begins serving time toward reduction of custody until final release. Custody reduction occurs as a result of reclassification hearings. All maximum- and medium-custody inmates must be reviewed at least once a year to evaluate their custody levels. Those who are within three years of their tentative release date or who have been scheduled for a parole hearing are reviewed at least twice yearly. Inmates normally are promoted from maximum to medium custody when they have the requisite number of points, unless there are overriding circumstances why they should not be promoted. Medium-custody inmates have their custody levels reviewed at least once per year. Those who have a history of sexual assault, violence, or other assaultive behavior, and those who have escaped (or tried to escape) or have been segregated cannot be promoted to minimum custody without being reviewed and approved by a special director's review committee. In these instances, it is imperative that the inmate have a positive psychological evaluation or custody promotion will be denied. Additionally, inmates eligible for minimum custody must be at the receiving institution for thirty days, regardless of the length of their sentence (Department of Correctional Services 1988a:28). If they have no history of violence or assault, and their crimes were against property rather than people, they may be reclassified to minimum custody after this period; however, inmates with histories of violent crimes must have a psychological evaluation before they are eligible to receive a custody promotion. This evaluation is also necessary for an inmate who has been convicted of a sex offense or other violent crime if he or she wishes to be eligible for community custody.

While there is no set amount of time that medium-custody inmates must remain at that custody level before they can be considered for minimum custody, it normally takes about nine months. Minimum-custody inmates are reviewed every ninety days for promotion to less restrictive minimum custody (level B) or to community custody. Once again, a psychological evaluation is required for those convicted of a violent crime. Receipt of misconduct reports may hold an inmate back from having his or her custody reduced, because disciplinary action numerically skews the score on the rating instrument used for this purpose.

Inmates track progress on their custody promotions with extreme interest and care. I have had numerous calls from prisoners requesting that I find out the reasons for denial of a custody promotion. An inmate's privileges depend on his or her classification, so any wrinkle in the process is terribly upsetting.

Beginning the sentence

Arrival at the designated institution and beginning the actual sentence means starting a period of adjustment—whether brief or lifelong—that

revolves around the sentence imposed by the court. The sentence is calculated quite specifically by the prison administration, and each inmate's parole eligibility date (the earliest possible date an inmate may be
allowed to leave the prison premises although he is technically still in legal custody) and release date are based on the sentence structure. Release
signifies departure from prison with no continuing legal bonds. In Nebraska, most sentences specify a minimum and maximum number of
days or years of incarceration, but the actual amount of time served will
be based on jail credit (the time spent in jail awaiting sentencing) and
"good time" credit. Good time is defined by statutory law and consists of
two kinds. *Meritorious* good time is awarded at the rate of two months
per year; in other words, every inmate's sentence is initially reduced
each year by two months. *Good behavior* good time is awarded at a rate
of two months for the first year of incarceration, two months for the second year, three months for the third year, four months for the fourth year
and for any year thereafter. The difference between meritorious good
time and good behavior good time is that while both are applied toward
the date of mandatory discharge from prison (when the inmate "jams
out," or completes the sentence in full), good behavior good time is applied only toward the date established for earliest parole eligibility.

Parole eligibility is calculated by taking the inmate's minimum sentence (one day is automatically subtracted so an inmate is not kept one
more day than required by the sentence) and subtracting from that whatever good behavior good time the individual has accrued. It's like a bank
account in that the good time is credited toward the balancing of the sentence. Taking into consideration all the calculations of good time, an inmate beginning a sentence can expect to serve approximately half of the
maximum sentence received (assuming he or she gets along well). Good
time can be lost, however, by being convicted of misconduct violations
during incarceration. So an offender can end up doing most or all of his or
her sentence if the good time initially credited toward the sentence is
lost. Good time can also be taken away if an offender violates the conditions of his or her parole and is returned to prison. Depending on the severity of the violation, some or all of the inmate's good time can be lost
and the inmate held to his or her mandatory discharge date, when the inmate must be legally released from custody. It is also possible that a prisoner on parole may lose some good time as a disciplinary measure but
will not have his or her parole revoked. This means the inmate's term on
parole will be extended. All good time loss is calculated not by the board

of parole but by the director of the Department of Correctional Services. The board may recommend that there be a loss of good time, but they cannot determine how much.

When inmates first arrive at their assigned location, they undergo an orientation to familiarize them with the Department of Correctional Services rules and regulations, which are the same for all institutions, and the daily routine at their new location, which may differ considerably from that to which they had become accustomed at the Evaluation Unit. Since this process is too long and variable to detail for each institution, the specifics will be provided for only one prison in the Nebraska system, the largest and oldest—the Pen. The arrival of an inmate is of course accompanied by the arrival of the inmate's jacket, or full evaluation. The prisoner attends an individual initial classification meeting, which is the first encounter with the new staff. While becoming acquainted with a unit manager and member of the mental health staff, the inmate is reminded of his or her custody level, given a housing location and the name of the housing unit manager, assigned to a job, and given instructions about appropriate channels to use for questions or problems. A mental health staff representative informs the inmate of the services available—at the Pen, for example, there is no long-term therapy, only short-term or crisis intervention counseling. Prisoners are told that they can request a visit with the psychiatrist who comes weekly to the institution. The programs in which inmates can participate include group therapy sessions, which deal with anger control, substance abuse, sex offense, general mental health issues, and special needs (this generally serves the socially and developmentally impaired, and this group operates separately from the others since participants are often low-functioning).

Inmates who come in with a recommendation from the Evaluation Unit that they take advantage of mental health programming because of a problem with drugs, alcohol, sexual offenses, or some other problem, are strongly encouraged to agree to comply. They are not obliged to do so; however, if they refuse services, they must sign a form indicating that they refused, and they are told that they will continually be pressured to take advantage of such programming. While becoming involved in mental health programming is voluntary, the parole board certainly looks at the recommendations and, if they have not been followed, may opt not to consider such inmates for parole. Prisoners often don't realize when they initially refuse mental health programming such as drug or alcohol counseling—and most inmates do refuse, for they are in denial about either their crime or their addiction—that this is likely to harm their chances for parole years later. By the time they come before the parole board, they may have forgotten their initial refusal of treatment, but the board has before it in the inmate's jacket a copy of that refusal of treatment signed by the inmate years before.

Prisoners go through a second, more detailed orientation the following day, which acquaints them with rules at the institution. The "bible" is distributed—a little beige book, entitled *Rules and Regulations*. Inmates are encouraged to read it carefully and be aware of its contents, for violation of the rules results in misconduct reports, which may result not only in punishment but in removal of good time, thereby lengthening an inmate's sentence. Disobedience of a correctional officer, they learn, is expressly forbidden; for example, if a guard requests a search or "shakedown," an inmate may not refuse without being written up for a misconduct violation. Prisoners are warned at orientation that they cannot have money on their persons at any time, only tokens, and only $7.50 worth. Any amount more than that is grounds for a misconduct report, and excessive sums may even be considered evidence of an escape attempt. Inmates learn that they may work and spend money from bank accounts, but if they owe the state money for damages related to their offense, the state will take money from their savings or earnings, usually at a rate of 25 percent to 50 percent. At orientation, educational opportunities at the school are first outlined, followed by a review of security issues, the location of jobs, prison policy about disposition of earned income, the location of services, and so forth. Inmates usually sit quietly through orientation, but acquaintances send each other glances and knowing looks as they endure this "first day of school" kind of lecture.

Misconduct reports

Since timely release from prison is contingent upon not losing good time, inmates are greatly concerned that they not receive misconduct reports, or write-ups of infractions of the prison's rules for which they are charged, go to "court," and suffer the loss of privileges or good time if found guilty. The Department of Correctional Services Code of Offenses provides the guidelines for disciplinary actions for breach of the code. Every inmate receives a copy of the Code of Offenses upon his or her arrival at each institution and so is aware of the consequences of rule infraction.

Offenses are broken down into three categories, according to the seriousness of the violation. Class I offenses are the most serious and include violent acts that result in the death or harm of other inmates or correctional officers, e.g., murder, mutinous actions, assaults, possession or manufacture of weapons, and escape. Class II offenses are somewhat less severe; they are generally violations that are not physically violent or dangerous, but cannot be tolerated in a prison setting, e.g., work stoppage or striking, refusing to submit to a search for contraband, use of drugs or trafficking, creating escape paraphernalia, property destruction, demand for payment for protection, being in an unauthorized area, sexual activities, or disobeying a direct order. Class III offenses, the least severe, are infractions dealing with unruly behavior and disregard for prison policy and regulations, such as failure to go to work, gambling, tattooing, possessing unauthorized articles (or transfer of them), swearing or using abusive language or gestures, and violations concerning visitors, mail, or telephone (Nebraska Rev. Stat. 83–173 and 83–186).

Once a correctional employee has witnessed a violation of the Code of Offenses, he or she has seventy-two hours to file a report with the chief executive officer of the facility, and an investigating officer then looks into the incident within twenty-four hours of the filing of the report. The officer then meets with the inmate within eight days and gives the inmate written notice of the allegations, providing him or her opportunity to discuss it, and informing the prisoner of their right to request representation and/or witnesses at the disciplinary hearing. The inmate must also be given notice twenty-four hours before the hearing that it will in fact take place, although this requirement may be waived in writing.

Inmates who are charged with an offense then come before the Institutional Disciplinary Committee, which, at the Pen, meets three times per week. Because of overcrowding, this "court" is often backed up, and two concurrent sessions may be held. At the hearing, inmates may offer in their defense their views on the events which transpired. Witnesses may be called either for the inmate's defense or to help substantiate the charge made by the person who wrote the report. If the charges are dismissed, technically the documentation of the charge is supposed to be destroyed or removed from the file, but inmates complain that dismissed charges continue to be held prejudicially against them. For example, if an offender had several drug write-ups and then stopped abusing substances but was charged with some other conduct violation, he might fear that he would be considered guilty because of his prior record. In 1989, a directive was issued to remove misconduct report charges from inmates' files if they are found innocent.

Drug and alcohol use are among the most frequent misconduct violations. Accusations of substance abuse must be disproved if the charge against the inmate is to be dismissed, so inmates submit to urinalysis. Drug tests are all performed in a state laboratory where the substances can be identified and the exact amount found in an inmate's system can be determined. If a test is positive, a second one is automatically performed for corroboration of results. Charges of drug or intoxicant use that cannot be substantiated are dropped.

If an inmate is found guilty of a Class I offense, he or she may be given up to sixty days in disciplinary segregation (going to "the hole" or "jail") for each offense, and/or may lose up to a year of good time if the offense involved assault or injury to another. This loss is not restorable, rather it means that up to a year may be added to an inmate's sentence. Class II offenses are punished by confinement in disciplinary segregation also, but only up to forty-five days are allowed for each offense. Up to forty-five days of good time may be lost for Class II offenses. Class III offenses are punishable by up to thirty days in the hole or loss of up to a month's good time. Other penalties may include extra duty, the assignment of extra work without pay for up to thirty days, restriction of specific activities for up to ninety days, or a reprimand. Inmates are encouraged to settle their misconduct violations within the Unit Disciplinary Committee, a lower court, rather than take them to the higher Institutional Disciplinary Committee. Since hearings at the housing units can only impose restrictions and extra duty and cannot send someone to the hole or take away good time, inmates may prefer to settle their problems there. They do believe, however, that the unit hearings in fact impose more onerous extra duty and restrictions than does the Institutional Disciplinary Committee. They also tend to believe that it is nearly impossible to get a fair trial before either committee and that the outcome is very likely to be in the prison's favor.

Receiving misconduct reports is very serious business for inmates, for they know that their chances for parole are severely compromised by the write-ups. Ideally, when an offender goes before the parole board, it is best to be clean and without any write-ups at all. In reality, life in prison is so fraught with stress that even the board does not expect inmates to be misconduct-free when they appear for their parole hearings. Minor infractions tend not to be held against the inmate; however, long histories of write-ups involving drug abuse or assault are definitely frowned upon and do indeed affect an inmate's eligibility for parole.

The hole

When offenders require segregation from the general population, either at their request or because there has been a disciplinary problem, they are temporarily moved to Housing Unit #5, the Control Unit—also known as the "adjustment center," the disciplinary unit, or, by the inmates, the hole or jail. Thirty-six cells make up this oldest building in the entire institution. Located on the south end of the prison yard, the Control Unit operates at full capacity most of the time now because of population pressure. The arrangement is the old, depressing cell-block style, with each cell having a narrow metal door rather than bars and a tray hatch for food service. Meals are brought in by the unit supervisor and correctional officers. New facilities are badly needed for this unit and were requested of the Nebraska State Legislature in 1989. Although funding was approved, Governor Orr vetoed such an appropriation. The Control Unit used to be seriously overcrowded, but current policy, meant to avoid more problems among an already problematic population, is against double occupancy in cells. While there is no court order that says inmates may not be double-bunked, the administration is trying to avoid conflict by sticking to a single-occupancy cell rule. When the demand for space exceeds the Control Unit's capacity, the overflow of inmates is housed in a special high-security area in Housing Unit #4, where death row inmates live.

The hole has its own rules and regulations, which are issued to each inmate who is held there. In order to avoid conflicts between inmates, the two galleries at Unit #5 are given separate yard time (and antagonistic inmates within a gallery may be separated for yard time as well). For extremely problematic prisoners, "no contact" orders may be posted, meaning they may not associate with any other inmates at any time.

At Unit #5, inmates fall into four categories. In *administrative segregation,* inmates are generally isolated because they have come into conflict with other inmates. An assaultive prisoner or an offender awaiting some kind of investigation might be temporarily housed there. Because inmates are being segregated rather than punished, they may have certain privileges, for example, they may have a radio. Inmates under *disciplinary segregation* usually have been so placed in response to the Institutional Disciplinary Committee's decision concerning a misconduct violation. Their television and radio privileges are withdrawn, but cigarettes are now allowed. The maximum amount of time an inmate can be housed in disciplinary segregation is sixty days per misconduct report; confinement is possible for longer periods if the inmate has been convicted of multiple violations. Inmates in *intensive management* are considered high escape risks or are extremely assaultive. Real management problems, they cannot live in the general population. These individuals may have television or radio privileges. Inmates who are in *protective custody* are separated from the general population because they are at risk there. If an inmate cannot be returned after a short period to the general population and requires long-term protection, he is normally transferred to the official protective custody unit at the Evaluation Unit of the Lincoln Correctional Center.

Because of the variety of types of inmates housed at Unit #5, potential for conflicts and hostility are great, so extra precaution is taken in management of these offenders. If an inmate has started a fire, for example, extra care will be taken to see that he has no access to matches. If two inmates have threatened or actually assaulted each other, they may be restricted to no contact with each other or with anyone else at all. A large display board informs officers which prisoners have what type of restrictions, with specific management details including names of persons with whom an inmate must not come into contact.

Employment opportunities

Inmates have a variety of employment opportunities within the correctional system. By far the largest number and the greatest diversity are at the Pen. In addition to institutional jobs, remunerative employment is available through Cornhusker State Industries or private venture companies, where inmates earn at least minimum hourly wage.

Prisoners wishing to work for a private company used to be able to seek employment with LaPen, a clothing manufacturer owned by the JADE company in Nebraska City. LaPen obtained contracts from other clothing manufacturers and hired inmates to produce garments to meet the manufacturers' specifications. In 1992, LaPen employed sixty-three inmates who received minimum wage and overtime for piecework; now, however, it has closed. Irwin Woods, the other private venture once available at the Pen, hired inmates to produce wooden lawn and yard ornaments, Christmas decorations, trellises, and the like. For both companies, inmates could work a forty-hour work week, receive regular lunch and coffee breaks, and get paid for overtime. Irwin Woods closed in 1990.

Prisoners who want to work for private companies notify their supervisors that they wish to apply for jobs. When positions open, they are sent to the training program offered by Southeast Community College behind the walls. Inmates receive instruction in good work habits, quality control, safety, machinery operation, garment work, blueprint reading, work philosophy, and whatever skills they require. Once they secure a paying job, inmates must pay room and board at the prison out of their salaries, and state and federal taxes as well. Some monies go into a victims' reparation fund, and a portion of their pay must be set aside for family support or savings. This money is not available to the inmate until he is released. He can, however, reserve a small portion to spend at the prison's store.

Prisoners may also work for Cornhusker State Industries, which comprises a variety of employment activities producing items for sale only to nonprofit organizations. Numerous CSI programs are available, including metal furniture production (chairs, desks, lockers, and beds for all adult and juvenile facilities in the state are produced), welding (for example, grills for all state parks are made here), wood furniture (desks and desk tops are made; staining, refinishing, and upholstery work are done), the print shop (forms for state agencies are produced, including license plate stickers), the braille department (inmates learn braille and transcribe books, maps, and even menus by hand and computer), a license plate factory (all steps of license plate manufacture, from beginning to end, are completed), and a soap factory (it manufactures cleaners and janitorial supplies and also mixes paint for state agencies). Inmates earn between $.38 and $1.08 per hour working for CSI, and may earn bonuses based on their productivity.

Inmates not assigned to private venture companies or Cornhusker State Industries are assigned mandatory institutional jobs. These pay between $1.21 and $3.78 per day for work in the kitchen, laundry, library, or yard (cleanup and gardening), as a porter (cleaning), or in athletics and recreation.

One final area of employment is actually part of the educational system, and that is food service, a training program run by Southeast Community College. Inmates learn not only basic cooking skills, but how to cook for large groups. They are required to study math and measurement, to enable them to plan food purchase and cooking for large numbers. Upon completion of the training program and release from prison, they are qualified to be hired as chefs, and local agencies do hire ex-offenders from this program.

Inmates completing Southeast Community College training programs—whether in cooking or in welding—receive certification upon completion of fifty-five credit hours and may receive a diploma from the vocational school upon completion of seventy hours of credit.

Employment opportunities are greater at the Pen because it is the correctional system's intention that those with longer sentences to serve be housed and gainfully employed there. The minimum-custody institutions at Omaha and Hastings both have more limited employment (and educational) opportunities, primarily telemarketing. The women's prison in York makes jobs (primarily sewing) and some education available to female inmates.

Educational services

All educational services at both the Pen and LCC are contracted through the Lincoln campus of Southeast Community College. Similar services are provided to the Omaha Correctional Center by Metro Technical School and to the Hastings facility through the Central Community College. The women's prison at York has an education department that manages classes for women without contracting out these services. Inmates at all facilities receive pay—$1.21 per day—for attending classes.

The Basic Studies program at the Pen consists of adult basic education and high school equivalency programs. Adult basic education provides reading, writing, and math skills through the eighth grade level, while the general equivalency diploma (GED) program serves those in the ninth- to twelfth-grade levels. In prison, the two programs are not openly distinguished so inmates do not feel stigmatized or embarrassed about the level of their work. Prisoners with diplomas take Basic Review (at LCC this is called the Expanded Learning Program). This course is designed for individuals who have earned a high school diploma but wish to review for themselves or for college preparation. Since work is highly individualized, offenders proceed at their own rate and are not put into competition with others.

In addition to the Basic Studies program, a Literacy/Language Training program is offered at the Pen, as well as a prerelease program. English as a second language is also available, and while there are non-native English speakers from several different cultures incarcerated, these classes are presently utilized only by Spanish-speaking inmates.

The correctional system employs five full-time instructors for the Pen and LCC. In addition to courses being offered at the school, satellite courses are taken to special needs groups, such as the socially and developmentally impaired or mentally retarded at the LCC Mental Health Unit, and to juveniles who are housed separately at the Evaluation Unit there. Because these individuals are too young to take the GED test to earn a high school diploma, special courses prepare them to take the test in prison when they reach sixteen (outside of prison the test cannot be taken until a person is eighteen and his or her senior class has graduated).

Because school has been a negative or even traumatic experience for many prisoners, every effort is made to provide a supportive learning environment. No judgments are made about skills or abilities. Instructors expect that the learning process can and must be different for adults. Educating inmates poses special problems because of high rates of learning disabilities such as dyslexia and functional illiteracy: while only 10 percent of the general population is considered learning disabled, it is estimated that in prison the figure is 40 percent to 50 percent. Similarly, while only 3 percent of the general population is mentally retarded, this rate is up to 10 percent of a prison population.

In addition to the high school equivalency or adult basic education programs offered during the day, inmates may take college courses after duty hours. College credits may be earned in a variety of subjects and are coordinated by a special office at Southeast Community College, which serves the correctional system.

Programs available to inmates

Beyond educational opportunities, inmates have access to self-betterment clubs. These clubs, which meet weekly, are geared toward helping inmates increase their business connections with the outside community, enhancing adjustment, facilitating successful interaction with the nonincarcerated world, and promoting interest in prison programs and affairs. Eight of these clubs exist at the Pen (and at most of the other institutions as well): the Mexican-American Through Awareness club (MATA); the Native American Spiritual and Cultural Awareness group (NASCA); Harambee, the African-American club; Vets, a veterans group; Toastmasters, a club to foster public speaking and personal communication skills; 7th Step, a club aimed at assisting inmates upon release from prison; the Stamp Club, a special interest group; and AA—Alcoholics Anonymous. All clubs are permitted to have one symposium and one banquet per year. Native Americans use their club structure to sponsor a number of Indian activities, including Hand Games and pow-wows or celebrations. The activities and concerns of the Indian group, NASCA, are the subject of the next chapter, which focuses on American Indian inmates within the correctional system.

2

Nebraska
Indian Prisoners

The Indian prisoners in the Nebraska correctional system do not comprise a very large group, at least in comparison to other ethnic groups; nevertheless, their numbers are disproportionately large considering their population in the state. In Nebraska, Native Americans make up only 1 percent of the population; however, in prison they account for 3 percent to 4 percent of the inmates (see Table 2, Inmate population by Gender and Race). For the last several years, the Nebraska Indian prison population has maintained that proportion—in 1989, Indians in Nebraska facilities numbered 78 (3.4 percent); in 1990, 91 (3.7 percent); in 1991, 100 (3.9 percent); in 1992, 93 (3.6 percent) (Nebraska Department of Correctional Services, Monthly Statistical Reports, 1989, 1990, 1991, 1992). These figures are somewhat lower than those for several years preceding this study; in my 1986–87 study of Indian substance abuse, the Native American population constituted 4.3 percent of the total population (Grobsmith 1989a).

Indian prisoners who are sentenced to the Nebraska penal system were taken into custody in either urban or rural areas, but always from off-reservation areas, for only tribal or federal (Bureau of Indian Affairs) police have jurisdiction on reservation (trust) land. Of the four Nebraska tribes—the Omaha, Winnebago, Santee Sioux, and Northern Ponca—only the Santee Reservation in northern Nebraska falls under the state's jurisdiction. The Omaha and Winnebago reservations located in Thurston County in northeast Nebraska were originally under federal jurisdiction, but as a result of government policy during the 1950s they were transferred to state jurisdiction. Unhappy with what they perceived as racist state attitudes, the tribes subsequently underwent retrocession—

Table 2

Nebraska Inmate Population by Gender and Race as of August 31, 1992

	African-American		American Indian		Hispanic		White		Other		Total
	no. of inmates	% of population	no. of inmates	% of population	no. of inmates	% of population	no. of inmates	% of population	no. of inmates	% of population	
Male	834	34.5	85	3.5	137	5.7	1,362	56.3	2	0.1	2,420
Female	69	39.7	9	5.2	6	3.4	88	50.6	2	1.1	174
Total	903	34.8	94	3.6	143	5.5	1,450	55.9	4	0.2	2,594

withdrew from state jurisdiction and returned to federal control. Both are currently under federal jurisdiction for all civil matters. The Northern Ponca, restored as a recognized tribe by Congress in 1990, do not have a reservation within the state of Nebraska and so fall under either state or federal jurisdiction of the area they inhabit, be it another tribe's reservation (federal), or urban/rural (state). Native Americans who commit major crimes (as defined by the federal Major Crimes Act of 1885) on trust land are charged in federal court and, if sentenced, serve time in federal prisons. Originally the "major" crimes included murder, manslaughter, rape, assault with intent to kill, arson, burglary, and larceny (Prucha 1984:679); today, the number of major crimes has been considerably expanded, and includes murder, manslaughter, kidnapping, maiming, felony sexual abuse, sexual contact, or assault, incest, assault with intent to commit murder, assault with a dangerous weapon, assault resulting in serious bodily injury, arson, burglary, robbery, and felony involving theft of property (U.S. Code Title XVIII, Section 1153: Crimes and Criminal Procedure, Offenses Committed Within Indian Country, 1988 edition). Tribal courts—whether on retroceded reservations or not—have jurisdiction only over misdemeanors and offenses punishable by a maximum of six months in jail and/or a $500 fine imposed by the tribe (see Deloria and Lytle 1983 for an extensive discussion of reservation jurisdiction).

The Pine Ridge and Rosebud Sioux reservations in South Dakota lie near the Nebraska border, and both reservations are technically dry (alcohol is prohibited by edict of the Tribal Councils), so many reservation residents travel to Nebraska towns for recreation that includes drinking. The small stretches of highway from Pine Ridge, South Dakota, to White Clay, Nebraska, and between Rosebud's towns of Mission and St. Francis and the Nebraska towns of Valentine and Kilgore, are notorious as highways of death or "suicide roads" (Lewis 1990: 31–32). Intoxication and its associated legal consequences—driving while intoxicated, disturbing the peace, assault—fall under the jurisdiction of the city and county police in Nebraska. Consequently, individuals from the Sioux reservations who commit legal infractions in Nebraska serve time in the Nebraska penal system. It is for this reason that many if not most Indian prisoners in the system are of the Sioux tribes. (The state penitentiary in Sioux Falls, South Dakota, also receives many Sioux prisoners—approximately one-quarter of the prison population is Indian). In my 1986–87 study of crime and substance abuse, of a subsample of forty-five Indian inmates (then about half of the Indian population in the Nebraska prisons), over half were of the various Sioux tribes—mostly Oglala, followed by Brulé, Santee, and Yankton—and the remainder of the sample were Omaha, Winnebago, Chippewa, Ponca, and of mixed tribal affiliation (Grobsmith 1989a). Although there is some variability in this breakdown from year to year, it is likely that the greatest numbers of Indian inmates will continue to be from the Western or Teton Sioux groups since they are the second-largest tribe in the nation and the most populous tribe in the plains, and because large numbers of Western (Lakhóta) Sioux originally from the South Dakota reservations live in northwest Nebraska. The Santee Sioux, Omaha, Winnebago, and Northern Ponca tribes of Nebraska are much smaller, and so have proportionally lower prison populations.

About a third of Indian prisoners claim they are from urban areas, a third claim reservation communities, and about a third indicate that they move back and forth from the reservations to the cities, considering themselves to be neither urban nor reservation Indians (Grobsmith 1989a:289). They are similarly varied in their degrees of assimilation. The majority of reservation Indians are native speakers of their indigenous languages and are equally familiar with their traditional cultures and religions. Indian prisoners from urban areas demonstrate less familiarity with their native languages and cultures, and it is not uncommon for an incoming offender to begin his or her familiarity with Indian language, culture, and values in prison. The nationwide increase in emphasis on Indian spirituality in prison has resulted in a strong political and cultural identification that plays a significant role in rehabilitation for Native American offenders (Hall 1986; Great Spirit Within the Hole 1983; Grobsmith and Dam 1990). This strong ethnic affiliation has been reinforced by a recognition in the courts—and consequently in the prisons—of their special legal status as Native Americans whose rights of religious freedom and cultural expression are protected by law.

Regardless of aboriginal tribal affiliation, family history, or place of origin, Native American prisoners become unified in prison by virtue of their unique cultural and religious activities during incarceration. Wearing bandannas in Indian headband style and sporting T-shirts with the NASCA logo of the Native American Spiritual and Cultural Awareness group, the Indian population is one characterized by strong ethnic markers, desiring to stand apart from other inmates. Their distinction from the general population is most significant, however, in their practice of native traditions.

History of the Consent Decree

The unique status of Indian prisoners in Nebraska is based upon their having sought special protection of their religious and cultural rights in a class action suit filed in U.S. District Court in 1972 against the warden of the Nebraska State Penitentiary (*Indian Inmates of the Nebraska Penitentiary v. Charles L. Wolff, Jr.*, CV 72-L-156). In 1974, "as a direct result of this suit, Judge Warren Urbom issued a federal Consent Decree, the result of negotiations between the Department of Correctional Service's attorneys and those of the Native American Rights Fund" (Grobsmith 1989b:136). In the twenty years that have elapsed since the decree was signed, all the litigation involving class action suits filed by Indian inmates has revolved around alleged violation of this decree. The prisoners request that the prison be held in contempt of court for violating the conditions of the decree and be required by the court to rectify the unsatisfactory conditions.

The original lawsuit grew from an incident in 1972, when a group of inmates in the Nebraska Pen, agitated by the prison's lack of regard for their religious or cultural needs, forced the prison's hand, so to speak, and had their hair cut into traditional Mohawk hair styles. They were told to cut their hair because it offended the deputy warden, or go to solitary. They all went to the hole. Another inmate had five days of good time taken away for wearing a headband. This denial of the right to wear their hair long or in Indian hairstyles was only a small, visible, symbolic expression of their substantive concerns, which involved constitutional issues: what they perceived as discrimination against them as Indians.

They argued that Catholic and Protestant clergymen had offices and salaries within the penal system, while Indians were denied their own church and religion. They stated that they had been denied the right to have an Indian culture club, although other special interest groups, including the Jaycees, Alcoholics Anonymous, the Stamp Club, and the Gavel Club (precursor to Toastmasters), existed in prison. They complained of having no Indian visitors or guest speakers. They stated that they were discriminated against with regard to parole considerations, work assignments, self-betterment programs, and in assignment to work release. They stated that instructors and drug or alcohol counselors were exclusively white, and that the Indian population could not relate to them as they had "no concept of the Indian or his problems, which are unique and different from those of the whites" (Consent Decree, CV 72-L-156). They complained of movies shown to the general prison population that were degrading to Indians and perpetuated stereotypes.

On behalf of twenty-seven Indian inmates incarcerated at the Nebraska State Penitentiary, Larry W. Cunningham, a prisoner, filed charges against Charles Wolff, Jr., then warden of the penitentiary, stating that the inmates had been denied substantial protection as guaranteed by the First, Eighth, Ninth, and Fourteenth Amendments (*Larry Cunningham on behalf of Indian Inmates of the Nebraska Penitentiary vs. Charles L. Wolff, Jr., Warden*, CV 72-L-156, originally filed April 12, 1972). When Cunningham was discharged later that year, Enoch Robinson replaced him as the plaintiff representing the class action suit. In November of 1973, Enoch Robinson's name was removed from the litigation and replaced with that of Jesse P. Rouse (now Tatanka SapaNajin), who became the new representative of the class. In 1974, when Joseph Vitek became the new warden of the penitentiary, his name was substituted for that of Charles Wolff, Jr., as defendant in the final decree. This substitution turned out to be extremely important, because while the original suit referred only to Indian inmates of the Nebraska Penitentiary, Vitek was named defendant as warden of the Nebraska Penal *Complex*, as it was then called. The implications changed; the defendant represented a state institution, not simply a single facility.

Now, over twenty years later, the court has indicated that the protections of the decree are afforded only those prisoners at the penitentiary where the original suit was filed; but inmates point out that in the substitution, all Indian inmates of the Nebraska correctional *complex* were under the umbrella of the decree and so were entitled to its protections, regardless of which facility they were housed in. This has yet to be resolved by the court.

In January of 1973, the plaintiffs sought assistance from the Native American Rights Fund (NARF) of Boulder, Colorado, acting as an *amicus curiae*—friend of the court. A relatively young Indian organization, NARF had been founded in 1970 and eventually located in Colorado, a convenient and central location providing tribes in all directions easy access to legal services. They had been formed to provide legal services to tribes who could not afford counsel, and were dedicated to protecting the rights and welfare of Indians. Their goal was also to help Indians maintain their cultural heritage within a penal institution and be free of racial prejudice. The issue of possible encroachment on religious freedom among Nebraska Indian prisoners brought them to Lincoln, where they assisted prisoners in the Pen in filing complaints against the correctional system alleging a number of forms of discrimination.

After a year of inmates' attempts to get their grievances into court and the prison's legal efforts to keep them out of court, a nonjury trial was set to begin on July 1, 1974, before the Honorable Warren K. Urbom, Chief Judge, U.S. District Court for the District of Nebraska. As a result of that trial, settlement was finally reached and the Consent Decree entered on the docket on October 31, 1974 (see Appendix A for full text). The Consent Decree, CV 72-L-156, the legally binding agreement between the state correctional system and the Indian inmates, addressed many issues (discussed below) and continues to provide the precedent for determining how Native American cultural and spiritual needs within the Nebraska prison system (as well as elsewhere) are to be met.

The Consent Decree set a new standard for Indian prison rights throughout the United States and has been regarded as a model by inmates from other states as well as the administrations that confine them. States wishing to resolve conflicts with Indian prisoners in their facilities have contacted the Nebraska correctional system and NARF, as well as the author, in order to learn how a settlement was reached in the Nebraska system.

After 1980, the court recommended that lawsuits filed by Indian inmates concerning alleged violations of the Consent Decree and pertaining to the original class action suit be screened (in principle, if not always in practice) by the Lincoln law firm Cline, Williams, Wright, Johnson and Oldfather to determine if the grievances did, in fact, stem from violation of any of the paragraphs of the decree and to make a recommendation to the court concerning the legitimacy of the grievances and whether the case should be heard. At this stage, it is sometimes feasible for the firm to serve as liaison between inmates and prison attorneys in negotiations and attempt a mutually satisfactory out-of-court settlement. If such negotiations fail and the grievances are determined to be legitimate and have relevance to a particular provision of the decree, the case is then assigned to a law firm which is requested to take the case as part of their pro bono work for the court.

If inmates file a suit directly in U.S. District Court without having it initially screened by Cline, Williams, then it is up to the judge to decide whether the issues are worthy of being litigated and whether or not the court will appoint an attorney to represent the inmates. Where the case is accepted by the court and an attorney is appointed, in most cases Lincoln attorneys have been assigned to the cases. And the majority of Indian inmates reside in Lincoln facilities. However, in order to prevent an unfair burden of cases being assigned to Lincoln firms, and because today there are three additional facilities (Omaha, Hastings, and York) housing Indian inmates, the court appoints firms from other parts of the state as well. While this distribution may relieve Lincoln attorneys from always having to bear this burden, it sometimes makes preparation for court more difficult because of travel time constraints on attorneys. Also, because of the continual re-evaluation of custody levels and inmate transfers, logistics become unwieldy as attorneys work with several inmates in one suit, despite their locations at prison facilities in different cities.

The assignment of different law firms to represent Native American plaintiffs may be fair to the attorneys in that the work load is distributed and no single firm bears the responsibility for representation. However, this situation places the Indian plaintiffs at a considerable disadvantage, because while the prison is defended by the State of Nebraska Attorney General's office (and the same lawyer has defended prison administrators in nearly all the lawsuits), every Indian plaintiff has a new attorney who is totally unfamiliar with Native Americans in general and the struggle for their religious rights in prison in particular. In the six instances where the author has served as expert witness for the Indian prisoner plaintiffs, all of the attorneys felt considerably disadvantaged by their lack of knowledge of Native American religious tradition. The inefficiency of this system results in an inordinate amount of time being spent by every attorney to learn the background necessary to try the case.

Implementing the Consent Decree

The Consent Decree asserted that Indian inmates were entitled to wear their hair long and in Indian styles as a matter of their religious right. The decree responded to the inmates' claims that their First and Fourteenth Amendment rights had been deprived, stating that "officials refused to permit an Indian culture club; that access to Indian religion, including the Native American Church, was denied to them; and that they were discriminated against in various ways in the rehabilitation process including work release, work assignments, and the failure to provide Indian counselors and instructors" (CV 72-L-156, Consent Decree Oct. 31, 1974, p. 1).

Specifically, Native American inmates wanted the right to form a club, to develop a religious program that allowed them to follow the religion of the Sacred Pipe, to hire a religious coordinator who would represent their group and develop activities for them within the correctional system, to have access to appropriate education and a proportional percentage of Indian counselors and instructors. They requested cultural training for other correctional employees. They further demanded that a portion of the prison's religious budget be dedicated to Indian spiritual needs, such as bringing medicine men into the facilities to worship, and building sweat lodges.

The Consent Decree required that more Indian employees be hired, as administrators as well as correctional officers or guards; however, the difficulties of recruiting and retaining Indian employees has precluded true increases in Indian staff. Fluctuations during the last twenty years have resulted in periods of increased Indian staff, and the prison administration has been successful in convincing the courts of the diligence of their efforts. Indian inmates do not believe that the prison has taken adequate steps to recruit qualified Indian personnel.

The Consent Decree addressed the issues of training and sensitization of correctional authorities as a way of avoiding unnecessary harassment of inmates by guards. Unfortunately, the decree has not totally resolved this problem either, as Indian inmates continue to feel that their cultural practices are not only not respected, but are subject to abuse and harassment. One 1989 lawsuit involved inmate claims of harassment in the sweat lodge area at the Pen. Other charges of disrespect toward religious objects involve mishandling of the Sacred Pipe and improper shakedown procedures used by correctional officers. Today, a pipe carrier and member of the Native American Spiritual and Cultural Awareness group must be present to observe all searches of the pipe and its associated materials. Violations of this religious requirement do occur and are deeply offensive to the Indian population, indicating what they perceive as correctional employees' disrespect and disdain for their religious traditions. In 1990, another lawsuit filed in U.S. District Court pertained to prison authorities' requirements that the sweat lodge ceremonial structure at the Hastings Correctional Center be dismantled between uses, despite the location there of ceremonial objects the inmates felt belonged at the sweat lodge.

Indian Studies curricula are another area specified by the Consent Decree that continue to be problematic. For almost twenty years, Indian classes have been offered, first by Northeast Technical Community College in Norfolk, Nebraska, and later by Southeast Community College in Lincoln. Inconsistency in course offerings and availability have plagued the stability of the education program, and sometimes when classes have been scheduled and their staffing arranged, inmates cannot be freed from their jobs to attend them. Receiving appropriate college credit is equally problematic. Credits for two-year colleges on the quarter system do not always transfer to a university system on the semester system, in part because of the lack of certification of some teachers, and in part because of the discontinuity in credit-hour transfer. As a result, continual revision and updating of college classes occurs, with huge disparities in the number of courses offered from year to year.

The Consent Decree required prison administrators to allow Indian inmates access to their spiritual leaders, as follows: "In order to meet the religious and spiritual needs of the plaintiff class, defendants shall allow inmates access to Indian medicine men and spiritual leaders and provide facilities for spiritual and religious services, *including but not limited to the Native American Church*" [emphasis mine] (CV 72-L-156, Oct. 31, 1974, p. 2). The last phrase has been subject to misinterpretation. While the court indicated that religious expression behind the walls should specifically include the Native American Church, the court did not realize that Native American Church services, by definition, necessarily include the use of peyote. Since peyote has never been permitted in prison anywhere in the country, it is unlikely that its use would have been sanctioned in the Nebraska penal system. It is possible that NARF deliberately omitted exact reference to peyote in the decree, leaving room for future legal interpretation. But the wording of the decree made it seem as

though it were to be allowed. Peyote in prison is an issue of religious freedom that is highly complex and not easily resolved; the details of negotiations between prisoners and the correctional system are discussed in a
later chapter on litigation.

Although the Consent Decree allowed "access to Indian medicine
men and spiritual leaders and . . . *facilities* for spiritual and religious services" (emphasis mine), conflict arose about what constituted a "facility" for worship. Soon after the decree was awarded, Indian inmates
objected that they were not permitted to construct a sweat lodge for ceremonies, despite their having been awarded the decree. They filed a second lawsuit requiring an elaboration of the initial provisions of the
decree. The Supplemental Consent Decree was awarded "because of a
dispute about what that sentence meant." (See Appendix B for the full
text of the Supplemental Consent Decree.) The court ruled: "Upon
agreement of the parties that a sweat lodge is a 'facility' for the worship
of Indian religion . . . it is: ORDERED, ADJUDGED AND DECREED
that the defendants, their agents, servants, employees and their successors in office are hereby permanently enjoined and ordered to . . . permit the construction of a sweat lodge . . . at the Medium Security Unit of
the Nebraska Penal and Correctional Complex" (CV 72-L-156, May 24,
1976, pp. 1–2). Furthermore, it was agreed that "the defendants will permit routine access to this sweat lodge at reasonable times to be agreed
upon by the parties" (p. 2).

Norbert Running, a Lakhóta Sioux medicine man from the Rosebud
Reservation in South Dakota, came to Lincoln for the dedication of the
first sweat lodge at a penal institution which was built at the Men's Reformatory (the old Medium Security Unit), and first used on May 21, 1976
(*Lincoln Journal*, June 19, 1976). The Supplemental Decree stated that if
there were no security problems with the sweat lodge at the Reformatory, an identical sweat lodge was to be constructed at the Penitentiary
within a reasonable amount of time. In 1976, shortly after the Reformatory sweat lodge was dedicated, the first sweat lodge at the Pen was constructed, and four years later, in 1980, upon his fourth visit to the Nebraska prisons, Mr. Running dedicated another, larger sweat lodge at the
Pen (*Lincoln Journal*, May 12, 1980). (In trying to reconstruct these historic events, inmates at the Pen argued with one another about which facility had the first sweat lodge, the Pen or the Reformatory, but newspaper reports clearly indicate that the first sweat lodge was at the Men's
Reformatory.)

In subsequent years, sweat lodges have been built at the Lincoln, Omaha, and Hastings Correctional Centers, and the Nebraska Center for Women and community sweat lodges have, from time to time, been available to Community Corrections inmates as well.

Although sweat lodges now exist at nearly all the correctional facilities, problems of access to them continue to plague some of the institutions. Although the Supplemental Decree guaranteed "routine access" to the sweat lodge at "reasonable times," correctional authorities and inmates do not necessarily agree on what constitutes such access. At the Pen and LCC, inmates may go to the sweat lodge area for private prayer even when ceremonies are not being held; however at Omaha, access to the sweat lodge is restricted to ceremonial occasions, a policy deeply resented by the Indian inmates. Efforts to negotiate with the administration have failed. A suit filed in U.S. District Court in July of 1990 requested a motion to show cause why the Hastings Correctional Center should not be held in contempt of the Consent Decree, alleging that "HCC violates the 1976 [Supplemental Decree] court order requiring prison officials to 'permit routine access' to sweat lodges 'at reasonable times' " (*Lincoln Star*, July 26, 1990).

Another issue of access to religious services involves the inability of inmates who are in protective custody to use the sweat lodge. Although there are protective custody units at all the prisons, long-term segregation or isolation of inmates is achieved by placing males in a separate gallery of the Evaluation Unit of the Lincoln Correctional Center. Offenders who fear physical abuse from others are housed there, where they cannot come into contact with those posing the threats. While such separation is desirable, it means they may not use the sweat lodge, because such use would preclude the correctional authorities' guarantee of safety. Lack of access to the sweat lodge for worship has caused anger and irritation among Indian inmates in protective custody, and some have sought redress through the courts.

At the Pen, sweat lodge ceremonies are held on Wednesday evenings during Daylight Savings hours and on Saturdays and Sundays year round. Occasionally, medicine men travel from a Nebraska or South Dakota reservation to conduct the ceremonies. Reimbursement of their expenses has caused considerable conflict between the institutions and inmates, and the Consent Decree is continually reinterpreted to establish whether the prison is obliged to fund those visits. In the original Consent Decree, inmates are promised access to medicine men and spiritual leaders, but no precise directive outlined how such access was to take place. However, it was specified that a certain percentage of the prison's religious budget was to be set aside, proportional to the percentage of Indians in the prison population, *"to payment of fees and expenses attendant to providing Indian religious services or ceremonies"* (emphasis theirs). Since that time, the Nebraska legislature has specifically funded a portion of the prison's budget to pay for inmate religious services and rehabilitation. But payment of Indian religious leaders has never been a smooth operation, and year after year medicine men are turned away from entrance into the prison system because of financial difficulties.

In response to one particular lawsuit concerning the prison's obligation to permit a variety of medicine men to enter the prison, the correctional system developed a plan to make all clergymen's visits dependent on their voluntary services. In other words, any religious or spiritual leader who entered the prison would have to do so on a voluntary basis and was not entitled to reimbursement for expenses or fees. The prison's proposal alarmed the Indian inmates, for they knew that while it might not be difficult to locate Christian or even Moslem clergymen to come into the prison to conduct services (especially in Lincoln or Omaha), getting indigent medicine men to travel 700 miles round-trip from the Rosebud Sioux Reservation, or 1,000 miles round-trip from the Pine Ridge Reservation without paying their costs would preclude their visits altogether. Although this plan has never been implemented, the court neither accepted it nor rejected it, ruling only that the plaintiff's right to have a medicine man of his choice enter the prison be upheld, with the understanding that if the prison did not permit this, it would be declared in contempt of court. Whether medicine men were to be recruited to come in on a voluntary basis or be paid by the correctional system was not determined by the court. In a lawsuit filed in U.S. District Court in July 1990 by Hastings Indian inmates, "reasonable access" to medicine men was again raised, as a medicine man arriving at the prison with two helpers was admitted, but the helpers (who happened to be female) were denied admittance. Because of room for interpretation of the Consent Decree wording concerning "reasonable access" to the sweat lodge, conflicts are bound to continue over this issue in the future.

Ceremonial practices of Indian prisoners

The majority of Native Americans in prison are followers of a generic
Plains Indian religion predicated on Lakhóta Sioux cosmological structure and ritual (Schneider 1984). Inmates refer to this as the "Pipe religion" because worship revolves around prayer with the Sacred Pipe, or
čhąnúpa. The Sacred Pipe is a ceremonial pipe made, owned, and used
strictly in prayer, in a ritually prescribed manner. It may belong to a specific individual or tribe (e.g., the Sioux), or it may represent the use of any
ceremonial pipe, by any Native American wishing to "carry" a pipe. Pipe
ceremonies are commonly held in prison, and individuals at each institution are designated pipe carriers for that facility, receiving special permission to retain the tobacco and sacred materials (tamper, red cloth in
which to wrap the pipe, sage) associated with its use.

Tribal legends vary in recounting how the original pipe in their culture came to be possessed by their people. According to Sioux legend, the
tribe's appearance on the plains was guided by instruction from the
White Buffalo Calf Pipe Woman, who gave the Sioux the Sacred Pipe and
instruction in the Seven Sacred Rites that constitute their ritual system
(Brown 1971; Grobsmith 1981). Use of the Sacred Pipe is thus an important foundation of Sioux beliefs.

The Seven Sacred Rites are the Sweat Lodge Ceremony, the Sun Dance,
the Vision Quest, Throwing the Ball, the Girl's Puberty Ceremony, Keeping of the Soul Ceremony, and the Making of Relatives. Seven is a sacred
number for the Sioux in that it represents the four cardinal directions
plus the zenith, the nadir, and the center or self. In addition to sweat
lodge rituals, contemporary Sioux actively conduct the Vision Quest,
the Sun Dance, and the Keeping of the Soul Ceremony, while the others
have become less widespread and consequently are less well known by
modern Native Americans.

Being a pipe carrier confers upon an Indian inmate certain respect. Because the pipe is associated with particular rituals, viewing, unwrap-
ping, and using the pipe must be accomplished in a particular ceremonial fashion. This requirement sometimes places pipe carriers in conflict
with correctional officers who do not recognize the pipe's sacred value
and in inspecting it violate some of the religious conventions regarding
its use.

The other Indian religious group of significance in prison, besides
those who follow the way of the Pipe, is the Native American Church. It

is also widespread in the plains, very prevalent among the Omaha and Winnebago tribes and, to a lesser extent, among the Lakhóta inmates. Predicated on the peyote cult of the Indians of Mexico and Central America, the modern Native American Church has century-old roots in the plains and is one of the strongest anti-alcohol traditions at work in Indian families. Although it has a distinctly Indian character, it is based on Christian belief, with some branches more Christian than others. Services involve prayer to the Great Spirit through the ingestion of peyote, the mediator to God. The Native American Church is probably the most misunderstood of Indian religions, in that its reputation for peyote use has left stereotypes in many non-Indians' minds of hallucinogenic drug use, excess, and intoxication. In reality, nothing could be further from the truth, as participation is extremely regulated and the Church is explicitly anti-alcohol. The Native American Church is, in reality, one of the strongest sobriety mechanisms available to Native Americans.

Although Native American Church spiritual leaders (called "road men") do occasionally come into the prison facilities to conduct ceremonies, no use of peyote, the required sacrament of this church, is permitted. (Upon one occasion, one peyote button was brought in for a ceremony but was not passed around or ingested.) Some inmates state that there are so few Native American Church followers in prison that the ceremonies are virtually nonexistent, so they have become followers of the Sacred Pipe. Without road men or elders coming into the prison system with any regularity, they feel they must do the expedient thing and take advantage of the spiritual guidance that does become available to them. While they may experience some guilt about switching Indian faiths, they understand that during their incarceration they must avail themselves of what religious services are provided. Similarly, inmates who are not Lakhóta become Sun Dancers, although they may have been raised in the Native American Church or other religious orientation.

Among followers of both the pipe religion and the Native American Church, participation in the sweat lodge has become an immensely important religious and cultural symbol of identification with Native American culture in prison. The Native American Rights Fund, following its success in obtaining the Consent Decree, documented the process and procedures it used in Nebraska by filming the sweat lodge and interviewing inmates concerning the victory they had achieved in getting the court to permit its construction. Sweat lodge ceremonies are not restricted to the Indian population; however, a person who wishes to attend generally is a member of the Native American Spiritual and Cultural Awareness group (i.e., one whose membership has been approved by majority vote of the group) and is sincere in his desire to learn the Indian traditions in prison.

The sweat lodge is a Native American practice that has become a nationally recognized means of religious worship for Indians, regardless of tribal affiliation. Since a great deal of contemporary Indian religious belief is predicated on the Lakhóta Sioux ideology and cosmology, it is to be expected that this most basic and fundamental religious system would become widespread. For the Sioux, the Sweat Lodge Ceremony is a purification rite that is a complete ritual unto itself and is also preparatory for the other sacred rites (Brown 1971:31–43). Its purpose is to cleanse and purify both the body and the spirit, and it has played an increasingly important role in alcohol rehabilitation (Hall 1986). Attending sweat ceremonies has become the single most important and widespread religious activity among Native American prisoners in the United States; it provides a unity of cultural and religious expression in prison, despite the variability in tribal affiliation.

Because use of the sweat lodge ritual is widespread throughout the plains area, it would be inaccurate to characterize this activity as strictly a Lakhóta ritual; however, the Sweat Lodge Ceremony *is* one of the Seven Sacred Rites brought to the Sioux by the White Buffalo Calf Pipe Woman, and the majority of inmates subscribe to a form of the sweat lodge ritual based on Lakhóta practice. Similarly, it is the Lakhóta deities who are invoked in prayer, both formally and informally, as inmates pray to the great grandfather, *Thųkášila* or *Wakhą Thąka*, and end each ceremonial activity with the required Lakhóta phrase, *mitákuye oyásʔį*, "all my relatives."

As in most sweat lodges throughout the United States, sage, cedar, and sweet grass are burned for purification, to bring supernatural spirits to the prayer ceremony, and to impart strength to the participants. Use of these herbs by prisoners in their cells used to be permitted, but because of the potential for mistaking the scent of burning herbs for marijuana, that practice is no longer permitted. Burning these substances within the sweat lodge area also has caused misinterpretation and has been challenged in court.

The other Lakhóta ritual that occurs in prison is the *yuwípi* ceremony, a healing ritual conducted by a visiting medicine man. *Yuwípi* literally means "they wrap him up" or "they roll it up," and in this healing ceremony the medicine man is wrapped and bound in a quilt (Kemnitzer 1970). The ceremony is usually held in a totally darkened room and lasts all night long. The medicine man, through communication with the spirits, is able to obtain supernatural instructions to aid the person for whom the ceremony is held. His success is usually indicated by his appearing free of his bonds at the end of the ceremony. *Yuwípi* has been characterized by anthropologists as a cult; it thrives today as the major ceremony to diagnose and heal illness. It is particularly relied upon to cure alcoholism (Powers 1982). *Lowápi* ceremonies (literally, "hymns," "a singing," or "a sing") are also healing ceremonies to diagnose, cure, and otherwise seek supernatural aid. The main difference between *yuwípi* and *lowápi* ceremonies is that in the *lowápi*, the medicine man is not wrapped in a quilt and therefore makes no attempt to demonstrate his supernatural contact through breaking his bonds.

The majority of medicine men who come into the prisons are Lakhóta, and so their ceremonies are Lakhóta as well. Since *yuwípi* ceremonies require that a room be completely darkened in order to properly entreat the spirits, the prison must accommodate the sacred requirement of darkness. Great pains are taken to effect total darkness, for proper performance of such rituals cannot take place without it. This is especially difficult to achieve in a modern prison, given lighting from fire exits and hallways; nevertheless, it can be accomplished. Outside guests who attend such ritual functions are put at ease in the very black room; their attendance at such ceremonies is a reflection of the relationship of trust they enjoy with the inmates. During such a ceremony I attended, I was particularly impressed with the strong relationship most of the inmates had with the medicine man, and with the complete solemnity of the occasion. It was indeed a moving experience.

One potentially troubling aspect of prayer or pipe ceremonies in prison is the offering of skin sacrifices by Indian inmates. This practice requires that small pieces of skin, usually from the upper arm, are lifted with a needle and cut off with a razor blade. Although the taking of skin is common practice and is routinely done, the presence of HIV-positive inmates within the general population poses a considerable potential threat to the welfare of all inmates, but especially Native Americans. Outside prison, disposable Exacto knives or surgical blades are used to obtain flesh offerings; however, in prison, lack of access to the knives or funds needed to purchase them brings the risk of infection to those sharing blades. Ceremonies in which twenty individuals share two or three blades are not uncommon. The use of sharp knives, scalpels, or Exacto blades during these ceremonies is not viewed as a security threat by the institution, and no problems with this practice have occurred with the Indian inmate population, but such traditional practices may have to be curtailed or proper sterile instruments supplied by the prison administration if the spread of AIDS is to be prevented. I seriously doubt that correctional authorities will make it official policy to distribute disposable blades to all participating inmates. The identity of individuals infected with the AIDS virus is known to the administration but not to the inmates. So even if no Native Americans in the institution were HIV-positive and therefore no risk of the spread of HIV infection among them existed, other inmates do attend the ceremonies and are regular members of the group. Consequently the risks of infection to all are increased since Native Americans who may not be HIV-positive could spread the infection through the practice of sharing blades with other prisoners.

There are other rituals accessible to Native American inmates, but only certain custody levels of inmates are permitted to take advantage of them. These are the Vision Quest (*haŋbléčheya*—literally, "They cry for a vision") and the Sun Dance. The Vision Quest is one of the Seven Sacred Rites of the Sioux, like the Sweat Lodge Ceremony and Sun Dance, and like them it is widespread among plains tribes as well as those of other areas of North America. Traditionally, a man or woman went to a solitary hill to seek a vision. Generally the quest lasted for four days, during which the individual fasted and prayed. Not everyone seeking a vision received one, but most returned with supernatural instructions from a guardian spirit or animal protector whose songs and prayers were then the individual's own spirit helpers. Because prisoners cannot go into the community to seek a vision prior to the Sun Dance, an inmate who has a low enough custody level to be allowed to travel to a Sun Dance will normally spend the first few days of his Sun Dance preparation going on "the hill" at the Sun Dance site, smoking his pipe, and praying. The Sun Dance, also one of the Seven Sacred Rites of the Sioux, has increasingly become a general tribal celebration that is becoming more and more pan-Indian (cross-tribal). The Sun Dance is primarily a ritual of self-sacrifice in that an individual, making a vow to the Great Spirit, will pledge to fast, pray, and dance for several days in hopes that his or her prayers will be answered. Participation in the Sun Dance requires a yearlong commitment to learning as well as physical and spiritual preparation. Many inmates regard the ceremony as the ultimate commitment they must make in their struggle to achieve sobriety. Prisoners who wish to participate must have a low enough level of custody for them to leave the prison grounds.

Both the Vision Quest and the Sun Dance may be attended by inmates who have minimum B or community custody. Although inmates with higher custody levels may wish to attend—and have brought suit against the correctional system for allegedly violating their constitutional right to religious freedom—they have not been successful in persuading correctional authorities to accommodate their desires, for they are considered too great a security risk to be allowed to travel out into the community. Having the proper custody level is not a guarantee of being allowed a religious furlough to participate in the Sun Dance. If an inmate was originally imprisoned for a sexual or other violent crime, unless there is a strongly supportive psychological evaluation and the inmate has demonstrated that he has been successfully rehabilitated through participation in the prison's mental health programs, permission to travel away from the institution is nearly always denied.

Inmates who desire to take part in the Vision Quest or Sun Dance must initiate a relationship with a medicine man coming into a prison facility and contract with him to participate. For a year before the Sun Dance, an inmate may attend sweat lodges frequently and strive particularly hard to conduct himself in a proper and religious manner, as part of his moral discipline in readying himself for the ritual. Presentation of a pipe to the medicine man is required, and this too can be accomplished behind the walls. When a prisoner knows he will have the proper custody level to make his participation in the Sun Dance possible, he must apply for a special travel pass to leave the prison and even the state. Because no prisoners besides Native Americans are permitted such travel, inmates claim that the procedures they must use to initiate a travel request are vague. Even if the prison agrees to permit an out-of-state furlough, unless such a pass is approved by the parole board, it will not be permitted. The parole board has the ultimate authority in permitting (or not) travel outside the correctional system. If the correctional system has opposed an inmate's travel plans (by not awarding the proper custody level, for example, so an inmate is not eligible to go), the request rarely goes forward to the parole board. However, there have been instances in which the correctional system was not in support of an eligible inmate's travel but the request was forwarded to the parole board anyway, and it *did* approve the inmate's request. In such instances, the parole board has the final say and can overrule the decision of prison administrators. Most of the time, however, the two agencies work in concert and only in the case of an appeal is the board likely to permit travel plans the prison has disapproved.

During the decade between the awarding of the Consent Decree in 1974 and 1984, when institutional policy changed regarding travel away from the prison, inmates attended a variety of functions within the community. Some attended powwows on nearby reservations; others went on Vision Quests. By the early 1980s inmates were obtaining travel orders to attend the Sun Dance in South Dakota.

Now (as of 1984, when the procedures for travel were revised) inmates wishing to travel away from prison grounds to participate in religious ceremonies apply for a medical/emergency furlough, since there is no provision for travel to attend religious ceremonies. Some offenders feel this is both confusing and misleading, and it puts new inmates at a considerable disadvantage because they are not familiar with the system.

Nebraska inmates generally travel to the Rosebud Reservation in South Dakota for the annual August Sun Dance; however, Sun Dances are now being conducted at Macy, Nebraska, on the Omaha Reservation, and on the Santee Sioux Reservation in Nebraska. Furloughs to attend these ceremonies may involve less difficulty since the parole board's involvement in out-of-state arrangements would no longer be necessary. Offenders who travel to the Sun Dance share a deep commitment to make sure that all inmates who have obtained the privilege to attend comply with the regulations and do not violate any conditions of their travel, lest they jeopardize similar arrangements for future inmates. In the decade since such travel has been permitted, no violations or escapes have occurred. Two Sun Dancers from the correctional system participated in the South Dakota Sun Dance in 1981; in 1982, five attended; in 1983, six went; in 1984, four attended; in 1985, four again; in 1986, four; in 1987, four attended, one of whom was on parole; in 1988, two prisoners attended, one of whom was on parole, and two ex-offenders who had discharged their sentences also attended. In 1989, several inmates applied for furloughs for the Sun Dance and all but one were denied. The individual who ultimately obtained permission to go had been paroled to an alcohol treatment program away from the prison, and while he technically was no longer an inmate, there was reluctance on the part of the parole board and the personnel of the alcohol treatment program to allow him to attend. Intervention by the author, emphasizing the importance of this native component of spiritual recovery, finally resulted in a reversal of the decision by the parolee's parole officer, the treatment program personnel, and the parole board.

My family picked the inmate up at the treatment facility in Winnebago and drove to the Rosebud Reservation for the Sun Dance. Dancers must arrive early, in time to cut down the sacred tree and carry it to the Sun Dance arbor. When we arrived, gatekeepers checked our names against a list, indicating we had been screened and approved as invited guests. Signs warned that absolutely no alcohol, drugs, or firearms were permitted. We were cautioned that all campsites would be regularly and randomly patrolled, and any violators would be banished from the ceremonial site. Our guest pitched his tent next to ours, and we began a week-long unforgettable experience. We had the opportunity to meet many of his relatives and friends, sharing quiet but extremely intense days. Friends and relatives who wish to dance behind a Sun Dancer must first participate in a Sweat Lodge Ceremony. I attended my first sweat with a female relative of the inmate—who had never been in a sweat lodge before either—and together we prayed for him and others. It was not until after the ceremony that I realized that a relative of another inmate for whom I prayed was also in that sweat. Upon hearing my words, she chose to identify herself to me later.

The closeness and spiritual involvement in these activities was deeper and more magical than any I had ever experienced. But another series of events was even more emotionally overwhelming: One of the dancers that year was a brother of a very close Indian friend I had met during my stay on the Rosebud Reservation, when I conducted field research for my dissertation. The dancer was a proud and successful young man, a spiritual leader and an individual everyone respected—in great contrast to his brother, my friend, who had just been sentenced to life in prison without parole for murder. Watching the successful man on the same reservation where my friend had succumbed to the problems of alcohol and crime could not have been more painful. In some ways, I felt I had come full circle, with the close friends I had made during my research now undergoing the tragedies that, in my later career, I was studying. The week was one of peace and friendship as we camped in a beautiful location, one in which hundreds of individuals had come together seeking solace, comfort, and an answer to their prayers. We returned the inmate to his treatment program, after which he was set free.

In 1990, two inmates with minimum custody applied for permission

to attend, and both were denied because of having minimum A (more restrictive) custody rather than B (less restrictive). One inmate appealed
the denial of his custody promotion to minimum B, stating that a positive psychological evaluation had been done and that no legitimate reason to deny the promotion had been given. Although the inmate would
have had only ten days left of his sentence to serve after he returned from
the Sun Dance, prison authorities refused to reclassify him to the necessary custody level because of the severity of this offense. The prisoner
contacted me for assistance and we filed an appeal based on a strongly
supportive psychological evaluation. That *did* result in a successful reversal of the decision to deny the required minimum B custody. However, the parole board refused to grant permission for the inmate to travel
out of state, despite the fact that I had agreed to assume supervisory responsibility for him, and despite the fact that the offender was within
one week of discharging his entire sentence. Although we appealed *this*
decision as well, our efforts were unsuccessful; consequently neither he
nor any other inmate Sun Danced in 1990.

Until 1985, even inmates from the Pen (medium and maximum custody) were eligible to apply for travel orders. However, in 1984 a change
in Department of Correctional Services policy concerning custody classification and procedures for travel into the community was initiated,
affecting Indian prisoners wishing to attend the 1985 Sun Dance. Custody levels previously categorized as minimum, medium, and maximum were altered so that minimum custody could be either A, B, or X.
The new regulations placed greater restrictions on the number of inmates eligible for such travel: only minimum B inmates and community
custody inmates could participate in the Sun Dance. Prisoners who had
attended the Sun Dance as minimum custody inmates in 1984 now
found themselves ineligible to apply for furloughs if they were classified
as minimum A. Deep resentment grew among those Sun Dancers who
had attended in the past without incident and planned to attend again
but were suddenly denied permission to do so because of a change in policy. One inmate in such a bind filed a lawsuit, and, coincidentally
enough, during the trial his custody was changed from minimum A to B,
thereby rendering him eligible to attend.

Because today the Pen and LCC are medium/maximum custody institutions, no inmates may apply to attend religious ceremonies away from
prison if they are housed at these institutions. Since 1985, inmates who
are housed at minimum-custody institutions (Omaha and Hastings), or

are on work release or education release or parole, may apply for furloughs (no longer travel orders) to attend the Sun Dance. Similar policies existed at the South Dakota State Penitentiary in Sioux Falls, but because of violations, the Sun Dance activities are now denied to them.

Native American Spiritual and Cultural Awareness group

One of the provisions of the Consent Decree permitted the formation of the Native American Spiritual and Cultural Awareness (NASCA) group or club (the prison classifies it as a self-betterment club and the prisoners consider it a religious and cultural group). Classification as a "club" as opposed to a "group" is problematic in that clubs and groups have different privileges in the programs they sponsor and the regulations that govern those functions.

The goals and character of NASCA vary as the membership changes with the prison population, and as the NASCA executive board in each institution changes its make-up as well. And of course there is variability in NASCA groups from institution to institution. Although the group at the Pen is considered the earliest, NASCA groups at the other facilities serve equally in meeting the needs of their Indian prison population, and the basic goals remain constant: to provide for the rehabilitation and welfare of members through increased Indian awareness, to support and reinforce spiritual values and activities, and to lend support, encouragement, and assistance to Indian brothers and sisters. Some of these aims are achieved through education (theirs and others'), some are accomplished through practicing tribal customs that emphasize Indian values.

Members of NASCA share an interest in their status within the penal institution and in how correctional policy affects their desire to maintain their religion and culture despite their incarceration. Grievances have sometimes turned into class action suits as NASCA members explored the ways their practices required accommodation by the correctional system. Group meetings can provide a forum for discussion of important issues—members' experiences of discrimination or lack of sensitivity by correctional employees, for example—and ultimately result in changes in prison policy concerning their activities. NASCA also plays an important role in leadership development. An executive board at each institution requires that participating individuals take charge of programming, budgetary matters, personnel issues, and a host of other concerns. Officers take their posts seriously and with pride, and often become elected leaders of NASCA groups at other, lower-custody institutions as they move through the system. Being on the board and being an elected official is certainly a position which, inmates hope, will be regarded by the parole board as demonstrating their commitment to self-betterment and personal growth.

At the Pen, at LCC, Omaha, and Hastings, NASCA groups are highly organized. In addition to meeting weekly, they sponsor special events twice a year (as do all other self-betterment groups), such as spring or summer celebrations or powwows and a fall/winter symposium or banquet. Formerly four such activities were permitted annually, but the penal system has now limited them to two and shortened the hours during which such activities are permitted. These limitations, supposedly due to security limitations such as insufficient guards, cause considerable resentment and engender lawsuits about the denial of religious freedom. The purpose of the cultural events is to increase the public's awareness of the group's existence and efforts, and to bring members of the community into active participation in club events.

At NASCA's annual symposia, guest speakers make presentations, friends attend and socialize, a festive meal is prepared, members who have been extremely helpful are recognized and given certificates of appreciation, and honorary members (outsiders) are inducted into the group. During the spring or summer, a powwow or celebration allows invited guests to join members in dancing, drumming, singing, hearing speeches by prison and community leaders, and enjoying a festive traditional meal cooked and prepared by NASCA members. Buffalo meat, pheasant, *wóžapi* (traditional Lakhóta berry pudding), and Indian fry bread are commonly served and relished, and leftovers are given out in *wathéča* (take-home bags) in the traditional manner. In order for an Indian meal to be prepared, the prison must make special arrangements and allow designated inmates access to the kitchen for meal preparation. Sometimes the request to cook an Indian meal is denied, and the club must instead arrange to have the cooking classes from the prison's Southeast Community College training programs cater the meal. This offends the Indian inmates, who consider the serving of traditional foods an integral part of ceremonial celebration. Hand Games, originally an Omaha ceremony associated with mourning activities but more recently considered a social event, are also held on occasion and are attended by outside guests. Like the request to cook Indian food, requests to hold Hand Games are meeting with increasing resistance and have been incorporated into recent litigation.

The NASCA group sponsors activities besides their two annual club functions: visits by medicine men (sometimes for special ceremonies), speakers, classes, parole board members, individuals supporting them from the community, Indian mental health counselors, and rehabilitative therapists who work with individuals or groups. As other prison clubs do, they derive their budget from a percentage of soft-drink sales from machines in the prison, as well as contributions and special grants.

One of the most serious concerns about club-community functions is the prison's change in policy governing the guests who may be invited to attend them. For Native Americans, family members are frequently their most important visitors, both privately and at their club events. Prior to 1985, all self-betterment groups were allowed to make up guest lists for their special events that included family members. But because of a mishap with another club involving an outside guest, the administration has forbidden the inclusion of people on an inmate's personal visiting list from being included in club functions. The Indian population has been extremely agitated about this policy, believing it is discriminatory. While from the prison's perspective no discrimination in policy exists, the special character and cultural style of Native American activities does seem to be more adversely affected by the denial of kin from participating.

The philosophical grounds upon which objections have been made, both by inmates and by outside community supporters, are that Indian prisoners are from cultural traditions in which no social events take place outside the sphere of the family. The concept of "self-betterment" as it applies to all clubs may be applicable to NASCA, but Indian self-betterment only occurs as a Native American prisoner rehabilitates himself first within his family and kin group and *then* beyond, with more distant kinsmen and community. The strong emphasis on family and kinship in the indigenous Indian tradition is contravened by prison policy that bars family members from attending ceremonies, and so accusations of discrimination are repeated. Inmates who have filed grievances and have attempted to initiate legal proceedings against the administration have failed, since a lawsuit can get to court only if the inmates can demonstrate that their group has been treated in some way differently from the others. That the policy may affect the Indian prison subculture more adversely has not been considered a sound enough basis for a claim of discrimination.

3

Litigation Involving Nebraska Indian Prisoners

The Consent Decree has become the Nebraska prisoners' legal foundation for Indian religious practice. It is the main rationale, the fundamental basis for justifying and defining all Indian cultural and spiritual activities in prison, and inmates who fault correctional authorities' efforts to comply with it can file a motion to show cause in U.S. District Court asking why the Department of Correctional Services should not be held in contempt of court for their alleged failure to comply with the 1974 Consent Decree and 1976 Supplemental Decree. Numerous challenges regarding the prison's compliance have occurred—and are still occurring. Change in prison policy or regulations at *any* of the Nebraska facilities may be seen by Indian inmates as a new violation of the Consent Decree. Such charges are reported to the news media in Lincoln and Omaha, they are reported and editorialized in the *Lakota Times*, an Indian newspaper with wide circulation in the plains, they are detailed in the *Iron House Drum*, an interprison Indian newsletter, and they become public issues long before they even get into court. Many lawsuits have been litigated, some resulting in further gains by Indian plaintiffs, some not. Regardless of the outcome, legal action has served to inform prison officials of the views of Indian inmates concerning their treatment in prison, to inform the public about issues of religious worship in prison, and to heighten Native American consciousness of their own religious freedom needs despite their incarceration.

Legally, the standard for evaluating claims submitted by inmates was set down in a federal case involving prisoners' allegations that the friends and families of American Indians were not allowed to participate in religious services although the friends and families of Christian inmates were allowed to do so. *Native American Council of Tribes v. Solem* laid down the very important precedent for a cause of action under both the equal protection and the free exercise guarantees of the Constitution:

> Freedom of religion is one of the federal constitutional rights of prisoners. . . . Although prison authorities may regulate the exercise of religion for legitimate institutional needs, those authorities may not unreasonably interfere with the inmate's exercise of his beliefs. . . . A prison regulation concerning the exercise of religion that is more restrictive than necessary to meet the penal system's objectives is impermissible under the free exercise clause of the First Amendment. (691 F2d 382 [8th Circuit, 1982])

The Nebraska lawsuits depended on this decision in establishing that Nebraska prisons could not interfere with Indian inmates' religious practices unless those practices compromised a prison's penological objectives. This, then, became the test.

The Consent Decree was broadly worded, and the leeway in possible interpretation has left considerable room for differences of opinion. Lawsuits frequently challenge an issue that was addressed in the Consent Decree but may not have been specific enough to permanently resolve a difference in perspective between prisoner and prison administration. A review of the litigation emanating from the Consent Decree and other lawsuits relevant to it is a necessary part of the important process of historic documentation. This information serves both as a record of what has occurred in the Nebraska penal system, and a point of reference for other prisons and inmates.

Difficulties in applying the provisions of the Consent Decree uniformly across institutions has plagued the ability of the correctional system to comply. Since each institution has its own executive officer, be it warden, as at the Penitentiary, or superintendent, as at the Omaha and Hastings Correctional Centers, it is up to the administration of each facility to operate in accordance with the Consent Decree. Knowledge of the specific contents of the decree on the part of the correctional authorities is variable, however; at the Pen and at LCC, where the original class action suit was filed, prison authorities are more cognizant of the provisions of the decree and the potential consequences of noncompliance. They make extra efforts to conform, having been forced by the court to be explicit as to exactly how they are in compliance.

At the Omaha and Hastings Correctional Centers, a more recent familiarity with the decree, combined with a shorter stay by lower-custody prisoners results in less liberal interpretation of the decree and consequently more unhappiness on the part of the Indian offenders. Inmates housed at those prisons have filed two of the most recent lawsuits. Problems regularly arise when prisoners at one facility have become accustomed to the exercise of certain rights of worship and, upon their transfer to another facility, find that such privileges are not allowed at their new location. Grievances may then be filed since the new facility is not, according to the inmates, in compliance with the Consent Decree.

Lawyers from the Lincoln law firm Cline, Williams, Johnson, Wright, and Oldfather, which was designated by the court in 1974 to screen grievances by Indian inmates, established two basic requirements to determine whether a grievance is worthy of litigation. If a correctional policy is discriminating against the Native American Spiritual and Cultural Awareness group by allowing other self-betterment clubs or religious groups privileges that are denied to NASCA, that may be grounds for pursuing litigation. If a grievance concerns privileges and rights inmates have been awarded by the court in the Consent Decree but those rights are being denied by a particular institution, the litigation will be pursued. In these instances class action suits are filed, as they reflect a group's collective complaint about their facility's noncompliance with the decree.

The Consent Decree, issued on October 31, 1974, referred to a "class" of Indian inmates within the institution where the lawsuit originated, the Nebraska State Penitentiary. This particular "class" was defined, by the 1973 order designating the class action, as "all Indian inmates presently incarcerated at the Nebraska Penal and Correctional Complex and those Indians who may be incarcerated there in the future" (CV 72-L-156, Order Designating Class Action, Nov. 21, 1973). Any class action suit poses tremendous difficulty in that it reflects all people of that defined class, whether or not they are or were party to the original litigation. Some inmates preferred not to be a part of the class and petitioned the court to remove their names as plaintiffs. Perhaps they believed that if they lost the litigation, there would be reprisals against them as prisoners. Indian offenders who enter the system today are, in effect, parties to the original lawsuit and are treated in accordance with it.

Litigation stemming from the Consent Decree

Since the Consent Decree was awarded twenty years ago, many grievances have been filed by Native American inmates. Of course, some lawsuits involve personal matters; those are not discussed here. In this
treatment I have attempted to trace only the litigation stemming from
the original provisions of the decree that involved the celebration of Indian religion and culture. I have tried to trace these lawsuits chronologi-
cally; however, as several cases were litigated simultaneously, such a
strict chronology is not altogether possible. Some cases filed early may
have taken longer to get to trial and so have been resolved considerably
later than lawsuits filed concurrently. See Table 3, Litigation Stemming
from Consent Decree, for a summary of suits litigated (not merely filed).

Indian Inmates v. Wolff, 1979

The first challenge to compliance with the Consent Decree occurred five
years after its issuance. In May of 1979, Indian plaintiffs who were members of the Native American Church sought legal protection for a ceremony they planned to hold at the prison. They petitioned the court not
to allow the prison to "search the medicine men who come for the service, nor disturb religious articles brought by the medicine men, or either confiscate or prohibit the use of peyote in the service" (CV 72-L-156,
Motion for Protective Orders, May 7, 1979). The plaintiff's request that
the prison not disturb religious articles including peyote implies that
prison administrators knew of and were in accordance with the use of
peyote in prison (in theory). The affidavit in support of this motion declared: "A part of the religious service is the use of religious articles and
the substance peyote, which would be used only for religious purposes,
and which would be brought by medicine men who would travel from
some distance to the Nebraska Penal and Correctional Complex for the
religious service" (CV 72-L-156, Affidavit in Support of Motion for Protective Orders, May 7, 1979). This statement clearly suggests that inmates were expecting that peyote be permitted and were seeking proper
treatment of their spiritual leaders. Improper procedures for filing grievances and lack of proper representation for the inmates resulted in chas-
tisement of the inmates by the court and a denial of their request: "The
absence of involvement of legal counsel in preparing such pleading

Table 3

Litigation Stemming from Consent Decree (CV 72-L-156)

Year	Lawsuit	Issues	Ruling
1979	CV 72-L-156* *Indian Inmates* *v. Wolff*	Confiscation of peyote. Search of medicine men. Disturbance of religious articles.	Documents not filed.
1980	CV 80-L-324 *Country* *v. Bolin*	Access to sweat lodge. Access to sweat lodge by inmates in protective custody. Prison's responsibility for setting up or simply allowing religious services.	Prison not in contempt (dismissed).
1983	CV 83-L-572 *Tyndall* *v. Benson*	Access to Native American Church. Access to sweat lodge by inmates in protective custody. Bringing in a variety of medicine men.	Dismissed.
1986	CV 72-L-156*	Use of peyote.	Dismissed.
1987	CV 86-L-720 *Weston v. Foster*	Attendance at funeral of relative.	Dismissed.
1987	CV 72-L-156*	Admittance of family members to NASCA functions.	Dismissed.
1987	CV 72-L-156* (SapaNajin suit)	Bringing in different medicine men. Access to sweat lodge by inmates in protective custody. Inadequate Indian Studies curricula. Too few Indian employees.	Consent Decree upheld. Prison must supply different medicine men. Dismissed. Prison admonished to improve. Dismissed.
1987	CV 85-L-459 *Wounded Shield* *et al. v. Gunter*	Denial of request to attend Sun Dance.	Denied, but prison admonished to consider travel by Minimum A inmates [as well as B on case by case basis].
1989	CV 72-L-156*	Airing of DCS plan for volunteer clergy.	Plan neither accepted nor rejected.
1989	CV 87-L-482 *Moniz v.* *Goeden*	Harassment at sweat lodge.	Denied, but court warned prison to remove dismissed misconduct reports from inmate's jacket.

Continued on next page

Table 3 (*continued*)

Year	Lawsuit	Issues	Ruling
1989	CV 72-L-156*	Removal of tarps [Spiritual Arbor] from sweat lodge area.	Dismissed.
1989	CV 89-L-321 *Thomas v. Hopkins et al.*	Interference with medicine men and ceremonies.	Not heard.
1990	CV 72-L-156* *Hastings*	Interference with medicine men and ceremonies. Failure to provide Indian Studies curricula.	Consent Decree not relevant.
1991	CV 72-L-156* *Omaha*	Access to sweat lodge. Lack of access to medicine men. Lack of Indian Studies curricula.	Consent Decree not relevant.
1991	CV 72-L-156*	Harassment at sweat lodge. Abuse of sweat lodge area. No traditional foods. Loss of services of club sponsor.	Dismissed.
1991	CV 91–3320 *Dick and Dillon v. Hopkins et al.*	Length of powwow. Classification of powwow as religious event.	Granted.
1992	CV 92–3129 *Dick v. Clarke*	Length of powwow. Classification of powwow as religious event.	Dismissed.

*All motions arising from the original Consent Decree are filed under the original court designation, *Indian Inmates of the Nebraska Penitentiary v. Charles L. Wolff, Jr.* (CV 72-L-156).

means that the work of preparing such pleading has been wholly nonproductive; the documents will not be filed" (CV 72-L-156, Memorandum and Order, May 22, 1979, p. 2).

Country v. Bolin, 1980

In 1980, Indian inmate Reginald Country filed a suit (CV 80-L-324) against Jerry Bolin (then director of the Department of Correctional Services), Robert Parratt (warden of the penitentiary), and Thomas Mason (deputy warden) and Harold Clarke (associate warden). It charged that inmates had been denied access to their sweat lodge and that inmates housed in administrative segregation (protective custody) for their own protection were being unfairly denied access to religious activities. Although *Country v. Bolin* was not a part of the original class action suit, the issues have appeared in subsequent litigation that *has* been a part of the class action suit (CV 72-L-156 re: Tatanka SapaNajin, 1987; 660 Fed.Supp. 394, aff'd 857 F2d 463 [1988]).

In the final ruling, the provisions of the original Consent Decree and Supplemental Decree were reviewed, focusing on the issue of whether the prison was required to *provide* services for Indian inmates or was simply required to *allow* inmates to obtain their own religious services and not interfere in that process.

> It requires . . . that there be no interference with the Indian inmates making arrangements to set up services. It directs that the defendants shall allow inmates access to Indian medicine men and spiritual leaders. It does not require the defendants . . . to go find those persons to come in, merely means that if arrangements are made by the inmates for religious leaders to come in the administration will cooperate with that by not interfering with it and . . . will allow the inmates to attend services that are set up by the inmates and their spiritual leaders . . . It in no sense puts the burden upon the administration to . . . go seek the leaders . . . That initiative and those details have to be worked out by the inmates or the religious leaders, not by the administration. (CV 80-L-324, Transcript of Ruling, April 1, 1982)

Additionally, the ruling declared that while inmates may prefer to use a tipi as the proper facility for a Native American Church service, this in no way obliged the correctional system to erect one at its own expense. The ruling concluded that it was not the burden of the institution to provide such services or structures and that the administration was not in contempt of the Consent Decree: "The obligation to get services going is upon Mr. Country and others of his church, not upon the administration." Although the suit was dismissed at the end of presentation of the plaintiff's case on April 1, 1982, this charge appears again in subsequent litigation.

Tyndall v. Benson, 1983

In 1983, Dennis Tyndall filed a suit (CV 83-L-572) against Charles Benson, then the director of the Department of Correctional Services, Charles Black, then warden at the Penitentiary, John Shaw, associate warden, Kenneth Bordeaux, the religious coordinator for NASCA, and Dr. Robert Fox, chief medical officer at the Pen. The charges revolved around denial of "free access to the rites and practices of the Native American Church, to spiritual leaders from his own tribe, and to other means of religious expression in violation of his rights under the First and Fourteenth Amendments" (CV 83-L-572, Memorandum of Opinion, Sept. 16, 1985).

Because Tyndall had been placed in protective custody, prison officials argued they would be unable to provide him with adequate protection were they to allow him to attend general religious ceremonies such as the sweat lodge or a local powwow. The plaintiff indicated that his religious freedoms were being abrogated, since the medicine men being brought into the institution were mostly Lakhóta Sioux, an entirely different linguistic and cultural group from his, the Omaha tribe. The two issues—access to medicine men other than Lakhóta Sioux and access to the sweat lodge by prisoners in protective custody—appear again in subsequent litigation (see CV 72-L-156, 1987). A jury trial was held in January of 1985 and, at the close of deliberations, the jury returned a verdict in favor of the prison administrators (CV 83-L-572, Proceedings, p. 3). (One other issue in this lawsuit was a medical problem suffered by the plaintiff, which is not pertinent here.)

Indian Inmates v. Wolff, 1986

Because of the diverse nature of the Nebraska Indian prison population, some being members of the Native American Church and others being followers of the Sacred Pipe religion based on Sioux belief, litigation began to be directed toward different issues depending on the tribal background and religion of the particular litigant. After the Lincoln law firm Cline, Williams, Wright, Johnson and Oldfather had been appointed to serve as a clearinghouse for grievances emanating from the Consent Decree, the court determined that any claims made by prisoners that were not reflective of the entire class of plaintiffs should be appointed to different attorneys. And so began a policy of appointing separate firms to deal with complaints of Indian prisoners according to the issue in question. As a result of this decision, Stephen Speicher and later Charles Humble, both Lincoln attorneys, were appointed to represent inmates in cases regarding the use of peyote.

On February 7, 1986, Dennis Tyndall filed a complaint under the origi-

nal Consent Decree (CV 72-L-156) against Gary Grammar, then warden
at the Penitentiary, because of the prison's lack of cooperation in permitting "a limited amount of peyote, subject to all adequate safeguards and
necessary inspections by the Nebraska Department of Corrections employees, and to remain at all times within the custody of a Road Man approved by the Native American Church" (CV 72-L-156, Motion for Order
to Show Cause, Feb. 7, 1986, p. 2). Because peyote is not actually mentioned in the Consent Decree, a pretrial conference was held with the
judge, lawyers for both plaintiffs and defendants, and me. The discussion
centered on whether or not we could use the word *peyote* during the
trial. The plaintiffs argued that since Native American Church worship
and peyote are inseparable, the term must be referenced. The defendants
argued that since there was no mention of the substance in the decree,
mention of it should not be permitted in court. My concern about how
difficult it would be to discuss the use of peyote in prison without saying
peyote met with little support. The judge ordered us to proceed to trial
with *no* mention of peyote and in fact stated that if we used the word in
our testimony, we would be declared in contempt of court. This was my
first time testifying in such a case, and the ruling greatly increased my
level of intimidation. In the first hearing we used words like *sacrament,
sacred substance, herbal plant,* and anything else we could think of, and
we succeeded in not violating the court's rule. (During the development
of this lawsuit, other issues surfaced that required further delineation,
and separate counsel was appointed to represent issues of Omaha Indians *other* than those concerning the use of peyote.)

The case went to trial in December of 1986 (649 Fed.Supp. 1374 [USDC
Nebraska 1986], aff'd in unpublished opinion, 831 F2d 301 [1987]); CV 72-
L-156, Dec. 16, 1986). The defendant, Warden Grammer representing the
penal system, was accused of failing to comply with the Consent Decree
by denying the plaintiffs access to peyote during Native American
Church ceremonies. As spelled out in a Memorandum of Decision filed
in U.S. District Court, the issue was "whether the appellee in approving
a consent decree . . . knew, or should have known, that the use of peyote
in the religious services of the Native American Church was such an integral part of that church that consent to access to medicine men and
spiritual leaders and the provision of facilities for spiritual and religious
services included the use of peyote in the conduct of such services" and
"whether the prohibition against the use of peyote . . . interferes with
the inmates' exercise of their religious beliefs under the First and Four-

teenth Amendments to the U.S. Constitution" (CV 72-L-156, Memorandum of Decision, Dec. 16, 1986, p. 2).

Because the Consent Decree stated that "the defendant shall allow inmates access to Indian medicine men and spiritual leaders and provide facilities for spiritual and religious services including, but not limited to, the Native American Church," it appeared to the plaintiffs that denial of the use of peyote in prison constituted noncompliance with the decree. The petitioners made numerous requests to have peyote included as part of their church service, but they were always denied by the prison. The summary of the argument of the Brief of Appellant states:

> The members of the Native American Church so incarcerated in Nebraska are denied the administration of their sacred sacrament. The denial of this administration is a clear violation of the Consent Decree. . . . The Nebraska officials, in approving the Consent Decree, *knew, or should have known*, that the use of peyote in the religious services of the Native American Church was such an integral part of that church's services that the consent to access to medicine men and spiritual leaders and the provision of facilities for spiritual and religious services *included the use of peyote in the conduct of such services*" [emphases mine]. (CV 72-L-156, Brief of Appellant, Dec. 16, 1986, p. 5).

During the trial, inmates indicated their desire to accommodate the prison's concern for security in allowing the use of peyote in prison by proposing to ingest peyote in tea form rather than the usual mashed paste, to permit correctional officers to be in attendance at the ceremony, and to hold the ceremony during the daylight hours rather than at night as is usually required. The inmates also indicated that they would restrict participation in the services to those whose membership in the church was legitimate, avoiding opportunistic individuals who might want to partake of peyote but were not legally entitled to as members of the Native American Church of North America. The history and legitimacy of the church, the substance and meaning of the tenets of faith, the use of peyote as an anti-alcohol substance and its rehabilitative value—all this was presented in court. Likewise were the penal system's security concerns about the use of a substance in prison that they feared would be subject to theft.

The plaintiffs' case was definitely compromised when a Native American Church elder from the Omaha Reservation at Macy, Nebraska, appeared in court and testified that the local chapter of the church was opposed to the use of peyote by inmates in prison and would not bring it in, despite the fact that a Native American Church elder had stated that a church service "without the use of peyote as its sacrament has no significance" (CV 72-L-156, Dec. 16, 1986, p. 11). Although the Brief of Appellant maintained "the record does not contain one bit of evidence to substantiate prison officials' concern that the use of peyote in Native American religious services is at all threatening to institutional security," the Memorandum of Decision stated: "I conclude that neither the Consent Decree nor the First Amendment . . . requires that the inmates be given access to peyote for Native American Church services in the prison setting. . . . Not permitting Native American inmates a full Native American Church worship service is a serious interference with their free exercise rights. Nevertheless, the potential threat that peyote use in the prison poses to security, safety, and discipline weighs heavy in the balance. Many accommodations have been made to facilitate the inmates' free exercise rights, but, in the prison setting, these rights must yield to the extent that the use of peyote is forbidden" (CV 72-L-156, Brief of Appellant, Dec. 16, 1986, p. 15; Memorandum of Decision, p. 30; see Grobsmith 1989b:139).

Since that ruling, no peyote has been used in the Nebraska correctional facilities. Debate continues about the court's understanding of the centrality of peyote at the time the Consent Decree was written and became legally binding. While the court has indicated that it did not realize that peyote was a part of the Native American Church services (Urbom 1989, personal communication), it is certain that the Indian inmates did and the Native American Rights Fund, who drew up the document, did. Although grievances filed by inmates in the late 1970s openly assumed peyote was to be allowed in prison, and inmates state that prison administrators *knew* and *accepted* the prospective use of peyote in prison (one peyote button was brought in for a ceremony in 1975), testimony by correctional officials in this particular peyote case summarizes the prison's point of view: "Gary Grammer, Harold Clarke, . . . and Frank Gunter . . . all testified that they believed that peyote *was not contemplated* by those agreeing to the Consent Decree" [emphasis mine] (CV 72-L-156, Memorandum of Decision, Dec. 16, 1986, p. 26). What the parties knew or didn't know now seems moot: peyote is not allowed in the Nebraska correctional system or, for that matter, in any other, and it is doubtful that it ever will be.

Weston v. Foster, 1987

In the fall of 1987, inmate Troy Richard Weston filed suit in U.S. District Court (CV 86-L-720) over the prison's denial of his request to attend his father's funeral, claiming a violation of his rights to religious freedom. William G. Blake of the Lincoln law firm Pierson, Fitchett, Hunseker, Blake and Loftis was appointed counsel for the plaintiff. The trial was originally scheduled for December 1987, but Weston, who had been released from prison, failed to appear in court. The trial was rescheduled for February 1 and 2, but once again the plaintiff failed to appear, so the case against the prison administration was dismissed. The attorney and I tried to locate Weston and actually succeeded in finding out where he had been, but we were unable to find him in time to arrange transportation to Lincoln to testify.

Indian Inmates v. Wolff, 1987

Family members were once allowed to join inmate relatives in prison for religious ceremonies, but a change in prison policy now forbids family members or anyone else on an inmate's visiting list from coming into the prison for any activity sponsored by a self-betterment club. The restriction created a great deal of resentment and bitterness on the part of Indian prisoners. On May 14, 1987, inmates filed a grievance under the Consent Decree (CV 72-L-156) contending that denial of permission for family members to attend their functions was a violation of their religious freedom rights as guaranteed by the 1974 decree. Protests to the warden had met with little success, and efforts by outsiders, including myself, senators, and other officials were equally unsuccessful in persuading prison officials of the harm to Indian activities such policy represented. The case was set for hearing on May 15, 1987. There is no formal evidence in the federal record for the disposition, but an appeal filed by the inmates on May 27 suggests that the preliminary injunction heard on May 15 had been denied. To date, no changes in prison policy have occurred to allow inmates' family members to come to their Indian club functions. Rather, inmates continue to harbor resentment and have continued their protest (another grievance filed in 1990 cited this issue again). Because the prison's policy is not discriminatory against the Native American group in particular, efforts to reverse the policy through litigation have been unsuccessful.

Indian Inmates v. Wolff (SapaNajin v. Gunter), 1987

While the use of peyote and attendance of family members at NASCA functions were being litigated, grievances filed by Indian inmates in 1986 concerning still different issues resulted in the appointment of the Lincoln attorney Dana Baker by the court to represent inmate Tatanka SapaNajin (a.k.a. Jesse P. Rouse, a plaintiff in the original 1972 lawsuit), a Yankton inmate, and other members of this Sioux tribe under the original Consent Decree (CV 72-L-156). Several concerns were at issue: first was SapaNajin's concern that the prison had come to depend on one medicine man to meet with all the Native American inmates' religious needs, constituting, informally, an "official" prison medicine man. Although Indian religious worship may appear uniform to non-Indians, of course tribal and linguistic variances mean that religious concepts and beliefs greatly differ between tribes. The medicine man who came in regularly was believed by some inmates to employ *heyóka* spirit helpers and employed a west-facing sweat lodge ceremony while SapaNajin's religious tradition mandated his use of an east-oriented sweat lodge.

Heyóka refers to a traditional cult of individuals who have become known as clowns or contraries (Carter 1966; Grobsmith 1981). These individuals have received a supernatural vision that has instructed them to act in ways opposite or contrary to the norm. Their power is obtained from the Thunder Being, which controls lightning and thunder. It is common to see individuals who possess this kind of power display lightning symbols on their clothing or ritual paraphernalia. *Heyóka* are expected to be different—they may dance in a way opposite to what is customary for their gender, or may smoke cigarettes or drink during periods of normally enforced abstinence, such as the Sun Dance. Although there are fewer *heyóka* than in the past, reservation residents continue to identify certain individuals in this manner and attribute their "differentness" to their being *heyóka*. The *heyóka* is not to be confused with the *berdache,* someone who demonstrates the behavior of the opposite gender. Today the traditional *berdache* is classified with the modern homosexual label, gay.

The second issue in the SapaNajin suit was one that had been raised in a previous lawsuit: the right to participate in religious activities while in protective custody or administrative segregation. Third was the failure of the Department of Correctional Services to uphold its Indian Studies curriculum offerings; and last was the issue of the prison's not having hired a proportional number of Indian employees in the capacity of correctional officer or administrator. In the Memorandum of Decision, the court indicated that "the prison's supplying only one official medicine man to serve the needs of all tribal members *was* a violation of the plaintiff's (and other inmates') rights to religious freedom as guaranteed by the First Amendment and that the Department of Corrections was to develop a plan within thirty days to remedy this situation" (Grobsmith 1989b:140). It was not until two years after this date that the correctional system aired a new plan in court and evaluated the feasibility of the plan to correct the situation.

The issue of practicing religion while in protective custody was quite complex because no reference is made to protective custody inmates in the Consent Decree. But the class action suit represented "any Native American who has ever been in prison or will ever be in prison" and "all Indian inmates presently incarcerated at the Nebraska Penal and Correctional Complex and those Indians who may be incarcerated there in the future," so the decree was certainly meant to apply to all inmates, even those segregated from the general population (CV 72-L-156, Order Designating Class Action, Nov. 21, 1973). The prison's argument was that an inmate segregated for security reasons at his own request could not then complain about not being able to participate in religious services with the other inmates, since in doing so he might come into contact with a potential enemy. Keeping him from mingling was their prerogative. However, because Native American religious worship involved attending the sweat lodge, such participation necessarily meant mingling with other inmates. The plaintiff agreed to sweat by himself, but the court determined that "confinement in a segregation unit *did* preclude the right to attend sweat lodge services which would require mingling with other inmates" (Grobsmith 1989b:140). So while the inmate had been prepared to perform the ritual by and for himself, the court upheld the prison's denial of his right to do so.

The issue concerning the decline of Indian Studies offerings involved a detailed accounting of what had happened to Indian courses since the education programs had been transferred from Northeast Technical

Community College at Norfolk, Nebraska, to Southeast Community College in Lincoln: "Prior to 1978, regular and varied Native American courses were available to inmates. Inmates were involved in course selection and content, and assisted in suggesting instructors for the classes. After SECC took over the inmate education program, officials sought inmates' input less often; by about 1982 inmates essentially had no involvement in planning courses or suggesting instructors for the Native American Studies program" (CV 72-L-156, Memorandum of Decision, May 19, 1987, p. 4; 660 Fed. Supp. 394, aff'd 857 F2d 463 [1988]). The court determined that the condition of the prison's education program was "not impressive," and while a violation of the Consent Decree technically had not occurred, the prison was admonished by the court to remedy the situation.

The final issue, concerning the prison's efforts to recruit Native American employees for both administrative and correctional officers' positions, was also determined not to be a violation of the Consent Decree's mandate for the correctional system to hire a properly proportional number of Indian employees. The prison administration's claim that they had made sufficient efforts to recruit Indian personnel was upheld by the court, which found them in compliance with the Consent Decree.

Only one of the contested issues in the SapaNajin suit met with a ruling in favor of the plaintiff: that of having a medicine man of the individual's choice brought into the institution to meet his religious needs. In his order of May 19, 1987, Judge Urbom ruled: "It is declared that the defendant's practice of providing only one official medicine man who is known to have beliefs and practices contrary to those of the plaintiff and of other Native American inmates violates the plaintiff's right to freedom of religious expression as guaranteed by the First Amendment" (CV 72-L-156, Order, May 19, 1987; 660 Fed. Supp. 394, aff'd 857 F2d 463 [1988]).

Wounded Shield et al. v. Gunter, 1987

Another case was heard in federal court on October 27 and 28, 1987, involving four plaintiffs desiring to attend the annual Sun Dance despite their status as inmates. In August of 1985, four inmates—Perry Wounded Shield, Rupert Dick, Laddie Dittrich, and Cornelius Black Bonnett—filed a grievance (CV 85-L-459) after the prison denied their requests to attend the annual Sun Dance on the Rosebud Sioux Reservation in South

Dakota. The four plaintiffs contended that in 1981, 1982, 1983, and 1984, inmates had been approved to travel to the Vision Quest and Sun Dance in South Dakota, but in 1985 some applicants had been denied approval to do so. Three of the plaintiffs were in maximum custody at the time of the filing; Wounded Shield was minimum A, the most restrictive of the minimum-custody levels. The prison denied all of the requests on the basis of a new policy that only individuals with minimum B or community custody were eligible to travel out of state on furloughs. While it was not really surprising that the prison would not permit the maximum-custody inmates to leave the prison facilities, the litigant who had minimum A custody was disheartened because he had previously been allowed to attend a Sun Dance as a minimum-custody inmate. Originally, there were only three major custody classifications: maximum, medium, and minimum. In 1985, minimum custody was subdivided into A, B, and X (the latter soon became obsolete). The plaintiff who once was eligible to attend as simply a minimum-custody inmate now found himself ineligible because he had been classified at the more restrictive minimum A custody level.

Because of the likelihood that the correctional system would not allow medium- or maximum-custody inmates to travel out of state for a religious ceremony, the attorney for the plaintiffs, Michael Higgins of the Omaha law firm Kutak, Rock and Campbell, with myself as liaison, initiated a discussion with the plaintiffs concerning the possibility of an out-of-court settlement, whereby the inmates would agree to drop their request for medium- and maximum-custody inmates to go to the Sun Dance if the prison were to allow minimum A inmates (who, after all, had once attended the Sun Dance) to go. Attorneys for the prison were unable to obtain a settlement, and on October 27 and 28, 1987, an evidentiary hearing was held under Magistrate David L. Piester.

The prison maintained that inmates with higher than minimum A custody posed too great a security risk to the public. Inmates offered to fund their own travel and pay the extra costs of necessary correctional officers and to be jailed in the evening if necessary at a nearby reservation jail, and they stated in court their commitment to "run down" anybody who tried to escape. They demonstrated that in all the years inmates had attended the Sun Dance, there had never been an escape or mishap, with all inmates returning to the correctional system on time and as required. Nevertheless, in January of 1988, the judge's Report and Recommendation was issued:

The interests advanced by the defendant in support of the policies at issue in this case are security of the inmate, safety of the public and the inmate, and financial considerations. There can be no doubt that these are legitimate interests in administering a penal institution. It is equally clear that the defendant's policy of not granting furloughs to inmates classified as minimum A or higher is rationally related to these legitimate interests. . . . In addition, the facts that such inmates have not demonstrated trustworthiness, would be in contact with members of the public, would be in an area which does not have an armed security perimeter, and in which some weapons are present, certainly bear heavily on security concerns. (CV 85-L-459, Report and Recommendation, Jan. 5, 1989, p. 8).

However, the court did also indicate that "regarding Minimum A custody inmates, it may be that some changes in the policy, or perhaps the allowance of individual case-by-case determinations regarding exceptions might be considered. Indeed the rehabilitative worth of the Sun Dance and Vision Quest would seem to provide reason for such changes" (p. 10). Ironically, two days prior to the Sun Dance, Wounded Shield's custody was changed from minimum A to B, and he was permitted to attend. No changes in the policy concerning other minimum custody inmates has occurred, but even now grievances continue to be filed by those Native Americans who feel they have been wrongfully denied their right to worship as guaranteed to them by the First Amendment, the Consent Decree, and the 1978 American Indian Religious Freedom Act (Public Law 95–341).

Indian Inmates v. Wolff, 1989

On January 6, 1989, the Department of Correctional Services presented a plan to obtain a variety of medicine men, which they had prepared in response to the court order two years before concerning Tatanka SapaNajin's right to have a medicine man of his choice come to the prison. The plan presented by the prison aimed to solve the problem of bringing in different clergymen at state expense in a uniform way: "It is the Department's position . . . that the most equitable way to treat all religions would be to implement a system of volunteer religious programs, not in-

volving the expenditure of state funds for religious ceremonies" (CV 72-
L-156, Plan, p. 2).

Their rationale was that because there were so many different religious groups in prison, it would be impossible to bring in a clergyman
suitable to each inmate, so state support should be eliminated entirely
for religious programming and only volunteer clergymen be recruited.
No attempt had been made by the prison administration to determine
whether such volunteers for the Native American community might be
locally available. In court, testimony revealed that few medicine men
resided in the Lincoln or Omaha area, that travel to Lincoln for a spiritual leader required a round trip of 700 to 1,000 miles, and that most
medicine men were indigent and would not be able to afford the expense
involved. The result would be, in practical terms, the total elimination
of visits by medicine men to Native American inmates.

While the court appreciated the prison's need to apply a policy uniformly to all prisoners, it also acknowledged that implementation of this
plan *would* adversely affect Indian inmates. Furthermore, the Nebraska
Legislature specifically allots money to the correctional system for religious rehabilitation, so it did not appear reasonable to alter the state government's stipulation about how state funds should be expended.
Finally, two years earlier, in May 1987, the court had stipulated SapaNajin's right to have a medicine man of his choice brought to the institution
because the prison was violating his right to freedom of religious expression as guaranteed by the First Amendment. The judge ordered the prison to submit a Plan for Implementing Judgment within thirty days.

Nearly two years after the plan was to have been submitted, the judge
indicated in his ruling that he accepted (sustained) the plaintiff's objections to it. However, he also determined that he would not ask the Department of Correctional Services to design yet another plan, nor would
he order that the plan not be implemented. Instead, he ruled:"For purposes of this case the critical feature is that the defendant must comply
with the order that it ensure that a medicine man or medicine men are
provided in a manner that reasonably accommodates the religious beliefs of the plaintiff. IT IS THEREFORE ORDERED: 1. that the defendant
has presented a specific plan in response to the order of May 18, 1987; 2.
that the objection to plan, filing 158, is sustained; 3. that the proposed
plan is neither approved nor disapproved" (CV 72-L-156, Memorandum
and Order on the Plan for Implementing Judgment, Jan. 10, 1989, p. 5).

The final admonition of the court was that the prison could go ahead and implement this or any other plan it wanted, but if the plaintiff's religious needs as required by the court order were not met, the defendant would be in contempt of court. As of this writing, the Department of Correctional Services' plan for a volunteer clergy system has not been implemented. The current practice of bringing in a variety of medicine men to serve the varied Indian population has been maintained as it has been done ever since SapaNajin's case first went to trial.

Moniz et al. v. Goeden, 1989

In 1989 inmates initiated a lawsuit in federal court involving claims of harassment in the sweat lodge area (CV 87-L-482). During a regular sweat lodge ceremony, which took place on January 1, 1987, a correctional officer who came to the sweat lodge area to do a count thought he smelled a substance resembling marijuana, and he reported to his superior officer his suspicion of drug use. The officer instructed him to write up the participating inmates. An incident report was filed by the correctional employee, the prisoners were charged with a misconduct report, and all inmates in the sweat lodge area were forced to submit to a urinalysis to detect drug use. The inmates were irate and insulted, believing that if the prison had conducted the training it had been ordered by the court to do, the guard would have recognized the burning of sage during the ceremony, precluding such accusations. Furthermore, they were infuriated that the guard made no inquiry about his concerns. Rather, he said nothing and left the sweat lodge area, and later that day all attending inmates received notice that they were to report for a urine test. To make matters worse, the guard was not informed by his superior officer of what might be going on, despite the fact that the superior officer had experience at the sweat lodge and *was* familiar with the scent of burning sage. The inmates' grievances stated that they had suffered irreparable damage and harm and their religious activities had been demeaned and degraded.

Thomas M. Maul, an attorney from the firm Leininger, Grant, Rogers, and Maul of Columbus, Nebraska, was appointed counsel for the plaintiffs on February 17, 1988. He pursued an investigation and prepared for trial, which was held on February 13, 1989. The prisoners' grievance had already been investigated by the state ombudsman's office, and full, transcribed interviews were available from the ombudsman's meetings with all plaintiffs and defendants. Urinalysis revealed that of the twelve inmates at the sweat lodge area that day, ten tested negative for drugs, one tested positive, and one inmate was convicted of the misconduct charge for refusing to submit to a urine test on religious grounds. The inmate who tested positive had been present to assist outside the with fire and rocks but had not been inside the sweat lodge at all that day. (Inmates who feel that they are not in the appropriate mental state may help out at a sweat lodge but will not go inside to participate in the actual ceremony.) The other inmates, who had been inside during a ceremony, were deeply angered that the ceremony and its participants had been suspected out of the guard's ignorance, and resented the fact that now their sweat lodge practices would come under exceptional scrutiny and suspicion because an inmate who wasn't even inside had received a "dirty UA" (urinalysis).

The main issues in court revolved around whether a correctional officer was engaging in activity that could be characterized as harassment, or whether his actions were fair in the performance of his duty to provide prison security: "Whether or not the conduct of the Defendant Goeden in the reporting and writing-up of the Plaintiffs for alleged drug abuse and the conduct of the Defendant Vinci in telling Goeden to prepare write-ups on said Plaintiffs, violated the constitutionally protected right of the Plaintiffs to exercise and practice their religious beliefs" (CV 87-L-482, Amendment to Order Pretrial Conference, Feb. 6, 1989, p. 1).

At the close of the plaintiffs' case, the judge indicated that there was not sufficient evidence to show that a violation of the inmates' constitutional rights to practice their religion had occurred, and the case was dismissed. The judge did declare that there needed to be more training of guards to make sure they understand what goes on at the sweat lodge and to enable them to differentiate between the scent of sage or cedar and the smell of illegal drugs. He also indicated his dismay at discovering, through inmate testimony, that misconduct reports which were dismissed against an inmate remained in his file for the parole board to see, thereby possibly prejudicing the board despite an inmate's innocence. So although the plaintiffs' case was lost, some of the issues motivating the suit—the need for increased awareness on the part of correctional officers about Indian spiritual activities, and the need to have dismissed misconduct reports removed from an inmate's file—were certainly addressed. Correctional policy is now to shred all dismissed misconduct reports in an inmate's jacket so that they cannot be seen or considered when an inmate appears before the board of parole.

Indian Inmates v. Wolff, 1989

On October 11, 1989, Michael Dillon filed a motion for an order to find defendants Harold Clarke, warden of the Nebraska State Penitentiary, and David Henry in contempt of the Consent Decree of 1974 and Supplemental Decree of 1976 (filed under CV 72-L-156). In July of that year, a group of inmates in the sweat lodge area had been ordered to take down a lean-to, which they referred to as a Spiritual Arbor, made of tarps provided to them to keep wood for the sweat lodge dry. The inmates were informed that the tarp posed a security risk and were ordered to take it down. Later, the tarps were returned, but the inmates were admonished: "Tarps have been returned for their original use of covering firewood from rain; however, if said tarps are used for a lean-to or shade, they will be confiscated" (response to Inmate Request, July 25, 1989). The inmates charged that the "defendants have interfered with and infringed upon the Indian inmates' religious rights by ordering the dismantling of the structure and refusal to allow the structure to be rebuilt" (CV 72-L-156, Report and Recommendation, Dec. 20, 1989, p. 5).

An evidentiary hearing was held before Magistrate David L. Piester on November 6 and 7, 1989. In his Report and Recommendation, the magistrate declared: "There is nothing in the language of either the 1974 decree or the supplemental decree . . . that would require the defendants to allow such a structure to remain on the sweat lodge grounds. There is no evidence that the structure was intended for the purposes now asserted by the plaintiff, nor is there evidence that the 'lean-to' is a necessary part of the sweat lodge ceremony itself" (pp. 4–5). The magistrate concluded that the removal of the Spiritual Arbor did not constitute a violation of the Consent Decree and consequently denied the plaintiffs' motion for an order to find the correctional officials in contempt of the court order. His recommendation, which was supported by Judge Warren K. Urbom, was based on the finding that the lean-to was an unauthorized structure that prevented one guard tower from seeing what was taking place under it and obstructed another guard tower's view of the area, both of which were believed to present a security risk.

Interestingly enough, the magistrate's recommendation included reference to the peyote issue as well: "As noted by this court in prior litigation concerning the use of peyote as a sacrament in the Native American Church, the substantial time lag, in this case nearly thirteen to fifteen years, between the consent decrees and the asserted necessity of the 'lean-to' suggests that the plaintiff's 'view is a recent invention' . . . and that such a structure was not contemplated by the parties to those decrees" (CV 72-L-156, Report and Recommendation, Dec. 20, 1989, p. 5). This statement is evidence that the court still believes that omission of the term *peyote* from the original language of the 1974 and 1976 decrees suggests that inmates had no intention of including its use in the provisions of the Consent Decree, when it has been shown elsewhere that the inmates' request for Native American Church ceremonies *did* include the assumption that peyote was a required sacrament in the Church, and indeed, the prison officials knew this as well.

Thomas v. Hopkins et al., 1989

Another 1989 lawsuit was filed on behalf of Indian inmates by Randy Thomas as next friend for the Native American Spiritual and Cultural Awareness group against Assistant Warden Frank Hopkins, Director Frank Gunter, Harold Clarke, warden of the penitentiary, Karen Shortridge, superintendent of the Omaha Correctional Center, and Major Naylors, a correctional officer. The suit, CV 89-L-321, filed on June 29, 1989, enumerates a series of grievances concerning the prison's alleged interference with inmates' efforts to bring in medicine men, have Hand Games, and conduct regular sweat lodge ceremonies. While inmates were once permitted four club events each year, now each club has been cut back to two, so a recent request to hold a Hand Game was denied, creating bitterness about being deprived of activities they once were permitted. The different NASCA groups are required to help share the costs of bringing in a spiritual leader, and a planned visit by a medicine man was cancelled by the prison because the club budgets were not able to afford these expenses until the new fiscal year budget began a bit later. The prison had denied the medicine man's visit, but the medicine man was also unable to attend due to the intensity of his preparations for the Sun Dance. This case was never heard in court.

Indian Inmates v. Wolff (Hastings), 1990

On July 23, 1990, Indian inmates from the Hastings Correctional Center filed a motion in U.S. District Court for the prison to show cause why prison officials should not be held in contempt of court for violation of the 1974 Consent Decree and 1976 Supplemental Consent Decree pertaining to sweat lodges. Filed by Richard Thomas Walker and Vernie Birdhead under the original lawsuit (CV 72-L-156), the petition stated that "HCC violates the 1976 court order requiring prison officials to 'permit routine access' to sweat lodges 'at reasonable times' " (*Lincoln Star*, July 26, 1990, p. 20). The class action suit—filed against Mike Kenney, the Hastings superintendent, Brian Gage, assistant superintendent, Gary Suhr, education department director, and Craig Jochim, captain of correctional officers—addressed a number of issues about which inmates were upset. Plaintiff Richard Walker had requested permission to conduct a special sweat lodge ceremony because of a serious illness in his family, making assurances it would not interfere with prison routine. Permission to conduct this ceremony was denied by correctional authorities as an "unreasonable request" because, in their view, there was no precedent for conducting such ceremonies. The motion also charged that prison officials continued to violate the Consent Decree by failing to provide Indian Studies courses; NASCA members stated that the Hastings officials denied their requests for ceremonial materials and hobby items. In a visit by a medicine man to the Hastings prison, the medicine man was admitted to the institution with no difficulty, but his assistants were denied entrance despite the fact that the inmates' approved requests were for the medicine man *and his helpers* to be admitted. The helpers who appeared at the prison happened to be female. "On July 14, 1990, there was a medicine man who arrived at the Hastings Correctional Center with three helpers, two of the helpers were female and Defendant Jochim did not let them in to participate in the ceremonies. The Plaintiffs allege that this is religious discrimination because the Christians have females at their Sunday Services and the Christian Fellowship Group during the week" (CV 72-L-156, Petition Requesting a Show Cause Hearing, July 23, 1990). Women assistants have, upon other occasions, been permitted to enter the institution and assist in healing ceremonies. On August 14, 1990, Judge Urbom denied the petition on the grounds that the original Consent Decree had been filed by plaintiffs from the *penitentiary* against the *Director of Correctional Services*, and therefore did not apply to Hastings inmates and administrators.

Indian Inmates v. Wolff (Omaha), 1991

On January 30, 1991, inmates of the Omaha Correctional Center filed a petition requesting a hearing to show cause why the prison should not be held in contempt of court over regular access to sweat lodge ceremonies (filed under CV 72-L-156). Inmates had requested permission to attend sweat lodge ceremonies but were told that unless there were nine inmates, they could not sweat. The prisoners claimed that this policy was discriminatory toward Indian inmates because no other religious group must meet a certain population quota in order to attend their religious services. Additionally, inmates were bitter about the fact that when they were told that they had insufficient numbers of inmates to allow them to sweat, they were also told that they should "go find one of the inmates who are wearing headbands around the institution" to make up enough inmates to sweat (CV 72-L-156, Petition, Jan. 30, 1991, p. 2). Such remarks were considered "poor in taste, very unprofessional and discriminatory towards the Plaintiff class" (p. 3). A second denial of a ceremony based on insufficient numbers resulted in the filing of this petition. Another issue addressed in the petition was the Omaha prison's refusal to allow inmates to hold sweat lodge ceremonies during the eleven o'clock count. Ceremonies had routinely been allowed during count since the prison opened, and inmates were accustomed to being accommodated, so reversal of correctional policy was upsetting to the prisoners. Finally, inmates stated that they continued to suffer "because of malicious persecution by the Defendants, which is racially and religiously motivated, through body and cell shakedowns, misconduct reports, and the constant intentional infliction of emotional distress" (p. 5.) Denial of access to medicine men and lack of Indian Studies curricula were also mentioned in this petition, as they were in most grievances filed. Specifically, the inmates requested that they obtain relief through removal of the prison's restriction requiring a minimum of nine inmates for a sweat; that sweat lodge ceremonies continue to be allowed through count; that medicine men be allowed into the institution as specified in the Consent Decree, and that harassment of Indian inmates cease.

The judge's decision rocked not only the Omaha prisoners but everyone in the state who was knowledgeable about Indian religious freedom issues. Reflecting his prior ruling on the Hastings suit, Senior United States District Judge Warren K. Urbom issued a Memorandum and Order on February 13, 1991, on the Petition that denied Omaha inmates' protections of religious freedom under the 1974 and 1976 Consent Decree agreements. His statement was: "I do not see any basis for obtaining relief from officials of the Omaha Correctional Center by Indian inmates of the Omaha Correctional Center. The only plaintiffs named in the decree and supplemental consent decree were Indian inmates of the Nebraska Penitentiary, which is located in Lincoln, Nebraska, and the only defendant was the director of correctional services. *There is not such a unity of parties to permit the relief asked for* [emphasis mine]" (CV 72-L-156, Memorandum and Order, Feb. 13, 1991).

Judge Urbom indicated that this statement did not mean that inmates couldn't make claims under the law, rather it meant that inmates in the Omaha (or for that matter Hastings or York) prisons who were not party to the original class action suit could not seek redress under the Consent Decree. The petition requesting a show cause hearing for Omaha Correctional Center inmates was denied. On the same day, a nearly identical Memorandum and Order was issued by Judge Urbom with the same decision concerning inmates of the Hastings Correctional Center in their suit from the preceding August. Inmates in both minimum-custody institutions in the state had decisions handed down indicating that they were no longer afforded protections of religious freedom rights as specified by the terms of the Consent Decree.

The potential repercussions of this decision are monumental: since only inmates in the Nebraska State Penitentiary and Lincoln Correctional Center were actually litigants in the original class action suit filed in 1972, all the protections afforded to inmates in Nebraska penal facilities (other than those from which the original suits were filed) are now at risk of being lost if the administration of those institutions wishes to remove them. Technically, only prisoners at the Pen and LCC can presently seek relief under the terms of the Consent Decree. However, at the time the decree was filed, only those two penal facilities existed in the state. Only in the 1980s were additional facilities provided at Hastings, Omaha, and York. Since all women are incarcerated in York, Judge Urbom's ruling may ultimately mean that women are at risk of losing the protections of religious freedoms afforded them under the Consent Decree. Minimum-custody inmates at Hastings and Omaha are also at risk, for those facilities came later.

While it may be technically true that inmates still have constitutional guarantees of their religious freedom rights, years of dispute between inmates and correctional authorities suggest that without the compliance enforced by the federal court, it is highly unlikely that prisons will feel compelled to abide by all the provisions of the decree. Reinterpretation of exactly which institutions enjoy the protection of the Consent Decree will be necessary because of another issue. While the original class action suit was filed as *Larry Cunningham on behalf of Indian Inmates of the Nebraska Penitentiary v. Charles L. Wolff, Jr., Warden* (later, Joseph Vitek was substituted for Wolff as the new warden and defendant), and referred specifically to the Pen, the suit *was generalized* to reflect "all Indian inmates presently incarcerated at the *Nebraska Penal and Correctional Complex* and those Indians who may be incarcerated there in the future" (CV 72-L-156, Order Designating Class Action, Nov. 21, 1973). This latter statement clearly indicates the intention that the provisions of the decree *should apply to all inmates within the state penal facilities.*

An article in the *Lincoln Star* covered Judge Urbom's decision on February 21, 1991 ("Judge denied Indian inmates court hearing"), but it caught only a few people's attention. It is bound to cause overwhelming problems for inmates in the next decade.

Indian Inmates v. Wolff, 1991

Another blow to Nebraska Indian inmates occurred soon after the Urbom decision was rendered. On March 8, 1991, James M. Bausch of Cline, Williams, Wright, Johnson and Oldfather, filed a motion to withdraw the firm as counsel for all Indian inmates. Originally appointed by the federal court in 1974 to screen inmate grievances emanating from the Consent Decree, the firm had provided this invaluable service to all Indian prisoners in the state, regardless of location, for sixteen years. Now, with no law firm appointed to serve in a similar fashion, inmates will have to act independently and without legal counsel in filing petitions. While that may not pose undue hardship, it is bound to compound the problems that will arise as a result of three of the five adult state correctional facilities no longer being able to claim protection of their political rights to religious freedom afforded by the Consent Decree. On March 11, 1991, Judge Urbom relieved James Bausch of any further responsibility in representing Indian plaintiffs. On March 15, Mr. Bausch officially withdrew as counsel to the Indian inmates of the Nebraska Penitentiary in the Consent Decree class action suit (CV 72-L-156).

Only two weeks later, on March 27, 1991, Michael R. Dillon and Wesley K. Buchanan filed a Motion for Contempt of the Court Order under the original class action suit (CV 72-L-156), requesting relief of problems encountered at the Nebraska State Penitentiary. Since both inmates were housed at the Penitentiary, there was no question of the legality of their filing under the original Consent Decree. The inmates claimed that numerous provisions of the Consent Decree had been violated, citing continual harassment and disrespect toward their religious activities, a change in prison policy that no longer permitted the Indian inmates to serve traditional foods at ceremonies, abuse of the sacred sweat lodge area both by correctional officers and by other religious groups such as the Odinists, denial of inmate requests to hold Hand Games as they once did, and the reconfiguration of the religious coordinator's position, resulting in a loss to the NASCA group of its special club sponsor. The plaintiffs demanded that "the Defendants be held in contempt of Court, for their neglect and refusal to comply with and obey the judgment" of the Consent Decree (CV 72-L-156, Motion for Contempt of Court Order, March 27, 1991).

One exhibit offered by Indian plaintiffs was a letter from Harold W. Clarke, the warden at the time, to inmate Dennis Lovejoy in which Clarke defended the administration's position on many of the charges. One complaint that had surfaced was the lack of a full-time religious coordinator assigned to the Native American Spiritual and Cultural Awareness group (NASCA). Since the reconfiguration of the religious coordinator's position, inmates have had increasing difficulty in management of their religious and club needs. While the coordinator still serves as liaison with the Indian community and provides supplies for ceremonies, club sponsorship is no longer one of his assigned duties. However, as all other self-betterment clubs share sponsors who have multiple responsibilities, charges of discrimination against the Indian club were refuted.

On April 2, 1991, a Lincoln attorney, John V. Hendry of the law firm Bruckner, O'Gara, Keating, Hendry, Davis and Nedved, was appointed by Magistrate David L. Piester to serve as counsel for the two Indian plaintiffs. A prehearing conference was scheduled for April 29, 1991, and a hearing on the motion scheduled for May 6, 1991. However, due to the attorney's lack of familiarity with the Consent Decree, with Indian inmate concerns in general and the specific grievances in particular, a continuance was granted. Jefferson Downing in John Hendry's office took the case to court finally on November 13, 1991. By then Buchanan had been removed from the litigation because of his release from prison. Magistrate Piester, in his final Report and Recommendation issued on February 13, 1992, concluded that Dillon's religious freedoms had not been violated in any of the instances cited and denied the motion to find the defendants in contempt of the Decree.

Dick and Dillon v. Hopkins et al., 1991

Mr. Downing was contacted by other inmates from the Penitentiary. In their preparation for the annual powwow, to be held on October 27, 1991, their request for an eight-hour period in which to hold the annual celebration had been denied. In *Rupert Dick and Michael Dillon v. Frank Hopkins et al.* (CV 91-3320) the inmates requested that the court issue a restraining order to stop officials at the Penitentiary from restricting the powwow to a three-hour event. An evidentiary hearing was held on October 25, 1991. The inmates expected the court to deny their request, and they were overwhelmed when Magistrate Piester stated: "From the affidavits submitted it appears that the powwow is a ceremony of important spiritual and cultural significance. The affidavit of Elizabeth Grobsmith, exhibit 2, instructs that a three-hour limitation 'would strip the event of most of its cultural and religious significance.' Further, I infer from the large number of outside visitors that typically attend this event . . . that the preparation . . . has required more than minimal planning. . . . Accordingly, I conclude that the plaintiffs have shown that a denial of their TRO motion would cause them irreparable injury" (CV 91-3320, Report and Recommendation, Oct. 25, 1991, pp. 3–4).

The magistrate recommended that the motion for a temporary restraining order be granted, thereby allowing prisoners to hold an eight-hour powwow. Judge Urbom signed the Memorandum and Order on the same day. The inmates were in a state of disbelief: they had forty-eight hours' notice, and permission to have a full eight hours available to them! But no institutional support was granted to call prospective visitors and inform them of the change; no dancers could be notified to bring their dance regalia, and no drummers could be invited to sing and drum. Many of us—myself included—had budgeted only three hours for the afternoon. Here was an occasion where the inmates had won the victory in principle, but in actuality they lacked the ability to find enough activities to fill the entire period. The victory was hollow in another sense as well: this restraining order was only a temporary one; when the next powwow was planned, the issue of length would have to be resolved again, perhaps permanently.

Dick v. Clarke, 1992

Inmates began to make plans in the spring of 1992 to hold their next powwow, knowing that the court had ruled in their favor for an eight-hour powwow six months before. In *Rupert Dick v. Harold Clarke* (CV 92-3129) inmates filed a motion for a preliminary injunction against the prison and requested that eight hours be set aside for their powwow. Echoing the documents and outcomes of the previous litigation, Magistrate Piester once again determined that the powwow was a religious event and, as such, was entitled to the full amount of time awarded to other religious groups for similar events. Magistrate Piester recommended to Judge Urbom that the plaintiffs' motion for a preliminary injunction be granted, as "no public interest is served in allowing state-condoned and purposeless discrimination" (CV 92-3129, Memorandum and Order, May 15, 1992, p. 7). This time Judge Urbom *did not* go along with the magistrate's recommendation and reversed the ruling. While he acknowledged that the annual gathering has religious aspects, he concluded that the religious elements were insufficient to warrant characterization as a religious event for the purposes of the lawsuit. He stated: "the plaintiff has not established his entitlement to a preliminary injunction. Accordingly, I shall grant the defendant's objection and shall deny the plaintiff's motion for a preliminary injunction" (CV 92-3129, Memorandum and Order, May 22, 1992).

On October 13, 1992, Judge Urbom upheld his previous decision to limit the powwow to a three-hour event, basing his decision largely on the "legitimate interest of maintaining a secure prison environment" (Memorandum and Order on Defendants' Motion for Summary Judgment, p. 4).

The impact of litigation on Indian prisoners

A review of the many issues presented to the court pertaining to the 1974 and 1976 decrees reveals that despite the initial "victory" experienced by Nebraska Indian inmates in the battle to exercise their religious freedom rights, the conflicts persist between what inmates perceive as reasonable and what correctional authorities allow. It is almost as though no gains in privileges (as they are called by correctional authorities) or rights (as they are perceived by inmates) occur without the inmates' forcing the prison to comply, through litigation, with the provisions of the Consent Decree. The initial decree was, without doubt, a landmark precedent, both locally and nationally; however, continuing grievances concerning the same issues being litigated over and over suggests that all is not well or by any means resolved. Since the Consent Decree was awarded, the issues addressed by each paragraph of the decrees have been litigated, some several times—except one: the right to wear long hair. The increase in prisoner litigation (not just Native American) certainly takes its toll on both plaintiff and defendant; and some correctional authorities may be more supportive of Indian religious expression because they know, from many years of working with Indian inmates, that failure to comply with the decree will end up in their being taken to court. Other institutions may be less enthusiastic, waiting to test the degree of compliance required by the court.

There is little question that the Consent Decree has had tremendous impact, on the prisoners and the prison authorities alike. For the institutions and administrators who are continually named as defendants, the litigation emanating from the Consent Decree has been a legally, morally, and politically efficacious directive, to ensure that they "stay honest." If for no other reason than to deter another bout in court, efforts at compliance are made. The level of compliance, however, is not at all uniform, and the unevenness across institutions frequently results in the filing of another lawsuit. Progress may be made at one institution only to be followed by a lawsuit alleging noncompliance at another.

For the inmates, the impact of twenty years of litigation is twofold. One part reflects the actual positive results that inmates have gained in the exercise of their religious freedom and cultural rights. The other part has less to do with the actual rights than it does with the more subtle political consequences, namely a stronger Indian identification, a tremendous rise in group solidarity, the notion of Native Americans being a political force to be reckoned with, and the pride they experience in being the only ethnic group in prison to have a special federal court order which dictates that the prison is compelled by law to allow their spiritual and cultural expression (Grobsmith 1989b).

A review of all the litigation suggests that despite the large number of lawsuits filed, there are some very basic issues that continue to be unresolved. The majority reflect the prisoners' beliefs that correctional authorities simply do not respect their religion or right to practice it. Confronted by ignorance about sweat lodge practices (which results in insensitivity to cultural practices interpreted by inmates as harassment), accusations of drug use (ignorance on the part of guards) or improper shakedown of the Sacred Pipe, Indian prisoners feel that the prison views their nonmainstream religion as lacking the legitimacy of Judeo-Christian faiths. Inmates try to rectify this situation by inviting correctional staff to sweat with them, or to attend their symposia or celebrations. But few correctional authorities are ever in attendance at these functions. The Indians take this as an affront, believing that if the prison wanted to learn more about Indian culture so as to better respect it, they would attend. They interpret correctional disinterest as disrespect.

Themes emerge in review of all the litigation filed by Indian inmates.

1. *Use of the sweat lodge* continues to be problematic at different institutions, whether the friction is over the odors of burning sage and cedar, orders to remove blankets, tarps, rugs, sage, flesh offerings, or other material at the sweat lodge, or interrupting the ceremony at an inappropriate and ritually unacceptable time to take count (the relevant cases are listed by year and document number; see Table 3. 1987:CV 87-L-482; 1989:CV 89-L-321; 1990:CV 72-L-156; 1991:CV 72-L-156). Indian inmates become angry that Christian prisoners are able to go to the chapel to pray at times other than when services are being conducted, but Native Americans are not permitted routine access to the sweat lodge area for contemplation or solitary prayer because the area is restricted except for designated ceremonies. At other institutions, inmates are frustrated by the lack of towels and blankets needed to sweat, and perceive the prison's lack of cooperation in supplying them with necessities as a message of disrespect and intentional resistance.

2. *Problems with spiritual leaders and medicine men (and women) being admitted to prison facilities for ceremonies* appear again and again in litigation (1979:CV 72-L-156; 1989:CV 89-L-321; 1990:CV 72-L-156). Paperwork always must be properly drawn up and well in advance, but arrangements for incoming medicine men who have no phones is sometimes difficult and the prisons do not seem to be able to demonstrate flexibility in responding to any last minute changes in plans. Funding and expenses allocated by the Nebraska Legislature for the religious needs of inmates have not precluded continual problems with reimbursement of visiting medicine men's expenses.

3. *Medicine men who come into the system may have beliefs different from some of the inmates,* and the prison has had to be educated on the differing cultural, linguistic, and religious traditions. This issue has been litigated on two separate occasions by two different Indian plaintiffs (1983:CV 83-L-572 and 1987:CV 72-L-156). Native American religion is often stereotyped as a single set of religious precepts, but the variety of different tribes represented in prison makes it clear that there are a number of different Indian faiths—they are not all the same. Those who

follow the way of the Sacred Pipe and attend sweat lodge ceremonies may be in the majority, but the prevalence of Omaha, Winnebago, and Chippewa Indians in prison (and many Sioux as well) means that an entire religious faith, namely the Native American Church of North America, is barely acknowledged. Inability of prisoners to have access to peyote within the ceremonies of the Native American Church is an extension of this problem, and has been litigated more than once (1979:CV 72-L-156; 1983:CV 83-L-572).

4. *Which inmates have access to the sweat lodge* has repeatedly provoked religious freedom issues. Although all inmates constitute the class in the original class action suit, protective custody inmates who are segregated from the general population have not gained support in the court for their participation in sweat lodge ceremonies (1980:CV 80-L-324; 1983:CV 83-L-572; 1987:CV 72-L-156). The prison's need to provide security to inmates in segregation is upheld repeatedly by the court and, in all the decisions handed down thus far, has outweighed the requests by this particular subgroup to participate in sweats.

5. *The lack of consistency or regularity in Indian Studies curricula* has continued to plague every correctional institution in the state (1987: CV 72-L-156; 1990:CV 72-L-156). Changing the schools that take responsibility for providing classes and instructors, and inconsistency across institutions once again has hindered the regularization of course offerings. Inmate institutional jobs have historically conflicted with class offerings, and poor attendance has weakened the prison's commitment to continue such offerings.

6. *The hiring of sufficient numbers of Indian personnel,* either as correctional officers (guards) or as administrators, has been litigated on several occasions, including the original class action (1974, 1987:CV 72-L-156). Although the prison has succeeded in demonstrating that it has made efforts to hire Native American employees, Indian inmates continue to point out resources that were not tapped in the institution's search for a suitable applicant.

7. *Privileges of the Indian group or club—NASCA—*also continue to be a sore point and has been repeatedly litigated (1974, 1987, 1991: CV 72-L-156). Although the Consent Decree requires that a religious coordinator be appointed to meet the needs of Indian prisoners, the tremendous growth in prison population has precluded the institutions' ability to provide sufficient personnel. Redefinition of the job description of the religious coordinator resulted in the LCC NASCA group not having a club

sponsor during 1988–89, requiring that it call upon volunteers on an ad hoc basis to come in and sponsor meetings; without a club sponsor, the group was not permitted to meet regularly. Although inmates considered this to be a violation of the Consent Decree, which guarantees them both a club and a religious coordinator, they were unsuccessful in convincing the authorities to hire additional personnel to enable the club to have regular meetings. Other club concerns are also upsetting to Indian inmates. Probably the most serious is the lack of family participation in the events staged by their club (1987:CV 72-L-156). This issue has been technically litigated only once, but it continues to symbolize to the Indian population the lack of regard for their culture by prison authorities.

In reviewing all the litigation filed since the Consent Decree was awarded, it is apparent that few formal rulings in favor of Indian plaintiffs have been entered. However, while gains appear to be minimal, they have, in fact, been quite significant. Successes are not necessarily reflected only in rulings made in favor of the prisoners—it is true there are few of those. But admonitions to prison personnel emphasizing their legal obligation to uphold the provisions of the decree have been crucial to the continuing expression of religious freedom in prison. When the court requires the prison to supply appropriate medicine men to different individuals, it is a symbolic indication of the court's appreciation for the cultural diversity of the Indian inmate population (1987: CV 72-L-156). The court's unwillingness to accept the prison's plan to meet the religious needs of all inmates by initiating a volunteer clergy policy is an indication of the court's validation of the inmates' rights to have a variety of medicine men rather than one "official" medicine man come in. The court *did* rule in favor of the Indian plaintiff SapaNajin concerning his right to have his religious needs met. Not accepting the prison's plan put the burden on the Department of Correctional Services to continue to comply with the provisions of the Consent Decree lest the prison be held in contempt of court. The fact that the prison has never implemented the volunteer clergy plan is a clear indication that they know that such implementation would result in a vast number of additional lawsuits filed by Indian prisoners in every institution. This is one way in which the court, without ruling in favor of the Indian plaintiffs, has nevertheless supported their assertions.

Similarly, while the court did not rule in favor of the Indian plaintiffs who petitioned to attend the Sun Dance, it did admonish the prison to consider minimum A inmates' requests to Sun Dance on a case-by-case basis. And the court did not rule in favor of the inmates in the cases of accusations of harassment at the sweat lodge, but it did reiterate the need for proper education of correctional employees and the need to remove dismissed misconduct reports from inmates' jackets lest they adversely affect parole hearings. In 1987, the court did not find the Department of Correctional Services in contempt of the Consent Decree, but it did urge the prison to revive its commitment to strong Indian Studies curricula. The court's actions "are a 'reminder' to the Department of Corrections to continue compliance with the Consent Decree lest they be found in contempt. . . . Continuing litigation keeps the prison administration 'on their toes' " (Grobsmith 1989b:143). In the debate over whether the powwow is a social gathering or a religious event, the victory of an eight-hour powwow was subsequently reversed. But the recognition by the court of the legitimacy of the Indians' claims continues to lend credibility to their assertions and hope to their cause.

In nearly all the cases, the most critical and frequently cited factor compelling the court to rule in favor of the defendants is the security issue. Whether the case involves inmates' wishes to sweat despite their being in protective custody, harassment at the sweat lodge, travel to the Sun Dance, or practices of the Native American Church, it is nearly always the risks such activities are believed to pose that ultimately give greater weight to the prison's concerns. Inmates are aware that it is terribly difficult for the court to rule in their favor when the state convinces the court that accommodation to Indian requests may compromise the prison's ability to afford security to all its inmate population. For the Indian inmates, it is nearly a no-win situation.

While the tangible gains from twenty years of litigation have been few in number, the overall impact of the collective suits has been a source of great pride, dignity, and integrity of the Indian prison population. If one views historically the efforts of Nebraska Indian prisoners, their vocal and highly visible political struggle is consistent with the national struggle not only for recognition but for religious tolerance. The Consent Decree was, in many ways, a local precursor to the federal law protecting the religious rights and practices of all Native Americans throughout the United States, the American Indian Religious Freedom Act. The Indian inmates in Nebraska had no intention of being deprived of their constitutionally guaranteed religious freedom rights despite their incarceration, and were willing to assert this in court years before the enactment of the federal law.

The drum belonging to the Native American Spiritual and Cultural Awareness group (NASCA) at the Pen bears a reference to *oyate wanji,* one nation. The drum is used at all NASCA activities. Photograph by author.

Indian inmates painted this mural on the wall of the visiting room at the Lincoln Correctional Center, symbolizing the Black Road to urban decay, as opposed to the Red Road or positive approach to life. The mural was later painted over during renovation of the visiting area. Photograph by author.

A portion of the Lincoln Correctional Center, a medium- and maximum-custody facility for men, includes the evaluation unit where inmates are initially brought before being assigned to one of the Nebraska institutions. Photograph by Jennifer Dam.

Inmates meet relatives and friends in the visiting room of the Lincoln Correctional Center. Photograph by the author.

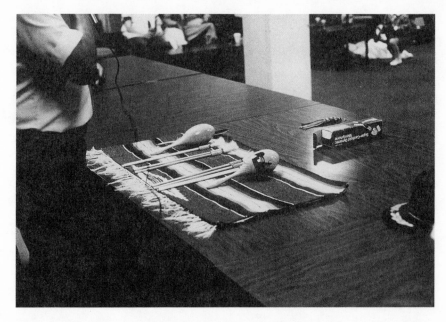

Items used in a Hand Game are set out for use during a NASCA activity at the Penitentiary. Photograph by the author.

NASCA club members sit around the drum and enjoy music during a Hand Game at the Nebraska State Penitentiary. Photograph by the author.

4

Alcohol, Drugs,
and Crime

Although Indian drinking problems and patterns have been and continue to be systematically researched, our understanding of how and in what ways substance abuse contributes to incarceration for Native Americans is not entirely clear. There is no question that alcohol abuse and the associated family disruption it engenders are principal causal factors on the path toward delinquency which affects both urban and reservation Indians. The use of drugs and alcohol is sometimes a pattern established so early that by the time children are exposed to health and alcohol issues in schools, they are fully addicted and on the road to dropping out.

Native Americans have historically been considered to have the highest arrest and crime rates of any ethnic group in the United States (Jensen, Stauss, and Harris 1977:252–53; Levy and Kunitz 1974:2). According to Cross (1982), these high crime rates have remained constant for the last forty years. Some studies have estimated that the Indian arrest rate may be eight to ten times higher than that for the remaining U.S. population (Stewart 1964). Rape, homicide, and suicide are serious crimes that occur with greater frequency in the Indian population, and the alcohol involvement in them has been well documented. Homicide is believed to be 90 percent alcohol-related (Lex 1985:150–54); the suicide rate for Indians is almost double that of the overall population (U.S. Department of Health and Human Services 1987:20), and, according to Indian Health Service estimates, is 80 percent alcohol-related. Both homicide and suicide appear to occur more frequently among the younger age groups. The rash of Indian suicides in the last two decades has captured national attention, and it is considered a function of the despair and hopelessness so characteristic of alcohol- and drug-addicted youth. Alcohol is involved in three-quarters of all fatal accidents among Indians, a rate three times greater than the rate for other races (Levy and Kunitz 1974:2). "Of the ten leading causes of death in Native American communities from 1978–80, alcohol abuse was implicated in four: accidents, cirrhosis of the liver, homicides, and suicides" (National Clearinghouse for Alcohol and Drug Information n.d.:5). On the Standing Rock Sioux Reservation, Whittaker noted in 1963 that no serious crimes had been committed by a sober Indian for the ten years preceding his study (Whittaker 1963:83).

It is not only the serious crimes that are increasing among Native Americans. The most visible rise in Indian crime appears to be in the less serious crimes, such as assault, liquor violation, and drunk driving (Greenberg 1981). Reservation crime is also believed to be on the rise (Harring 1982).

The disproportionately high alcoholism, arrest, and crime rates among Native Americans are reflected by the high percentages of Indians in prisons. Indians comprised 1.6 percent of the federal prison population in 1992, somewhat of a decline from the 2.2 percent to 2.8 percent for the previous several years, despite the fact that they comprised only 1 percent of the nation's population (Mail and McDonald 1980, Camp and Camp 1989, Camp and Camp 1992). For all state and federal penal institutions in the United States, the incarcerated Indian population averaged 3 percent (Camp and Camp 1992:5).

The Indian population in the United States is very young, the birth rate is high, and the teen-age pregnancy rate is among the highest in the country. Fetal Alcohol Syndrome (FAS) is epidemic; "twenty-five percent of all Indian mothers who bear a child with FAS give birth to another one similarly damaged" (National Clearinghouse for Alcohol and Drug Information n.d.:5). With alcoholism endemic, contact with law enforcement begins early—by about age fifteen—and drops off again after age forty. Since most alcohol consumption is done by males between the ages of twenty-five and forty-four, the vulnerability and susceptibility of this group to crime is exceedingly high (Lex 1985:153, Grobsmith 1989a:287).

Many theories attempt to account for the high incidence of alcoholism among Indian groups, citing as causal factors poverty and economic depression (Dozier 1966), lack of economic opportunities as a result of acculturation (Graves 1967), efforts to reduce anxiety (Horton 1943), loose (bilateral) family structure and weakened kin ties (Field 1962), and lack of control over their own society as a result of living under a paternalistic governmental arm (Stewart 1964). Lurie suggests that Indian alcoholism is "the world's oldest on-going protest demonstration" and attributes excessive drinking to a method of asserting and validating Indian identity (1974:55–59). Mohatt (1972) believes that excessive drinking represents a quest for personal power and draws analogies to psychological states of ecstasy and religious highs as well as quests for personal prestige and power such as those achieved by Plains Indians in the Vision Quest or Sun Dance or in being a successful warrior. Myths of "firewater" (alcohol mixed with tobacco juice, hot peppers, or opium) have suggested a stereotypical addictive impulse to drink that most Native Americans supposedly found irresistible (National Clearinghouse for Alcohol and Drug Information, n.d.) This early European interpretation of Indian drinking was based on what was thought to be racial or constitutional differences between Indians and whites (Leland 1976; see also Joy Leland's comprehensive review of theories concerning Indian alcoholism in Mail and McDonald 1980:1–56).

Theories of genetic predisposition or susceptibility to alcohol abound, with general agreement that Indians (like other Asian peoples) lack an enzyme that aids in the absorption of alcohol. Physiological symptoms such as facial flushing, rapid heart rate, and lowered blood pressure indicate that Asians metabolize alcohol up to 30 percent faster than do Caucasians (National Clearinghouse for Alcohol and Drug Information n.d.). Consequently, Indians require less alcohol to become inebriated. (Native Americans are generally classified with Orientals in such explanations since Indians represent descendants of Asians who crossed the Bering land bridge into North America from Asia.) There is no universal agreement, however, about the etiology of alcoholism; in fact, several studies have been published that refute the metabolic studies' findings, and so cast doubt on a genetic or biological argument for widespread Indian alcoholism (Fenna, Mix, Schaefer, and Gilbert 1971:23). "To date, reviews of the research literature reveal no consensus on why Native Americans drink [and] under what circumstances" (National Clearinghouse for Alcohol and Drug Information, n.d.:5). What is lacking in data is certainly made up for in the public stereotype that somehow Indians are born drunkards who have mysteriously inherited the disease of alcoholism. They are frequently considered to be genetically as well as socially predisposed to addiction.

No single explanation can account for the epidemic of alcoholism among Native Americans or the endemic nature of reservation alcoholism. Certainly getting drunk faster contributes to overall intoxication; however, the widespread alcoholism prevalent on America's reservations can only be attributed to the culturally learned and accepted behaviors (norms) of drinking, for recreation and general social activity. Most explanatory theories point to stress as an inducer of alcohol consumption and drinking behaviors as attempts to escape from stress. But such explanations do not account for the addiction rates so characteristic of Indian children, many of whom are addicts before they truly know the stresses of adult life such as poverty and unemployment. It may be that individual Indians drink because of stress; but I believe it is more likely that drinking induces stress and results in crises that undermine life's normal flow. Drinking is a behavior pattern children learn on their parents' knees; from the earliest ages, children learn that many activities are responded to with excessive drinking, and the stigma of overconsumption and its legal consequences become accepted hazards of daily life. Consequently, Indian youth do not regard early alcohol consumption as especially dangerous or deviant, but more as routine, the culturally appropriate response. Those not wishing to participate in drinking activities are ridiculed and excluded and are considered by peers to be "too good" for the rest of the crowd.

The metaphor most frequently cited by Indian offenders who leave prison is the bucket filled with crabs. Any attempt by one crab to pull itself out of the bucket is hindered by the remainder of the crabs pulling the one crab back down to the bottom. Indian inmates see this as their biggest challenge when they get out of prison. One offender who continually failed parole and was returned to prison told a tale of being pressured to go drinking with another parolee to help celebrate the latter's daughter's birthday. He simply did not feel that he could refuse. He joined the celebration, got drunk, failed to return to his residence, was turned in to his parole officer, and was returned to prison as a parole failure. There is so much social pressure to consume alcohol that anyone refusing is stigmatized, ridiculed, and ostracized by the community. And without a sense of community, Indian identity is threatened. Most believe it is better to return to drinking than to reject (or be rejected by) one's peers. And so the cycle of failure persists.

It must be remembered that theories rely on generalizations, and generalizing about Indian alcoholism is difficult because of tribal variation:

theories that are relevant and meaningful for one particular Native American cultural group may not apply all that well to another. Variation in tribal size, custom, language, circumstances of contact and subsequent level of acculturation, history, and tradition can render one tribe's response to alcohol quite distinct from another's, and "no single style or pattern of drinking [is] manifested by all Indians" (Lex 1985:158).

Alcoholism in Native Americans does not appear to be restricted to members of certain socioeconomic classes, and yet there is a commonality of experience drinkers from different parts of the country will attest to, particularly if they share a reservation history. Among many Indian families, courts are now seeing fifth-generation addiction (Flute 1985, personal communication). Parental alcoholism, weakening the fabric and integrity of the family, all too often results in inadequate parental supervision and subsequent termination of the parents' legal custody of their children (Flute et al. 1985). In a study of juvenile problems of Indian tribes in the Plains, the majority of reservations reported that Indian youths who ran away from home and subsequently were taken into custody were returned to their parents despite heavy parental drinking, because of a lack of appropriate facilities to house them (Grobsmith and Flute 1985). In interviews with forty-five Nebraska Indian inmates, this phenomenon was corroborated: prisoners stated that even if parents held steady jobs and went to work during the week, binge drinking on weekends was heavy (Grobsmith 1989a). They discussed the dilemma of getting into trouble with the law for drinking yet being returned to parents who were unable to discipline them due to their own alcoholism (Grobsmith 1989a). Parents not only drank themselves but were significant factors in the introduction of alcohol to their own children. Inmates told horrifying tales of legal guardians in institutions, foster parents, and even supervisors in detention homes supplying them with intoxicants during their stay in such facilities.

The pattern that emerges in many Indian families is echoed again and again in offenders' personal histories. During ninety hours of interviews with forty-five male and female offenders, each visited privately for a period of two hours, the pattern emerged of childhood involvement in alcohol and drugs, disintegration of the family, commission of small delinquent acts in the beginning, and eventually a prison sentence (Grobsmith 1989a). Most notable is the exceptionally early age at which these individuals came into contact with alcohol and drugs. Studies done throughout reservations in the United States show that Indians become familiar with marijuana, alcohol, and inhalants far earlier than other children in the country. May (1986) conducted a survey of different tribes in which he reported that 56 percent to 89 percent of all Indian youth had experimented with alcohol. The National Indian Health Board Reporter (1986) similarly found in a nationwide survey that 70 percent of Papago high school students used alcohol on a regular basis, 80 percent of Navajo students at Shiprock, New Mexico, used alcohol and drugs, and 90 percent of Cherokee students in Oklahoma said they used alcohol and drugs frequently.

The drugs used the earliest by many Indian children are substances known as inhalants, stimulants that are breathed in. Most often it is small children who become "huffers," because they cannot afford to purchase drugs. Inhalants are easily available to Indian youth, for they come in the form of over-the-counter products that contain solvents, such as Lysol spray, spray paint, correction fluid, mimeograph and ditto machine chemicals, Scotchgard, lighter fluid, and model airplane glue, as well as nasal aspirators such as Benzedrix and Wymine, and gasoline. May (1986) stated that 17 percent to 22 percent of Indian children have used inhalants as opposed to 9 percent to 11 percent of the general U.S. population. Goldstein (1976) showed that among the Pueblo Indians, twice as many Indian children had tried inhalants as in the national sample of adolescents, and my research with Nebraska Indian inmates indicated that fifteen times as many continued their use into adulthood (Grobsmith 1989a). In an Association on American Indian Affairs (AAIA) survey of Indian reservation youth conducted in 1985, some tribes reported use as low as 13 percent, while others reported that 90 percent of their youth had tried inhalants.

Inhalant use commences at a very early age and usually decreases with maturation, but its lasting effect is the habituation of the child to getting high and beginning the road to drug dependence (Cohen 1977, Westermeyer 1986, Grobsmith 1989a). Children who use inhalants normally come from homes where their parents have abused alcohol and where the child has been abused or neglected (Carroll 1977, Grobsmith 1989a). Use of these substances causes massive brain damage, atrophy of the central nervous system, and kidney dysfunction, and produces a depressed state in which users are more likely to commit suicide or homicide (Korman 1977, Grobsmith 1989a). Cohen found that "the physiological damage to children is compounded when emotionally immature users begin turning to solvent use rather than developing strategies of problem-solving" (Cohen 1977:5). Finally, inhalant use has been associated with excessive aggression and violence (Korman 1977, Grobsmith and Flute 1985, Grobsmith 1989a). Neglect is an almost inevitable by-product. In his work with juvenile justice concerns of Plains Indians, Jerry Flute, community development director for the Association on American Indian Affairs, described an incident one winter when a couple who had been using inhalants were arrested, and their baby was discovered with a diaper frozen to its bottom.

The inhalants used most often by inmates I interviewed were spray paint, lighter fluid, nasal inhalers, glue, and gasoline (Grobsmith 1989a). Mixing inhalants with alcohol is quite common when alcohol can be obtained. Inmates told of spraying paint in plastic bags and inhaling the fumes, of placing their nose and mouth over gas tanks and cans, and of stealing cases of correction fluid from schools to get high (I had documented a police report of such a theft on the Omaha Reservation in Nebraska during my work with Jerry Flute for the Association on American Indian Affairs).

Data gathered in 1986 and 1987 from 106 Nebraska Indian inmates suggest that early drug and alcohol abuse played significant roles in the onset of juvenile criminal activity. It was not uncommon for inmates to have begun smoking marijuana as early as age eight or nine—the average age was about twelve—with continuing access to inhalants (Grobsmith 1989a). Inhalants like Lysol spray are not illegal, but increasingly these items are not to be found on the shelves in reservation stores; rather they are behind the counter, much like X-rated magazines). Children poke holes in the can, drain the fluid, then fill the can with Kool-Aid and drink it to get high. Sometimes gaining access to inhalants does require a criminal act, such as petty theft, vandalism, or breaking and entering. By the time these children reach their early teens, they are well on their way to regular delinquent behavior and not unaccustomed to participating in minor illegal activities.

Based on the forty-five inmates in my subsample, the profile of the typical incarcerated Native American in Nebraska is as follows. The average age is 30, but most individuals had significant encounters with the criminal justice system as teen-agers and had experienced their first arrest by the age of fourteen and a half (Grobsmith 1989a:289). This is consistent with a Canadian study of incarcerated Natives for whom the average age of first arrest was between fourteen and fifteen, depending on what kind of community they were from (Lane et al 1977:313). In the Nebraska penal system, inmates had had an average of nearly nineteen arrests prior to incarceration, while the average inmate had had twenty-nine arrests so far in his lifetime. If twenty-nine arrests is "average," this means that about half the inmates had arrest histories well over this number—some numbered in the hundreds. Even so, such arrest rates are underestimates and poor reflections of the real extent of such activity, because these numbers reflect only actual arrests and don't begin to reflect all the criminal activities that were not reported or recorded. Typically, inmates had already served time in a county jail or prison, on average about twelve times apiece (Grobsmith 1989a).

For the majority of Indian inmates, incarceration (theirs or a relative's) was not a novel experience. From my subsample of forty-five prisoners who were personally interviewed, more than a quarter (28.3 percent) had a relative who had gone to prison. For an equal number of respondents, such data were unknown, leaving only 43 percent who had no relatives with a previous sentence. In Lane's study of incarcerated Canadian Natives, 50 percent "had relatives who had been in jail while they were growing up, and 66 percent had friends who had" (Lane et al. 1977:313). This phenomenon reinforces the notion held by most inmates that there is nothing unusual or necessarily deviant about coming from a family where several people have done time.

For the forty-five Nebraska inmates I interviewed, the instability of the family environment was even more apparent when life histories were obtained. It was the norm for an inmate's parents to have suffered from alcoholism, with over two-thirds reporting that their parents "drank to excess" and nearly 90 percent indicating that their parents used alcohol or drugs or both. It was not uncommon for inmates to share that one of their parents had indeed died from alcohol-induced cirrhosis, or had been killed in an alcohol-involved car accident, or had even committed suicide. Such data are clear indicators of the intergenerational and endemic nature of family alcoholism. Heavy parental drinking had a definite impact on the physical abuse inmates suffered, but it was not only parents who engaged in such abusive behavior. Nearly one-quarter (24.4 percent) of inmates told of having been abused by parents or other relatives, 9 percent said they suffered abuse from foster parents or guardians, another 9 percent indicated that they were physically abused by a combination of parents and foster care providers/guardians, and almost 5 percent told of physical abuse they suffered at the hands of house parents in boarding schools and teachers. Altogether, nearly 47 percent of inmates in the sample indicated that they had been physically abused by primary care providers (Grobsmith 1989a:293).

One inmate told of an incident in which his father, having misplaced his jug of wine, accused him (the child) of having stolen it. When the child denied it, the father kicked him over a fence. The inmate stated: "When I was four or five, I already knew what alcohol did to people. My grandmother used to make home brew . . . dad used to drink while he was working. He was a quiet drunk until someone was abrasive towards him. Then he kicked me over the fence. Psychologically it did something to me, because I lost the ability to speak. I went from age four or five to ten years old without speaking . . . I could only use guttural sounds. No one ever took me to the doctor. I started to drink when I was about twelve years old." Another inmate's story of his abuse is a reflection of the lessons that inflicting cruelty teaches to victims: "I took a spoon and heated it up and burned my dog; he died. My mom couldn't figure out who put the spoon marks on him. She found out I did it so she heated a spoon and burned me on the shoulder" (Grobsmith 1989a:292).

In a personal letter a Native American inmate in an Ohio correctional facility wrote of similar acts of cruelty suffered, which had lasting effects on the building of rage within him and eventually caused him to strike back:

> My mother is a white woman, my father was a quarter white and three-quarters Oglala (Sioux). My father died when I was three. My mother remarried a white man when I was six. He didn't like Indians. . . . I climbed a tree in my school clothes and he called me down . . . and beat me with a stick all over my body, from my ears to the soles of my feet. . . . I still have the scars. He made me climb back in the tree . . . and made me stay up there (overnight) without any food or water. I was isolated from other children. When I asked why, I was locked in an underground cellar. I had a dog, and she was the only friend I had. When (my father) asked me if I loved that dog more than I loved my family, he made me live in the dog house, with no blankets or anything. I stole a blanket but got caught . . . and he tied me to a big oak tree, naked, facing and hugging the stick, and I passed out from the pain. (condensed)

The treachery of this tale goes on and on; but the point is that incarcerated Indians who have endured the hatred of non-Indian step-parents carry far more than just physical scars. Eventually, this inmate killed his step-father and received a life sentence.

Often drinking and instability led to the termination of parental rights, leaving the children to be cared for either in institutions or in foster care, particularly if relatives were unavailable to help out. Only about a quarter of the inmates in my sample were raised by their parents. Although it might appear consistent with Indian tradition that the remaining three-fourths were raised by extended family members (not parents), it was not extended family members who often took custody, but non-Indian foster parents and adoptive families, youth homes, and institutions. In the Canadian study, it was not uncommon for people to have "been in ten foster homes in the same number of years"—79 percent had lived either in foster homes or institutions, and 66 percent had been in multiple institutions or foster homes (Lane et al. 1977:313). Nebraska inmates frequently reported a mother's remarriage to a step-father who was especially abusive. The problems of step-families are well known, and in cases where friction existed between a step-father and step-son, the result was often physical and emotional abuse. It was not uncommon for inmates to have had numerous successive foster (or even adoptive) families, causing the youngster to experience name changes, denial of his or her Indian heritage, or physical or psychological cruelty. Beatings, being burned by cigarettes, being locked out of the house, and total lack of emotional support were commonly reported.

Being raised in such environments is, of course, a major contributing factor to delinquency. Indian youths form habitual patterns of minor criminal activity, which become well-established patterns in their teens. Confrontation with law enforcement during childhood and teen years was commonplace for the inmates in the sample, with arrests a frequent occurrence by the age of fourteen or fifteen. The arrests were usually for relatively minor offenses—breaking and entering, truancy, driving while intoxicated, or stealing. But by the time they reached the late teens, alcohol and drug dependence had become so heavy that the criminal activity had escalated to meet the alcohol or drug needs or turned to the more serious crimes such as assault, robbery, and homicide. Table 4 illustrates the breakdown of 154 offenses committed by 106 inmates in 1986–87 (Grobsmith 1989a). Since the majority of Native American offenders cannot afford private counsel, they are appointed attorneys from the public defender's office. Plea bargaining is the rule, with nearly 73 percent pleading guilty to lesser or fewer charges (Grobsmith 1989a:289).

Table 4

Offenses Committed by 106 Inmates, 1986–1987

Crime	First Offense	Second Offense	Third Offense
Burglary	23	6	2
Theft	9	3	
First-degree sexual assault	8	2	1
Robbery	8	5	
First-degree assault	7	3	3
First-degree murder	5	2	
Third-degree assault	5	1	
Second-degree murder	4		
Escape	4	6	1
Second-degree assault	3	2	1
False imprisonment	3		
Second-degree forgery	3	3	
Breaking and entering	2		2
Criminal mischief	2		1
Resisting arrest	2	2	
Motor vehicle general violation	2		
Use of firearm to commit felony	2	2	
Driving while intoxicated	2		
Criminal attempt	1	1	
Manslaughter	1		
Failure to appear		2	
Kidnapping		1	
Third-degree arson		1	
Criminal trespass		1	
Carrying/possession of concealed weapon		1	
Possession of firearm by a fugitive/felon		1	
Habitual criminal		1	
Conspiracy			1

SOURCE: Elizabeth S. Grobsmith, "The Relationship Between Substance Abuse and Crime Among Native American Inmates in the Nebraska Department of Corrections," in *Human Organization* 48, No. 4 (Winter) 1989:290. Reprinted by permission.

From the subsample of forty-five respondents I interviewed, the crimes occurring with the most frequency were (1) burglary, followed by (2) theft, (3) first-degree sexual assault tied with robbery, (4) first degree assault, and (5) first-degree murder tied with third-degree assault (Grobsmith 1989a:289). While these numbers reflect the first offense for which an inmate was doing time, the breakdown is comparable for the

second and third offenses. The most frequently occurring second offenses were: (1) burglary and escape, (2) robbery, (3) first-degree assault
tied with theft and second-degree forgery. For third offenses, the most
common crimes were (1) first-degree assault, followed by (2) burglary
tied with criminal mischief. Burglary, robbery, and theft are common in
all three categories; all three also contain violent crime—murder, assault, or sexual assault. Clearly, the Indian population in prison is serving time for very serious felonies.

Several inmates revealed during interviews that they had killed a
member of their immediate family. One prisoner spoke of his murder of a
baby he did not know, during a period of heavy intoxication; another
spoke of his murder of an elderly woman, also unknown; one spoke of
having murdered a parent. They had no recollection of these acts—they
had occurred during alcoholic blackouts. Several inmates were serving
time for vehicular homicide; one individual had accidentally killed his
own wife, another a high school student. These, and other examples like
them, were all cases of drunk driving, leaving the offender largely un-
aware of what happened. It is difficult for individuals to truly experience
remorse when they cannot recall their acts or the reasons they committed them. Of course they suffer deep regret, not just about the crime but
about the consequences of it on their lives.

All of the forty-five inmates I interviewed in 1986–87 claimed that
they suffered from alcohol and/or drug addiction and had begun their
substance abuse as small children. As one informant stated: "You don't
have to tell a six-month old baby what a beer can is; they already know.
You see little kids drinking whiskey. Their mom knows they're doing it
but she doesn't do anything because she is drinking too" (Grobsmith
1989a:292). Substance abuse was a part of child's play, worsening and
deepening with the influence of street life for juveniles. Thirteen percent
of my informants indicated that they used inhalants alone or in combination with other drugs, 49 percent claimed to be addicted to alcohol, 22
percent considered themselves drug abusers, and nearly 16 percent considered themselves both alcohol and drug addicts (Grobsmith 1989a).
Drug use was more characteristic of those coming from urban backgrounds and alcoholism more prevalent among those from reservation
areas. For this subsample within the Nebraska prison system, a total of
100 percent claimed chemical addiction.

The role alcohol and drug use play in promoting criminal activity was
also apparent from the subsample of forty-five offenders. Regardless of

whether a crime was an inmate's first, second, or third offense for which he was doing time, the criminal act was alcohol- or drug-related between 91 percent and 100 percent of the time (Grobsmith 1989a). These data are corroborated by a 1985 survey of Plains tribes: "Thirteen of the fifteen [tribes] or 87 percent believed that juveniles involved in pranks had been drinking or were high on drug/alcohol combinations. Even more serious is the belief of seven tribes that 90 percent or more of the criminal activity [on their reservation] is alcohol-related" (Grobsmith and Flute 1985:2–5).

A study of Canadian Indian inmates revealed a similar pattern of the involvement of alcohol and drugs in crime commission: of 316 inmates sampled, "only 10 percent of offenses had occurred without the influence of either drugs or alcohol"; 90 percent of inmates claimed that their crimes were related to the use of alcohol, drugs, or alcohol and drugs (Lane et al. 1977:311). Little Rock Reed echoes these findings: "Dale Smith, a former spokesman for the Tribe of Five Feathers, the Indian cultural/spiritual group at the Lomoc Federal Prison in California [stated], 'If we have, say fifty guys, forty-nine of them are here because of alcohol problems' " (Reed 1989).

Reed also cites Native Americans from other areas who agree: "An Idaho/Montana prisoner who expresses the general feeling among Indian people [stated]: 'I feel that [with regard to] our Native people, the percent who are in prison on alcohol- and drug-related crimes [is] 99 . . . if not 100.' " Another inmate Reed quotes, from a New Mexico facility, also concurs: "Out of any twenty Indians incarcerated, nineteen are in for alcohol- or drug-related offenses."

In Nebraska, inmates spoke freely about how they came to establish a pattern of criminal involvement and the role alcohol or drugs played in it. In most instances, they were first introduced to alcohol and drugs by friends and relatives. While it is not surprising that 31 percent said these substances were introduced by a friend, it is rather alarming that 24 percent were introduced by a relative (cousin, uncle, or grandparent). An additional 20 percent said they learned of drugs or alcohol directly from their parents, and 7 percent learned about such substances from siblings (Grobsmith 1989a). Altogether, family members exerted considerable influence on teaching younger family members about drugs and alcohol—in approximately 51 percent of the cases. These figures are consistent with the respondents' claims that two-thirds of their parents had alcohol problems.

While some may believe that heavy drinking among Indian groups oc-curs following social, recreational, or even illegal activity, the pattern identified more readily by prisoners was that they began their drinking prior to other events, and later "things got out of hand." The lack of recre-ational facilities on most Indian reservations is quite well known, and Indian prisoners told of heavy drinking as the main pattern of social rec-reation. Unfortunately, this pattern is established by the early teens, and by the time they are licensed drivers, most Indian teens are already well on their way to being chemically addicted. The involvement of vehicles in early offense commission was notable, with charges of DWI (driving while intoxicated), drunk and disorderly conduct, or even vehicular ho-micide or vehicular manslaughter. Although only four of ninety-six "first offenses" committed by Indian prisoners in the 1986–87 survey (about 4 percent) were for vehicle-related offenses, most offenders ex-pressed during interviews how drinking and driving with a group of friends ("joyriding") was nearly always the setting for commission of a delinquent act (breaking and entering or petty larceny, for example). Le-gal infractions such as stealing a bicycle, checkbook, or BB gun, robbing a gum machine, or stealing a VCR from someone's home were common, with courage coming from peer pressure and a jug.

Without question, as alcohol consumption increased, criminal behav-ior escalated. Often during such a group drinking-and-driving episode, one individual knew where to find a weapon and would involve friends in robbing a service station or breaking into a building to see what they could find. Another common pattern was the alcohol-induced escala-tion of disagreements into fist fights and true assaults (especially in bars), and, if a weapon were involved and a member of the group injured, felony charges might result. Fights not uncommonly resulted in assault charges and, upon occasion, when a group of friends committed an armed robbery or assault resulting in a fatality, an inmate's first serious felony charge of manslaughter, armed assault, or even murder might result.

Sexual assault charges were also not uncommon, although this may come as a surprise to a society which has viewed (and stereotyped) In-dians as placid, reticent, passive, and withdrawn. Of the 154 crimes com-mitted by 106 Native American offenders during 1986–87 (actually more were committed, but only first, second, and third offenses were used in the computer analysis), 7 percent were for *first-degree* sexual assault. Sexual assault was the third most frequently occurring crime among these Native Americans during this period, exceeded only by burglary

(20 percent) and theft (7.8 percent). Since sexual assault is not a crime of sex but one of extreme violence, complete intoxication might result in rape or attempted sexual assault. Inmates who had been convicted of first-degree sexual assault did not deny that they had committed such crimes, but they were in total disbelief that they could have done such a thing, not remembering any details of the act, only awakening in jail following a blackout and being told of the charges which had been filed against them. Several inmates interviewed told of their conviction for sexual assault on their own daughters or other minor children. At least three individuals told me of rapes they supposedly committed but could not recall. It doesn't seem reasonable that a severely intoxicated individual could successfully complete sexual intercourse with the victim; but the aggressive violence of the acts of someone totally inebriated by alcohol or drugs can be limitless. Inmates who had victimized others through sexual assault were generally remorseful and were deeply pained at the thought of the atrocities they had committed. Other acts were not always seen as criminal. One inmate was serving a life sentence for the murder of two men who had raped his sister and niece, one of whom was in a wheelchair. The rapists had not been punished—so the inmate went after them himself, castrating one and killing them both. He hardly sees himself as a logical recipient of rehabilitative therapy.

One interesting aspect of sexual crimes is the inefficacy of treatment for sex offenders, in terms of national success rates as well as offenders' unwillingness to participate in inmate rehabilitative treatment. The sex offenders inpatient treatment program at the Lincoln Correctional Center is severely underutilized by Native Americans, despite the requirement of the parole board that sex offenders demonstrate involvement in such programs if they wish to be eligible for parole.

Alcohol and drugs are commonly still used in prison despite their being forbidden and despite the fact that inmates receive misconduct reports for such use. Forty percent of inmates interviewed in the 1986–87 survey indicated that they still used drugs and alcohol in prison, and evidently there is no mystery about how it gets behind the walls. Guards or correctional officers are known to bring in alcohol and drugs in return for favors from inmates (sometimes sexual). Visitors are also able to bring in drugs, by hiding them in hair, shoes, or body cavities (no body cavity may be routinely searched without the presence of a physician and only under special circumstances). The other common method of obtaining alcohol is making homemade hooch. As I was awaiting an inmate's arrival for an interview, a guard showed me a gallon jug of hooch which officers had just confiscated. It had been made with sugar and oranges, and had a pungent smell from fermentation. Any food substance that will ferment is used in making hooch, and can easily be obtained by working in the kitchen or removing food from meals. Water, sugar, and yeast (or wadded-up bread) are used if no fruit, juices, or tomato puree are available. Place them in a gallon container, a trash bag, or even a foot locker, and after four or five days a powerful brew is ready for consumption.

Drugs and alcohol (Indian inmates refer to marijuana as *pheží*, the Lakhóta word for grass) also easily enter the system via inmates who go out into the community on work release or detail and, in their contacts with "the outside," obtain substances they smuggle in supplies, laundry, or other work materials. This is most easily accomplished when community custody inmates have jobs bringing supplies to a medium/maximum facility like the Pen or LCC, with designated inmates waiting to receive the goods. Over-the-counter drugs as well as prescriptions can be purchased by inmates, and certain inmates are well known in each prison as being the major suppliers. In 1976 an Indian inmate was killed in a knifing by other inmates; it was attributed to a bad drug deal. Inmate substance abuse was certainly clear to me upon a number of occasions in which respondents in interviews were nearly incoherent.

Inmates who wish to remain sober in prison express pride in their doing so. While outsiders do not regard sobriety in prison as a real accomplishment (after all, inmates are locked up), inmates say it *is* a real accomplishment because alcohol and drugs are so easily obtained.

Weapons are also relatively easy to obtain, or they may be fashioned out of available materials. Nebraska, probably like most prisons, has an impressive display of homemade weapons such as shanks or knives made from kitchen utensils that were confiscated from inmates after a fight. At a powwow one year, my children found a fork whose tines had been bent to form a sharp point, in the bleachers in the gym. It had obviously been stashed for safekeeping. (I dared not touch it, and admonished my children to put it back where they found it. I guessed that if I brought the "weapon" to the correctional authorities, the powwow would be shut down.)

When inmates discuss their lives—and many of them see their lives as failures because of alcoholism—they know that the only path to living a fruitful life is sobriety. They make promises to themselves that when they are released from prison, they will not return to drinking and living on the streets, because they know that is the shortest route back to prison. Yet when asked point blank whether they have made a commitment to actually *not* drink when they are released, very few are willing to state that. In personal interviews, I spoke with inmates about increasing their chances of remaining sober on the outside, and whether or not a plan or intention of being sober might dictate a course of action when they found themselves in a pressured situation. In other words, if one thought about refraining from drinking and knew that one would certainly encounter such a situation, one could be prepared for it by knowing in advance how to handle it. But given such a scenario, very few inmates were actually willing to state that they would fall back on this plan to help keep them sober. It was far more common for inmates to respond that they would "see what happens." This seemed to me a statement of resignation or acceptance of the inevitable—a return to drinking. Inmates know the risks of temptation, for while they are in prison they see others returning for the exact same set of reasons they are in prison. Yet this does not seem to provide enough incentive to make a commitment of sobriety.

Inmates are very critical of each other's failures, and while they may not actually confront a fellow inmate about his or her return (the reasons are obvious), they suffer the consequences of humiliation in watching another failure. They know that such failures reflect poorly on the group, that they feed stereotypes of Indians who can't resist drink, and they fear that their religious quests for sobriety in prison will be undermined— which they are—because prison administrators will see them as opportunistic: being religious only in prison, but shedding the cloak of religion when faced with the harsh realities of the outside world.

5

Substance Abuse Treatment for Prisoners and Ex-Offenders

In chapter 4, the endemic nature of Indian alcoholism and the extent of its involvement in Indian offense commission was reviewed. This chapter will focus on the various ways in which alcohol and drug abuse are treated in prison, how inmates perceive these rehabilitative programs, and what the unique responses of Native American prisoners are to them. The treatment approaches available to inmates upon release from prison will also be considered, focusing on their appropriateness in serving the Indian ex-offender population. Ultimately, of course, success in treatment or rehabilitative therapy is determined by the rate of recidivism, both into drinking (or using drugs) and into criminal behavior. This is very difficult to establish, since treatment programs define in different ways what constitutes sobriety. But establishing return to prison is far less difficult to document, since the inmates who fail in their attempts at sobriety and get caught again breaking the law reappear in the correctional system (although not always in the same state). One can establish minimum recidivism rates for incarceration, and can discover from the inmates themselves what it was that caused their downfall. Almost universally, it is a return to substance abuse, and the drug of choice is nearly always alcohol.

Treatment options in prison

When offenders begin their residence in a penal institution, they are asked repeatedly about their possible use of or problem with alcohol or drugs. The majority of inmates readily admit having alcohol or drug problems, and it is unusual for an inmate to have no history of substance abuse. Inmates are steered toward the correctional institution's mental health programs, and are encouraged to become participants sometime during their sentence. When the psychological evaluation has assessed that there is a chemical abuse problem, they are informed that the recommendation to take mental health programming will be a part of their record, or jacket, and will ultimately be considered by the board of parole. Since counselors and mental health professionals make recommendations about the psychological status of the prisoners and their readiness to return to society, inmates know that not following the recommendations of the mental health staff may cost them their release.

Within the first year of a sentence, and every year thereafter if the sentence is under five years, inmates appear before the board of parole for a review. At this meeting, the board discusses the prisoner's criminal history, sentence, and plans for rehabilitation in prison. If alcohol or drug abuse has been a part of the inmate's history (as revealed during the presentence investigation or at the individual's divulgence) and the counseling staff has recommended treatment, the board will generally recommend that the individual address his or her problems by taking advantage of whatever mental health programs are available at their institution. Inmates do not always take these recommendations seriously, or sometimes they are in a state of denial about their alcohol or drug problems. They may be cavalier about becoming active participants. But time and again, inmates who have not addressed the nature of their crime in some form of mental health programming are frequently passed over by the board for parole.

When an inmate applies for custody promotion or a special furlough into the community (to attend a Sun Dance, for example), if the recommendation of the prison counselors *and* the board was for treatment and the offender did not opt to take it, chances of the inmate's request being honored are slim. Often, even a custody promotion will be denied for lack of participation in mental health programs, meaning the inmate may never even receive the custody level necessary to establish eligibility for parole. An inmate's regular and committed participation is normally required before parole is finally granted as well. The unwillingness to participate in correctional mental health programs may, in part, account for the tendency of Indian prisoners to shy away from parole, preferring to "jam" their sentences and be totally free.

Availability of programs to inmates depends, in part, upon the custody they have received (as a result of their custody classification hearing) and the subsequent assignment to the appropriate custody institution. Since not all programs are available at all institutions, an effort is made to place the inmate where the program he desires to participate in is housed. Overcrowding has, of course, reduced the options for most inmates.

Inpatient Programs at LCC

At the Lincoln Correctional Center, where medium- and maximum-custody inmates are housed (and a few minimum- and community-custody inmates are assigned to work details around the facility), two inpatient programs are available to inmates, one for substance abuse and one for sex offenders. An inmate expressing a desire to participate in intensive inpatient therapy might inform his counselors while at the Evaluation Unit that he desired placement at LCC. If a bed were available, he would be placed there. If not, he would go to the Pen, where no inpatient programs exist. Since LCC tends to house younger, less "hardened" criminals and the Pen houses older repeat and multiple offenders, placement of the programs at LCC gives newer, first-time offenders the opportunity to receive intensive help in hopes of deterring future involvement in drugs, alcohol, or crime.

The inpatient substance abuse program at LCC, a 90-day voluntary program, is available at the inmate's request or upon the recommendation of counselors at the Evaluation Unit or the board of parole. While the inmate has the option to attend or not, the parole board may have stipulated that if he does *not* participate, he will not receive parole. An inmate whose parole has been revoked because of drinking may be told by the board that subsequent parole will occur only upon completion of the program. Naturally, inmates interpret this as mandatory, not voluntary participation.

The LCC inpatient program constitutes a co-residential therapeutic community—that is, participating inmates are housed separately from all other inmates (in Unit D-2) for the duration of the program, with the exception of sex offenders, who are housed on the same unit, but on a separate "pod" (Unit D-1). Each unit has a capacity of thirty-three.

The program relies heavily on the concept that alcoholism is a disease and is based on an Alcoholics Anonymous approach. Inmates have group therapy and access to readings, tapes, films, and outside speakers, and they are required to keep a daily log or journal. No individual therapy occurs. While some Indian inmates participate (there may be only two or three Indians in the inpatient program at any given time), they are less than enthusiastic about it, and the staff suggests that they are more passive and less vocal than other participants, contributing the most "during the early group sessions where individuals initially speak out about their alcohol histories and the impact substance abuse has had on their lives" (Grobsmith and Dam 1990:413). Some Indian participants have said that while there is supposed to be a treatment team, two weeks may pass without their having been seen a single time by any of the staff. One inmate indicated that his orientation to the program was having a packet of information thrown at him. This situation is certainly exacerbated by prison overcrowding: Where demand for limited resources may increase, additional funding has not been forthcoming to increase staff. Indian participants are encouraged to attend sweat lodge ceremonies available to the general population at LCC.

The mental health staff recognizes that Indian inmates may not feel comfortable in the structure and atmosphere of their inpatient program, and acknowledges that Indian offenders may prefer to address their alcohol problems through attendance at sweat lodge ceremonies. The lack of participation of Indians in their program concerns the staff; however, their belief in the group process (as opposed to individual therapy) results in few Indian prisoners joining this program. Native American prisoner preference is for an exclusively Indian group, however, restriction of programs based along cultural/ethnic lines is difficult for a state-funded facility to endorse. The Judeo-Christian orientation of the AA model creates a conflict for some Indian prisoners as well (see detailed discussion of these issues at the close of this chapter).

The sex offender program at LCC is a long-term inpatient treatment program available for individuals who have committed such crimes as sexual assault, child molestation, and incest. Inmates in this program have admitted to being sexually assaultive and are admitted to treatment because they have expressed a desire to change. The program is voluntary. Some sex offenders have requested assistance from this program but have been told either that they cannot be helped or that they are not suitable participants for the program.

Treatment of sex-offenders is quite complex, as offenders have rarely committed only one assault. Most adult rapists have committed assaults on children, and about one-fourth of child molesters have committed adult rape (see Grobsmith 1989a). The LCC sex offender program overlaps with that of the Lincoln Regional Center, where mentally disordered sex offenders are treated. Inmates whose treatment began at the Lincoln Regional Center, a state psychiatric facility, may be transferred to LCC to finish their sentences. Occasionally, a serious sex offender who refuses treatment at the Regional Center is housed at LCC simply to serve his time, since he is not amenable to treatment. Mentally disordered sex offenders must go before a mental health board before they can be released back into the community; but a sex offender at LCC, one not classified as mentally disordered, may be released upon completion of his sentence or upon parole.

Inmates in this program deal with all facets of their assaults in therapy—how they were planned, their perceptions of the act, the effects of their crimes on the victims and their families, re-offense prevention, and all other possible factors that contributed to their crimes. The mental health staff meets with inmates every three months to review their progress.

Not all inmates complete the program; some drop out, others are asked to leave. The staff believes that those who leave early are at high risk for re-offending.

Indian inmates have historically chosen not to participate in the sex offender program, although their involvement in sexual assaults is relatively high (of 106 Indian inmates in the 1986–87 sample, 10 percent had been convicted of first-degree sexual assault, the third most frequently occurring cause for conviction; see Table 4). Reluctance to discuss personal issues or self-disclosure may account, in part, for their failure to take part in the program. The program is reputed to be quite confrontational, and this may contribute to Native Americans' disinclination to participate as well.

Mental health programming at other institutions

Since only the Lincoln Correctional Center has inpatient programs, mental health programs at all other institutions are outpatient services, generally designed for groups; individual counseling is available only on an emergency basis. At the Pen and Omaha Correctional Center, mental health group therapy sessions help the inmate to deal with whatever issues are involved for him—substance abuse, violence, family problems, anger control. One group which serves mentally impaired inmates is offered separately. The prohibitive cost of offering individual counseling has made it impossible to provide genuine psychological therapy in prison except on a group basis.

In addition to group therapy, Alcoholics Anonymous meetings are available to the general population, and while some Native American prisoners would like to see an Indian AA get started, none exists at this time. The general AA meetings are not well-attended by Indian prisoners for a variety of reasons: they feel conspicuous as minority members; they dislike the Judeo-Christian orientation of AA and feel it is not relevant to their Native American practices; they are often shy and reticent about speaking up in front of others, thereby drawing attention not only to themselves but to shameful acts in which they may have engaged; and finally, they do not feel that genuine self-growth can occur in an environment where correctional officers are present. Confiding personal things about one's activities—whether past or present—is too risky in a prison setting where inmates suspect that guards will not keep their confidence (Grobsmith 1989a:295; Grobsmith and Dam 1990:412). Indian inmates may participate in AA, but they say their heart isn't in it; they attend because they don't believe they will be paroled without it.

Dissatisfied with the opportunities for therapy offered by the correctional system, Indian inmates have, from time to time, been successful in setting up counseling programs specifically oriented to the needs of their group. Counselors from the community Lincoln Indian Center periodically come into the prisons to conduct alcoholism classes, group therapy, or weekly anger group sessions. The anger group (run by non-Indian staff from the Indian Center) consists of outpatient therapy, a highly structured workbook session dealing very specifically with anger, appropriate and inappropriate ways to express it, causes of anger, and learning effective means of coping with it. While these have been ongoing for several years at the Penitentiary, inmates in other correctional facilities have not been successful in getting such counselors into their institutions, although they continue to work toward this goal.

A second group oriented to Indian needs is an alcohol class or support group run by a Native American counselor. It deals with problems resulting from alcohol abuse—guilt, powerlessness, family problems, and other issues participants wish to share. This group is less formally structured than the anger group. Such programs receive considerably more support from Indians since they are not attended by correctional officers and are geared toward Indian clients. Inmates feel assured that confidences are better kept, and they feel more willing to make disclosures about themselves in the safety of a meeting with their Indian brothers.

The majority of trained counselors who come into the penal system are non-Native American. Employees of the Indian Center, however, are trained and sensitized to the issues involved in minority and particularly Indian substance abuse and family problems, and they have been readily accepted by the Indian prison population. The success of Indian paraprofessionals who are recovering alcoholics, or perhaps even ex-offenders, has been noted by a number of researchers (Weibel-Orlando 1989a:138). Some counselors come into the prison to meet with inmates individually for brief periods, as their caseloads permit, and offer private therapy at no cost to the offender. Because this represents an overload for them, most cannot sustain the burden of long-term clients.

Male and female prisoners housed at the Community Corrections Center in Lincoln on work release can avail themselves of counseling services at the Lincoln Indian Center. Because of their lower custody levels (community custody), they are transported to the center two evenings a week for counseling. One evening clients participate in a domestic violence group, and the other session is an anger group. Although Indians may take part in these programs, they are not designed exclusively for them and the group is ethnically mixed. Often individuals who have been referred by the court for outpatient counseling are participants in these groups.

At the Nebraska Center for Women at York, no therapeutic counseling is available. Women prisoners seem to have fewer educational, vocational, and rehabilitative options than male prisoners, a situation many in the community would like to remedy. No psychological therapy is available through prison mental health or the Indian Center. At the two minimum-custody facilities (Hastings and Omaha), mental health services are minimal. Since the Indian Center is not in the same city, no special programs geared to Native Americans have been established for these institutions.

Although Indian Center programs certainly enjoy more popularity with American Indians, some inmates do not wish to participate in any prison mental health counseling, preferring to address their addiction, family problems, personal difficulties, and offense commission in an entirely Indian fashion. Such rehabilitative activity has become more common and prisoners are insisting that the prison and parole board learn about their preferred methods of addressing their crimes—through personal prayer, with or without the Sacred Pipe, through attendance at *yuwípi* or *lowápi* healing ceremonies conducted by medicine men, through preparation for and attendance at the Vision Quest and Sun Dance ceremonies held in South Dakota, and, most often, through attendance at the sweat lodge.

Inmates claim that regular attendance at the sweat lodge is extremely important for their maintaining sobriety. By far the majority of imprisoned Native Americans believe such attendance is preferable to any prison programming. For traditional Indians who were perhaps raised in a reservation area, attending the sweat lodge is a necessary part of the psychological goal of attaining mental health, purification, and personal integrity. The sweat lodge is where answers to difficult questions are sought, where private prayer can be spoken and sung and supported by one's brothers, where no ridicule or negative attitudes can prevail, and where ultimate communication with the spirits can be accomplished. This is the area where purification of body and spirit occurs, without which rehabilitation cannot occur. One inmate, frustrated by his repeated efforts to stay clean and tired of returning to prison, reflected on what hope there was for him: "They sent me to treatment centers, and those things don't work for us skins. I want to be in the Sun Dance this August and get my life in order and continue taking care of my family. I sincerely believe that my religion is the only way I'll straighten up and fly right."

Relying on traditional values and healers, native ceremonies and being in balance with oneself and one's community is the only hope most Indian inmates have for recovery, and that is the predominant value they share.

For Indian prisoners only marginally familiar with such native ceremonies, prison life offers a full encounter with sweat lodge ceremonies and many become fully absorbed in this method of prayer and rehabilitation, whether or not they knew of it before their incarceration.

In all the Nebraska penal facilities but York, sweat lodges exist, and sometimes more than one lodge structure exists at a single facility. Sweat lodge ceremonies are held with regularity and are always a part of the activities planned when a medicine man visits one of the facilities. All the necessary materials to prepare for a ceremony are obtained for the inmates by their religious coordinator or club sponsor, including firewood, rocks, and tarps. Use of the Sacred Pipe, sage, cedar, and sweet grass are all permitted for such worship. Most prisons allow inmates to use the sweat lodge area for solitary prayer and meditation with minimal lead-time requests; however, difficulties of access at some institutions have caused bitterness among Indian prisoners and have been the focus of concern in a number of lawsuits from 1972 to 1983 (CV 72-L-156, CV 80-L-324, CV 83-L-572).

Since the sweat lodge was first built at the old Men's Reformatory in 1976, other correctional facilities have watched Nebraska to see how an institution accommodates Indian religious freedom without compromising security. Officials from Nebraska have even served as consultants to other prisons. In Utah, for example, the first sweat lodge was finally built in 1989. The Native American Rights Fund film describing the use of the sweat lodge by Nebraska inmates has served as an informational model to other prisons throughout the country. (Another film, *Great Spirit Within the Hole*, produced by KTCA Public Television in Minneapolis in 1983, presented the ways in which Indian prisoners in the Oregon penal system depended on the sweat lodge for prayer and rehabilitation.)

The success of traditional Native American ceremonies in alcohol recovery has been noted by researchers examining substance abuse rehabilitation efforts outside prison walls. Roberta Hall (1986) examined the use of the sweat lodge throughout the nation. Powers (1982) has noted the reliance on *yuwípi* healing ceremonies for alcohol recovery for the Oglala, and similar ceremonies are held at Rosebud to seek spiritual assistance with efforts to obtain sobriety (Grobsmith 1981).

Commitment to the sweat lodge strengthens in prison as Indian inmates are drawn to its unifying and affirming effects. Sweat lodge ceremonies are uniquely theirs (or at least they have been until recently, when a group called Odinists have begun to request access to a sweat lodge as part of their religious service; this has caused tremendous conflict between them and the Indians, and has been the focus of one lawsuit). Non-Indian inmates (other than Odinists) may be permitted to sweat with Indians, but participation of outsiders is discouraged for two reasons. First, motives for outsiders wanting to participate in the sweat lodge are suspect. If non-Indians are largely ignorant of Indian ways, why would they want to embrace them? Some inmates, as taught by their religious leaders, feel that any individuals who desire to follow the Indian path in prayer and recovery ought to be allowed to do so; others believe that outsiders know too little about the meaning of the rituals to properly commit themselves. Second, Native Americans are rightfully extremely protective of their right to sweat and make every effort to prohibit any abuse of such ceremonies. The sweat lodge is vulnerable to exploitation by others because of its potential for privacy and secrecy. And, with correctional officers being poorly trained in identification of the smells of burning sage, cedar, and sweet grass, inmates believe they are harassed through the ignorance of guards. Indian inmates further protect the sweat lodge because of rumors about its use for sexual activity and illegal drug use. For these reasons, they are disinclined to let outsiders join them, unless the outsiders have adequately demonstrated their sincerity and commitment to follow the Indian way.

While many Indian inmates are expressing their desire to experience self-growth and rehabilitation through the sweat lodge, prison authorities and the parole board have difficulty accepting the idea that the sweat lodge offers an *equally valuable* method for addressing the nature of their crimes. When an inmate enters prison, he is encountered by a staff not trained in Native American spiritual expression, so any recommendations made about the individual's rehabilitation will generally be in keeping with mainstream mental health programming. An offender's review with the board of parole further outlines what will be expected in order for him to obtain parole, and normally those recommendations refer him to the prison's mental health program. So an Indian inmate who does not feel comfortable in non-Indian programs staffed by non-Indians, who have little or no understanding of Indian problems and culture, will have little recourse but to join the prison's mental health program, if he wishes to be eligible for parole one day. Failure to comply with such recommendations usually is noted in the inmate's psychological evaluation (done for custody promotion), so when it comes time for an inmate to proceed through the custody levels or when he nears the end of his sentence, it is no surprise that Indian offenders are turned down for furloughs into the community, perhaps to attend a Vision Quest or Sun Dance.

The alternative to this bind is for inmates to try to educate all their jailers in the Indian spiritual methods of rehabilitation—no easy task. Such cross-cultural training and sensitization efforts are required in Nebraska by the 1974 Consent Decree, which specifically requires that correctional employees be educated in Indian religious and cultural needs. However, training has been piecemeal and occasional, and turn-over of correctional employees results in the level of training of officers at any one time being slim to nonexistent. But such training for correctional officers is only one aspect of the difficulty: employees, counselors, psychologists, and all mental health staff at *all* institutions in the Department of Correctional Services would have to receive similar training for changes in programming recommendations to have any consistency across institutions.

The other major area where understanding of the sweat lodge, Native American Church, use of the Sacred Pipe, and other rituals outside the walls must occur is with the board of parole. It does no good for a psychologist during evaluation to recommend that an Indian inmate attend outside sweat lodge ceremonies with regularity, if the board indicates that an Inmate will not be considered for parole unless he or she completes a mental health program (e.g. an alcohol abuse or sex offender program) with which Indians have little success. Sensitization of the board of parole *is* occurring, but of course with only five members on the Board, that is a task far more readily accomplished than working with the entire correctional staff. Whereas once, over a decade ago, former parole board members might have chided Indian prisoners for the rebelliousness expressed by wearing long hair, today the board's respect for and appreciation of Indian religion has enabled them to alter their recommendations for rehabilitative programming and discuss with the inmate the way he or she would prefer to address the crime and any substance abuse problems related to it.

Several actions in recent years reflect the board's willingness to adjust their recommendations based on sensitivity to cultural issues. They permitted early release of an Indian inmate to attend alcohol treatment *and* the Sun Dance in South Dakota. Since the Sun Dance is offered only in August, the board accommodated the calendar and moved up the inmate's parole hearing. They have permitted an inmate to travel to a nearby reservation to attend the funeral of an extended family member, despite the correctional administration's regulation that only funerals of immediate family may be attended by inmates. And they have begun to accept the sweat lodge *in place of* participation in prison alcohol treatment as a means for an inmate to achieve recovery.

Such accomplishments should not be minimized. Yet problems still arise in implementation of such culturally sensitive recommendations. For example, the board of parole may recommend that an inmate be allowed to go to the Sun Dance; but an inmate on parole has to work through his parole officer, who generally has received no training in Indian religious issues and lacks understanding. So an inmate completing paperwork to attend the Sun Dance, knowing he will have the board's support, may have to lock horns with a parole officer who believes that attending "some other church some other weekend" would be adequate. Or the board might grant an inmate parole with the recommendation that he attend outpatient counseling "at the discretion of his parole officer." Once again, the decision is in the hands of the parole officer; if he or she recommends that the inmate attend AA, little choice exists, for noncompliance with the directives of the officer will result in a recommendation to the board that the inmate's parole be revoked.

Despite the increase in culturally sensitive decisionmaking, there are many more instances where the board upholds its requirement that any inmate whose offense involved substance abuse go through the conventional treatment approaches, whether or not they have been demonstrated to be effective. Parole officers do still prevent Indian offenders from completing the rehabilitation program that they believe is in their best interests and turnover in membership on the board threatens to impede progress in cultural accommodation.

Alcohol treatment for parolees and ex-offenders

Since the majority of inmates' crimes are alcohol- or drug-related, some kind of rehabilitative programming is usually built into parole requirements. For many inmates, placement in an inpatient treatment program upon parole is greatly desired; for some it is simply a place to go upon release from prison. For others, inpatient treatment is regarded as a requirement that must be met before they are eligible to go to a halfway house. Halfway houses in Nebraska will not accept residents unless they have completed a treatment program, so placement in a facility may be motivated by practical concerns.

Of the forty-five inmates interviewed in my 1986–87 study and subsequently followed-up, twenty-six were released from prison on parole by 1989. Of these, eleven were paroled to an inpatient treatment program (42 percent); eight of them successfully completed the program and two did not. Of the eight who completed treatment, five had come into new contact with the criminal justice system. It does not appear, then, that completing treatment was sufficient to keep Native American prisoners out of trouble with the law. The two who did not complete the treatment returned to custody as well (Grobsmith and Dam 1990:408).

The programs available for offenders on parole reflect a wide range of therapeutic alternatives. At one end of the continuum a Western medical model makes no particular use of the clients' religious or cultural background; at the other, a native approach relies heavily on traditional healing and curing techniques (Weibel-Orlando 1989a:132–34). The programs between vary in the degree to which they incorporate Indian culture and spirituality, the length of stay required or recommended, the philosophy around which the program is designed, whether it is publicly or privately funded, and the employment of Indian personnel to run the program (Grobsmith and Dam 1990:414, 421–24). The "non-native" oriented programs are generally located in hospital settings or clinics and are staffed by medical practitioners who may use drug therapy (e.g., Antabuse or antidepressants) in addition to education and counseling. Generally these programs do not have Indian staff and are not sufficiently familiar with Native American or minority issues to tailor their treatment to meet special needs.

The biggest single factor in selection of an alcohol treatment program upon release from prison is funding. While private treatment centers exist throughout the state of Nebraska, they are under-utilized by the Native American population because they are not within the financial reach of this group. Privately funded centers such as Lincoln General Hospital's Independence Center or Valley Hope have few or only occasional Indian ex-offenders because of the prohibitive costs. State-funded programs such as those at the Hastings Regional Center and NOVA (see below) receive Indian prisoners as conditions of their parole, but neither program addresses addiction issues from the perspective of the Native American addict. The Veteran's Administration hospital in Lincoln accommodates Native Americans coming from the penal system; it is federally funded, but of course it accepts only veterans.

Hastings Regional Center

The Hastings Regional Center Alcohol Treatment Unit is an inpatient, fully funded state program that accepts clients who are on parole. Their approach is highly Western/medical, and they employ a philosophic orientation that regards all addiction—alcohol, drugs, or cigarettes—as maladaptive symptoms of altered neuro-stress adaptation (Grobsmith and Dam 1990:415–16). Treatment aims are to address all aspects of addiction: physiological, psychological, behavioral, nutritional, and spiritual. An Alcoholics Anonymous or Narcotics Anonymous approach is utilized at Hastings, and patients attend several meetings each week both during and after their inpatient stay. Clients are expected to participate in exercise programs, recreation, library, and individual and group therapy sessions. Hastings' clientele is normally around 10 percent to 12 percent Native American, but the high number of Indian participants is more likely due to the institution's being funded than to their particular success with Indian clients. No opportunity to incorporate Indian spiritual practices exists with the Hastings program, one reason that Indian offenders choose it only as a last resort.

NOVA: New Options, Values, and Achievements

The NOVA program, like Hastings, is chosen by Indian parolees not because of its unique accommodation to Indian cultural activities but because it is state funded. Agreeing to go to NOVA requires a commitment to participate for a year, even if the inmate has just six months remaining to serve on his or her sentence. For some, this year is too great a commitment. For others, the promise of drug or alcohol recovery is sufficient motivation to join.

NOVA is a residential therapeutic community in which clients are treated as a family that shares responsibility for its well-being. Group pressure is positively applied to clients to help them learn how to cope with the stress and anxiety of daily life without resort to addictive substances. NOVA utilizes a transactional analysis approach and depends on a personality disorder model with a goal of restructuring the client's lifestyle.

The family is arranged into hierarchical levels, with senior members imposing moral and ethical sanctions upon junior members. Infractions of the rules result in loss of privileges and penalties suffered by the offender. Commitment to the group is reinforced through confrontation, through prohibition of intimate relationships or exclusive friendships, and through individual sacrifice for the well-being of the group. The Game is a group therapy confrontation session at NOVA in which family members are required to confront a single individual. Failure to join in the confronting may result in non-confronters becoming the focus of the group. Participation in the Game is extremely stressful—clients feel ganged up on, because they *are*—and it may be especially difficult for

Native Americans, who do not see themselves as verbally aggressive, nor do they feel comfortable as the focus of confrontation. While serving the needs of the group may be laudatory, Indian clients sometimes feel lost in this group process and resent the loss of their private thoughts and acts. The direct aggressive confrontation is sorely disliked by Indian clients, who cite this most often as the cause of their leaving.

I participated in one session of the Game and found it very uncomfortable (I knew if I didn't participate in the confrontation process, I was risking becoming the focus of the confrontation). I observed the group ridicule an Indian client's long hair, and while I appreciated that participants were trying to get the client to reveal his deeply held if unconscious values of self-identity, I could see where the entire process would just make him want to flee. An ex-offender who became a counselor at NOVA once revealed to me how he used his knowledge of the pain associated with the cutting of long hair as an aid in helping a client to more fully understand the symbolic meaning his long hair represented, and how he could reach within himself for the strength of identity formerly expressed by his hair. Since cutting the hair is an Indian way of expressing mourning, the client was made to see his haircut positively—as a symbolic gesture of leaving behind the identity of addiction and beginning the process of recovery from the loss of his good friend, alcohol. (Although this was a brilliant approach to culturally sensitive therapy, the counselor was unable to apply equally useful strategies to his own circumstances and ended up as a recidivist, both to addictive substances and to incarceration).

NOVA is reputed to enjoy greater success with urban Indians than with traditional/reservation Indians, as it makes no attempt to accommodate Native American cultural baggage (except as in the previous example, when a particular Indian counselor made use of his own cultural knowledge). Although having a Native American counselor there from time to time may make the program more acceptable to some Indian clients, the lack of incorporation of spiritual elements makes the program less attractive to Indian parolees and ex-offenders.

Funded native programs

The treatment programs preferred by Indian prisoners are, of course, those that make some attempt to accommodate the Native American spiritual and cultural worldview and practices. Such programs are generally federally funded by the Indian Health Service and so are, in practical terms, available to indigent clients upon release from prison. Most popular are the Inter-Tribal Treatment Center of Nebraska (formerly Four Winds) in Omaha and the Winnebago Drug Dependency Unit at Winnebago, Nebraska. Other native-oriented programs less utilized include the Santee Sioux Alcoholism Center on the Santee Sioux Reservation in northeast Nebraska; the Macy Alcohol Counseling Center on the Omaha Reservation in northeast Nebraska; the Native American Alcohol Treatment Program in Sergeant Bluffs, Iowa; and the Lincoln Indian Center.

The Inter-Tribal Treatment Center of Nebraska, sponsored by the Nebraska Urban Indian Health Coalition, offers a six-week inpatient program for men and women, permitting those requiring a longer stay to have one. The majority of counselors are Native American, which has great appeal to Indian clients. The program is oriented around an AA format and provides individual, group, and family counseling that addresses issues of co-dependency. This is especially important since the return of a client to an environment where family members have not been a part of the therapeutic process is likely to diffuse efforts at sobriety. While not as confrontive as NOVA, Inter-Tribal does incorporate mildly confrontive techniques in therapy and believes that street language elicits deeper participation from the client. Because the program is Indian-oriented, incorporation of spiritual elements such as the sweat lodge is encouraged. Today, Inter-Tribal has a long waiting list for admission, further reflective of its popularity with Indian clients.

The Winnebago Drug Dependency Unit, located in the Indian Health Service Hospital at Winnebago, Nebraska, is a forty-five-day inpatient program for men and women. Like Inter-Tribal, it enjoys great popularity with Indian clients (both from prison and not) because it addresses issues of Indian culture and spirituality along with other medical and psychosocial approaches. Winnebago functions on the premise that the experience of being Indian and the demands of living in a bi-cultural world are factors that must be incorporated rather than ignored in the recovery process. Because Native Americans have suffered difficult and often demeaning social experiences, recovery stresses issues of pride and integrity in maintaining an Indian heritage. Additionally, clients wishing to attend Native American Church services or sweat lodge ceremonies in the community may do so.

Like most treatment programs, Winnebago depends on an AA-style support group, but because meetings are held in an Indian social context where all clients are Indian and share similar cultural backgrounds, the difficulties of participating are greatly reduced. Individual and group therapy, family counseling, relaxation and biofeedback, exercise, and nutrition are all part of Winnebago's varied approach to recovery.

The Santee Sioux Alcoholism Center is an outpatient treatment program located on the Santee Reservation in Nebraska. It offers individual, group, and family therapy, and education and referral services. No inpatient facility exists, so the program operates only to support those coming out of inpatient treatment or needing referral to locate one. Because of this, the program is geared more toward prevention than cure, and serves youth more than adults.

At Macy, Nebraska, on the Omaha Indian Reservation, the Macy Alcohol Counseling Center is a halfway house to assist clients awaiting or coming out of inpatient treatment. Individual and group therapy, films, and AA meetings are available to clients. The program is striving to obtain approval by the Federal Bureau of Prisons so that male offenders coming directly from a federal prison can be paroled to the program.

The Native American Alcohol Treatment Program in Sergeant Bluffs, Iowa, like Winnebago, is a forty-five-day cycled inpatient substance abuse center (all patients enter as a class or unit and complete treatment together). Only fifteen beds are available, but only Native American clients are accepted. Because the program is funded by the Indian Health Service, treatment is available to indigent clients. Ex-offenders from Nebraska may apply to go there, but because the program is located in Iowa, arrangements have to be made with the board of parole to transfer legal authority to the state of Iowa.

The program at Sergeant Bluffs adopts the philosophy of a corporation entitled Medicine Wheel, Inc., whose aim it is to bring Indian clients to recovery through resolution of difficulties in their family histories that resulted in their becoming chemically dependent. Family alcoholism, sexual abuse, incest, and domestic violence, which all play a part in many Indian home environments, are seen as contexts that must be explored and the problems resolved before they can be put in a client's past. The philosophical approach divides the world into "natural" (Indian) and "unnatural" (non-Indian) spheres, and clients are encouraged to observe their maladaptive behaviors as dysfunctional ways of coping with an alien world. Once the experiences of an individual's past have been confronted and understood, new coping skills can be learned. Because the program revolves around a strongly Indian orientation, incorporation of religious and spiritual practices is considered an important component of the recovery plan.

Valley Hope in O'Neill, Nebraska, and the Independence Center at Lincoln General Hospital are so underutilized by Native American offenders that their programs are not detailed here. (For a discussion of these programs, see Grobsmith and Dam 1990.)

The rough road to recovery

All of the treatment programs consider working with ex-offenders or parolees difficult to some degree; some prefer not to accept clients coming straight from prison. Prison life places so much stress on individuals it makes them less receptive to and suitable for alcohol treatment. Some clients who have had little or no mental health counseling in prison arrive at treatment still in a state of denial concerning either their crimes or their chemical addiction. Often the difficulties of prison life have left them in a state of helpless rage, an anger that probably began before they committed their offenses and has not been addressed much less resolved. Consequently, these individuals may be reluctant to reveal themselves, be candid about their addiction, or acknowledge their culpability or responsibility for their situation. To the contrary, in fact, many prisoners see themselves as the victims and leave prison angry at "the system." Having been discouraged from expressing anger, or viewing anger as a negative emotion, these offenders sometimes have difficulty even identifying their anger or understanding where it is directed. Such individuals only go to treatment because it is the quickest way to obtain parole. But they do not stay out of prison, and frequently do not make it through treatment.

Entering a treatment program in such a state or with this kind of attitude makes treatment especially difficult. Staff indicate that the majority of their time is spent trying to break down barriers the individual has created and overcoming his or her state of denial. At treatment, ex-offenders often form a clique, making it harder for the treatment team to penetrate. Such groups tend to reinforce defense mechanisms and keep the inmates isolated from the recovery process. Lack of trust on the part of ex-offenders, also learned in prison, carries over into treatment and makes establishing a strong bond between client and therapist especially problematic. Since any alcohol therapy can be effective only if the client is receptive, ex-offenders present a genuine challenge for treatment agency personnel.

On the other hand, some parolees leave prison with an enormous commitment to recover and surmount any obstacles to have the opportunity to go through treatment. The potential for recidivism to prison life is so large and frightening that nothing can deter them from total involvement in a program. Unfortunately, adjusting to re-entry into the community is so difficult—restoring family roles and relations, picking up a marriage or parenting where they left off—that the chances of staying sober and staying free are abysmally low, even though treatment may have been successfully completed.

The issue of what treatment is most effective with Native American clients, coming from prison or not, is a difficult one. According to Joan Weibel-Orlando, the high rate of return to drinking among Indian alcoholics is, in part, a function of the "lack of fit between the client's worldview and life experience and the program treatment modality" that serves them (1985:220). Philip May has found that "traditional Indian strengths and treatments have been ignored even though some have proven effective for many individuals" (1986:193). Kemnitzer (1972), Jorgensen (1972), Parker (1988), Hall (1986), Powers (1982), and many others have commented on the importance of incorporation of some elements of the traditional culture into therapy, an attitude certainly consistent with the Native American perspective. Between 1981 and 1983, Dr. A. Logan Slagle, Dr. Kenneth Lincoln, and Dr. Joan Weibel-Orlando constituted a project team that, under the auspices of a grant from the National Institute of Alcoholism and Alcohol Abuse (NIAAA), visited fifty-two alcoholism treatment programs, recovery homes, and traditional Indian healers in California, Arizona, New Mexico, Oklahoma, and South Dakota. Weibel-Orlando indicates that programs "with the highest rates of sustained client sobriety are those that integrate a variety of spiritual elements and activities into their treatment strategies" (1985:223).

However, lack of systematic measurement of treatment successes has prevented anyone from saying with any real confidence that native-oriented programs are in fact more successful than Western-oriented, more conventional modes of therapy. Weibel-Orlando cautions: "Most alcohol intervention projects suffer from inadequate treatment evaluation procedures" (1989a:126), and she bemoans the difficulty of measuring sobriety success rates because of poor tracking of a mobile population. (Nebraska prison research certainly concurs, for it is doubly difficult to measure not only recidivism to drinking but recidivism to incarceration as a result of the loss of sobriety; see Grobsmith and Dam 1990.) Advocates for Native Americans can further complicate the issue by expecting indigenous approaches to treatment to be superior to Western modalities. Weibel-Orlando (1989b) points out the considerable amount of romantic appeal in asserting that native styles of treatment are more effective than non-native, and warns that we as scholar/advocates must resist the temptation to make such unsubstantiated claims.

While it *appears* that adoption of a combined strategy—using the "white man's medicine" in conjunction with issues of Indian culture and spirituality—may be the most effective, some treatment program personnel say they fear that programs that depend heavily on native ritual, such as the sweat lodge, may be contributing to the individual's refusal to face his or her alcoholism. Spirituality is seen as one of many important components in recovery, but not as a panacea promising full recovery. It was definitely noted by agency personnel that some ex-offenders used the sweat lodge to avoid discussion of their own problems in therapy. But inmates are reluctant to join programs that do not incorporate the sweat lodge into their recovery plan, so many programs offer sweat lodge facilities if only to avoid accusations of cultural insensitivity (Hall 1986:168; Grobsmith and Dam 1990:422).

The style, mode, or type of treatment could be less critical a factor than the individual's commitment to recovery. An ex-offender deeply committed to recovery may be able to do it himself, with little or no assistance at all. Support from family and friends can play a significant role in helping the parolee to avoid the people and contexts that are bound to bring him down. Without question, Indian ex-offenders say that pressure from their so-called friends is usually what causes a breakdown in their resistance, and when they finally capitulate results in a drinking episode that leads to violation of many conditions of their release and parole (alcohol use is an automatic violation).

Some inmates say that they know they must avoid returning to the environments that fostered their drinking habits and contributed to their offending. Others long to return to their reservation communities and feel that only when they go home can they return to really being themselves and rebuilding their lives. In either case, pressures to join friends and relatives in drinking activities are immense, and many fall prey to these pressures. Because parolees whose offense involved alcohol or drugs are, as a condition of their parole, prohibited from going to any bar, returning to that former circle of friends invites trouble. Refusal to join former buddies in drinking activities may result in ridicule of the parolee, ostracism, loss of friendship, and real social isolation. Inmates with the best of intentions to stay sober find themselves in compromising situations, and a single breakdown is often sufficient to return a parolee to custody and cause revocation of parole and loss of good time, resulting in an extension of time to be served before release. Additionally, a return to drinking raises questions with the board of parole about a questionable commitment to sobriety or lack of sincerity concerning staying free of trouble with the law. As one inmate whose parole had been revoked for an alcohol-related arrest indicated, "I forgot there was a chain around my neck; I forgot I was a prisoner." Life on the outside becomes private and comfortable, and a parolee can lose track of the fact that even the slightest violation can have dreadful consequences.

Inmates who promised that they would *never* return to prison find themselves back at the Evaluation Unit awaiting parole revocation hearings. They had no intention of drinking; they certainly did not consider that a minor infraction of the conditions of their parole would result in a return to prison. However, follow-up of the forty-five Indian offenders in my 1986–87 study revealed that after a period of three years, nearly two-thirds of the individuals who were paroled—seventeen of the twenty-six—had been returned to custody; more than half (52 percent) of those released from prison with or without parole *had been returned to custody* (Grobsmith and Dam 1990:408). Even more depressing are the recidivism statistics for Native Americans who successfully complete alcohol treatment. Without the imposed structure of prison life or the regimentation of an intensive recovery program, return to drinking is the norm.

Why does this breakdown occur? There is no single answer, but many contributing factors. First, without question, *inmates do not receive adequate alcohol or drug therapy behind the walls.* Overcrowded and underfunded, the correctional system makes no pretense of being able to offer genuine rehabilitation. Prison is a temporary holding tank where inmates are housed until they have served their sentence, compensated society for the injustices they have done, or demonstrated that they no longer pose a risk to public safety. Inpatient programs are available only to a few, and are rarely selected by Indians. The lack of individual counseling is the most damaging. For Indian prisoners, for whom participation in the prison's mental health program seems alien and frightening, those groups do not even seem legitimate options. Prison AA meetings, large racially mixed groups where the orientation is largely Judeo-Christian, where correctional officers are in attendance, and where tremendous self-consciousness exists about being Indian, are not an acceptable alternative either.

If prison mental health programs are not the ticket, then perhaps commitment to sobriety through the sweat lodge contributes to the answer. However, the double bind is that the correctional system—unit managers, housing counselors, authorities, parole officers, and the like—understand so little about its significance that they are suspicious of its rehabilitative value. Only recently has the parole board even begun to recognize its value in recovery. Yet those inmates who espouse participation in the sweat lodge as the only reasonable means of attaining recovery from alcoholism will be carefully scrutinized once they get out to see if they maintain sobriety. The political struggle to achieve acceptance of the sweat lodge in prison as an alternative to other forms of therapy will place special burdens on it. Naturally, *some* followers of the sweat lodge and Sacred Pipe have failed their efforts at sobriety, just as *some* followers of AA or medical approaches have failed. Conversely, some adherents of the sweat lodge have succeeded both in maintaining sobriety and in staying free of law enforcement contact, just as adherents of more conventional approaches have likewise succeeded.

Within the Nebraska penal population, the numbers of native religious practitioners who succeed in achieving sobriety and avoiding reincarceration have been extremely low. While a return to drinking may not be uncommon for any alcoholic, Indian inmates do comprise a unique population. Many of these individuals have been raised in alcoholic homes, have been physically and sexually abused, have had long histories of legal entanglements, and have become accustomed to the use of alcohol as an accompaniment to nearly all social activities. Community reservation culture has not provided a supportive environment for ex-offenders wishing to remain sober; in fact, returning home is fraught with perils for those choosing not to drink. And few make it. Additionally, the majority of offenders have long alcohol histories with involvement of alcohol or drugs in prior offenses; many have served time in penal institutions before. As a group, then, Native American prisoners may suffer the same problems as other chemically dependent individuals; but even those who gain a strong sense of a spiritual identity in prison, who become deeply religious and discover a new religiously based sense of self-worth, are seldom able to overcome the histories that initially led to their incarceration.

6

The Parole Process

Parole is probably one of the most confusing prison procedures, for inmates and the public alike. Not all inmates take parole, and in fact many Indian prisoners make the decision not to seek release from prison through parole. Of those who seek and receive parole from prison, successes are fewer than failures. The actual failure rate is unquestionably higher for Native Americans than corrections statistics estimate, because only first offenses are figured into recidivism rates (including leaving the state on parole, a new felony for which parole failures may serve additional time).

Parole refers to the physical but not legal release of an inmate into the community. Generally, paroled inmates return to home and work but must meet certain conditions to which they have agreed, including lawful and responsible behavior and specified check-in with their parole officer. They are still in the legal custody of the penal institution. *Discharge* refers to an unconditional release from prison, both physical and legal.

Parole has existed in the state of Nebraska since 1893—for a century. Originally, the governor had the authority to parole any prisoner who had served the minimum amount of time for the crime he or she had committed (Sixteenth Annual Report of the Nebraska Board of Parole 1984–85). Parolees could be returned to the penitentiary at any time, without notice or hearing and for any reason deemed sufficient by the governor. In 1911 the state legislature created the State Prison Board, consisting of three members appointed by the governor for a period of three years. One member had to be a practicing physician and one a practicing attorney. This board also served in an advisory capacity to the Board of Pardons. It was not until 1968, when a state constitutional amendment was passed, that the state Parole Board was established. In 1969, the Nebraska State Legislature passed LB 1307, which created the Division of Corrections, the Board of Parole, Office of Parole Administration, and Board of Pardons. Today the Board of Parole, under the direct authority of the governor and not formally a part of the corrections system, consists of five full-time positions. Each appointment is made directly by the governor, subject to legislative confirmation. The fact that the parole board is an autonomous political entity, connected only in a cooperative, consultative fashion to the Department of Correctional Services and in no way obliged to conform to the directives of DCS is a great source of confusion for inmates who see that the board's recommendations must be implemented during their incarceration. Naturally they assume that the two administrative authorities are under one umbrella; but they are not. They do, however, cooperate in their recommendations concerning programming, rehabilitation, scheduling of parole hearings, and, ultimately, release. The Adult Parole Administration, which *is* directly under the authority of the director of the Department of Correctional Services, supervises parole agreements drawn up by the Board of Parole by assigning parole officers to parolees and governing parole infractions.

Of the five full-time positions on the board, one individual must have a professional background in corrections, and one must be a minority. (These two characteristics had inadvertently been collapsed into one position, but shifting appointments to the board resulted in clarification of this policy and separation of these appointment characteristics in the early 1990s.) Each board member is appointed to a six-year term, and one member is appointed to serve as chair. The members of the board must be "of good character and judicious temperament" (Rules and Regulations of the Nebraska Board of Parole 1986, p. 5). Their responsibilities include conducting reviews or initial meetings with inmates, determining when an inmate shall be released, outlining the conditions under which parole is granted, handling the return of inmates to the correctional system when the parole agreement has been violated, and deciding when the sentence and parole should be discharged.

When an inmate is sentenced by the court and has been through the evaluation process and has arrived at the appropriate facility, he or she meets with the board of parole for an Offender Board Review. Even if the inmate's sentence is such that he or she is not eligible for parole, a review must take place within the first year of incarceration. Even lifers whose sentences carry the stipulation that they will never be eligible for parole

must have a review—after all, commutation of a life sentence may occur; even the death penalty may ultimately result in commutation and
parole. After the initial review, the decision to have annual reviews (or
not) is based on the length of the inmate's sentence and the parole eligibility date, which has been established after the computation of good
time has been made. If an offender is within five years of parole eligibility, he or she will be reviewed annually. If an offender is not eligible for
parole until more than five years after the initial review (but within ten
years from the date of incarceration), the board may defer the next review
until the inmate is within three years of the parole eligibility date. If an
inmate has been sentenced to serve between ten and thirty years, he or
she may be deferred every five years until five years before the eligibility
date. For those serving more than thirty years, the board may defer visits
every ten years until the offender is within five years of the eligibility
date, at which point the prisoner is reviewed annually. Lifers can be deferred every ten years until the sentence is commuted and the offender is
within five years of the parole eligibility date, at which point reviews
will be scheduled on an annual basis.

Reviews, which are not open to the public—are critical to the inmate's plan for release. It is at the initial review that the board first
becomes acquainted with the offender, the crime and his or her perceptions about it, the pre-sentence investigation, social history and criminal record, and any test results and evaluations that have been made by
the correctional staff. The board discusses with the inmate what he or
she feels will be necessary for rehabilitation and what kinds of programs
or goals the inmate has set. "The purpose of the Offender Board Review is
to provide the Board with a personal profile about you; to briefly discuss
the circumstances surrounding your offense; to evaluate your progress
and conduct to date; to make recommendations for your involvement in
needed treatment programs, vocational/educational programs; and to
determine your readiness for release in society on parole" (*Rules and
Regulations of the Nebraska Board of Parole* 1986: 4).

Later the inmate may not recall precisely what he or she promised the
board would be accomplished during the incarceration; but the board records on tape all inmate meetings and refers to the inmate's statement of
intent. If the inmate discussed an alcohol or drug problem and indicated
willingness to become involved in mental health programming, but
then failed to do so, five years later or whenever the inmate next comes
before the board, either for another review or a parole hearing, the board

board will ask what was accomplished in the way of rehabilitative programming. If the inmate indicates that no programming was undertaken or completed *as originally promised in the review,* the board may not feel assured that the underlying causes of the original offense have been addressed, and may very well defer the offender another year or until such time as the inmate has demonstrated some effort to address the nature of the offense. Inmates get frustrated when they are deferred a year, or discover that their parole hearings have been put off; but the board can review an inmate's jacket and if they see that the inmate has not taken advantage of programming or has been involved in a number of misconduct reports, they may save everyone's time by postponing the hearing.

At their reviews, all inmates are given a copy of a pamphlet, "Getting Ready for Release," prepared by the Board of Parole. They are expected to read it. The pamphlet emphasizes that parole is a privilege, not a right, and may be granted when all the conditions of parole have been met and when the board has reasonable assurance, through the inmate's prior behavior and future plans, that the inmate will comply with the agreement. The pamphlet reads: "Parole is a RIGHT of society and a PRIVILEGE for the offender. The purpose of parole is to protect the rights of society and to provide you assistance through a gradual resocialization, under a period of supervision, into the mainstream of society as a productive, law-abiding citizen. Parole does not release you from your court sentence. It merely provides you with an opportunity to complete your sentence under supervision in a community setting or to begin satisfying any outstanding detainers" (page 2). Additionally, the pamphlet emphasizes that parole is considered only for those who demonstrate positive growth and development by dealing with the nature of their offenses and by taking advantage of self-help programs in prison, and staying out of trouble—in other words, by obeying prison regulations and staying "misconduct free."

An offender who has served the minimum sentence may be set for a parole hearing if the board has determined that the individual appears to be ready to complete the sentence in a community setting, where he or she can work, go to school, support family members, and otherwise begin the readjustment to being a productive citizen. Inmates fear parole hearings, for they recognize the control the board has over their freedom and future; this realization causes them to be intimidated by direct questioning about their offenses, rehabilitative programs, and future plans. All the work habits, behaviors, misconduct reports, psychological evaluations, personal conflicts, and attitudes an inmate has experienced are taken into consideration in the board's deliberations, as well as the inmate's personality, potential for being a law-abiding citizen, employment history, history of narcotics use or alcohol abuse, the recommendations of the sentencing judge or law enforcement officers, and, of course, the perspective of the victim of the crime.

Parole hearings are by necessity public affairs, to afford an opportunity for all who wish to be heard to express themselves concerning an inmate's release, whether in favor or against. Notice must be made in the newspapers announcing the date, place, and time of each inmate's parole hearing, providing ample opportunity for the public, the sentencing judge, and the prosecuting attorney to present evidence. Not uncommonly, victims and their families appear to testify under oath concerning their views of the offender's prospective release and the impact it may have on them. They may request that the board delay or deny parole for an offender who brought harm to them or members of their family through theft, assault, sexual assault, domestic violence, incest, or other crime. Such hearings are dramatic and tense affairs where offender and victim may be together in the same room for the first time since the offense was committed.

There is nothing comfortable about a parole hearing. It begins with an inmate's entry into a room in which the board is seated around a table with microphones placed where the offender and board members sit. A tape recorder and operator are present along with a member of the Adult Parole Administration and any members of the public who wish to observe or testify. The authority of the parole board is undoubtedly intimidating. The board member presiding that day will initiate the hearing by asking the inmate to identify himself or herself for the record. The entire criminal history is reviewed, which naturally brings all parties in attendance to focus on the inmate's criminal acts. The board reviews the time at which the inmate was set for this hearing, the history of any prior paroles or releases, parole revocations, and behavior in prison. Psychological evaluations are discussed and the mental health counselor's recommendation are read in detail. The board weighs how and in what ways an inmate poses a parole risk and whether the concerns of the therapists can be resolved. Additionally the board indicates that they have notified the county attorney, sheriff, and police where the inmate was arrested and invited them to appear or write a letter expressing their views on the offender's prospective release.

After all these details are reviewed, the inmate is asked directly why he or she feels entitled to parole. The inmate may be fully expressive about the years spent in prison, about plans to resume a place in society and return to being a productive, law-abiding citizen. But it is equally likely that the inmate will be extremely frightened, soft-spoken (barely audible), and inarticulate. The inmate's offense and how he or she has addressed the causes of its commission are then reviewed, with no tiptoeing around the issues. If the inmate is serving a sentence for sexual assault, he will be asked how he feels about his crime, and to describe programs in which he has been involved (if any) and what his performance in those programs has been. The board must assess his empathy with the victim and whether he has fully considered and resolved the harm suffered by the victim and his or her family. Any indication that the offender has either not fully dealt with these issues or is still denying involvement or intent in the crime unequivocally results in denial of the parole and deferral to some future date.

The parole board also discusses the offender's behavior in prison. If previous reviews indicate that the prisoner was convicted of a misconduct violation during incarceration, that will be discussed. Perhaps, for example, the inmate had been written up for some minor infraction such as being in an unauthorized area or possession of unauthorized articles. Normally the board will not consider such transgressions sufficiently serious to warrant denial of parole. However, if the inmate was initially involved in an offense that involved alcohol or drugs and then received *any* misconduct report that involved substance abuse, the board most likely will not believe the inmate is sincere in his or her desire for rehabilitation and will deny parole. Violent acts or drug and alcohol use are the two behaviors most likely to interfere with the granting of parole. Inmates fear that any misconduct report on their record will harm their chances for release, but in fact minor infractions are not serious threats.

The board's discussion with the offender may be quite in-depth, probing into what the individual has learned about himself or herself during incarceration, into reasons for not having complied with former board recommendations, or even into the inmate's personality characteristics, especially if the board believes they will be a detriment to successful parole. Prisoners are warned that as quickly as parole is granted, it can be taken away. They are confronted with the heartache they have caused their families, the disappointment they have brought to their loved ones.

If the inmate responds satisfactorily to this portion of the hearing and has demonstrated a commitment to straighten out by remaining misconduct free, the board asks questions about future plans: where the inmate expects to go (for example, to reside with a relative, to go to a treatment program or halfway house, to return to a wife and children), where he or she intends to work, and other details of the release. Inmates may not be released unless they have secured employment. If there is no commitment of a job, only "house parole" will be granted, meaning activity will be restricted to job-seeking and remaining at home until employment has been established.

If this set of conditions has been met, the board presents the inmate with a copy of the parole agreement. The provisions of the document are extremely specific, and the inmate is required to follow each one exactly. Failure to do so may result in a separate charge for every violation of the agreement. The board asks the inmate if, knowing the conditions explicitly outlined in the document, he or she is still interested in parole, and of course the inmate responds positively. Discussion of the offender's prior parole problems and the board's expectations or admonitions may follow, with the board cautioning the individual that if another failure results, the board will revoke parole without hesitation. If there appear to be concerns, the board may opt to go into executive session to discuss these issues privately, and all are excused. If not, a member of the board will make a motion to parole the individual as specified. If the motion is seconded, a majority vote (three out of five) must then be obtained. The roll is called, the votes are taken, and the die is cast. If the necessary votes have been obtained, the inmate's parole is authorized. Both inmate and the Board of Parole sign and date the agreement, upon which the offender is sent off with wishes of good luck.

While the parole agreement may appear straightforward, compliance with all the provisions is difficult for many offenders and a kind of disbelief exists among inmates that an infraction will in fact result in revocation of parole. Not all infractions do result in revocation. Violations of the agreement are reported immediately by the parole officer to the Adult Parole Administration and, if the charges are minor or if the offender has been doing well for the most part, infractions are dealt with in an administrative hearing. Such a hearing is attended by the supervising officer, the parolee, and a member of the parole administration—the parole administrator—who follows guidelines in determining what if any sanctions should be imposed on the parole violator. The seriousness of the violation is considered and the number of charges that have occurred as a result of that single violation. For example, if a parolee is arrested for intoxication and not returning to the approved residence that night, he or she technically may be charged with several counts—but since failure to return to the residence is likely a result of intoxication, the parole administration attempts to be charitable and deal with the violations as a single incident.

Normally when such a violation occurs, the parole administrator will recommend that the parolee suffer a loss of a certain amount of good time, at the discretion of the director of the Department of Correctional Services. Only good behavior good time can be taken away (it is the only kind that is applied toward parole), not meritorious good time, which applies toward the discharge or "jam" date. Removal of good time is a form of discipline that results in the inmate's having to remain under supervision longer, although it does not require a return to custody. The additional time is considered ultimately to benefit, not simply discipline, the offender, in that the time period during which he or she receives structure and discipline is extended. If an inmate suffers only a loss of good time, a certain amount will be taken away depending on the infraction; but if the inmate is also returned to custody—a loss of freedom— the inmate will lose *less* good time. Because of prison overcrowding, pressure exists to keep an offender on parole (although it is not likely that a parole violator will see it that way). If it is at all reasonable to continue parole and keep an offender out on the streets, where he or she is learning to cope, that is preferred by parolee and parole administrator alike. The philosophy of the parole administration is that it is preferable to keep the program stable and allow the inmate to work through the conflicts he or she has encountered. If the violations are minor and technical, the inmate will be returned to the streets. If, however, the number of violations are too many or have been repeated too often, the inmate will be returned to custody to await a parole revocation hearing.

Public parole revocation hearings are scheduled to deal with offenders who continue to violate the conditions of their parole agreement and are getting along poorly and/or have had several administrative hearings already that have evidently not been sufficient to enforce the inmate's compliance with the agreement. Naturally, the inmate is extremely nervous, fearing the worst—a return to custody and possibly a loss of good time. Added to the fear of re-incarceration is the fear of being chastened by the parole board. At revocation hearings, the board does not mince words. If the inmate has failed and disappointed the board, that is expressed. If the board took a chance when the offender was initially released and the board feels their faith in the individual has been betrayed, the offender will be told. In cases where the individual has numerous charges against him or her, members of the board may be quite confrontational and demand that the offender explain what has been happening to cause such abysmal failure.

When the inmate is sworn in, once again, as with the parole hearing, the individual is identified for the record and the initial crime, parole eligibility, and results of the hearing are all reviewed. The inmate is asked whether representation by an attorney is necessary, and in some cases one is already present. The offender is then given a copy of the summation of charges, and the parole administrator is asked to read the allegations filed against the offender. Then the inmate's response to each charge is requested. Admissions of guilt to various violations usually precipitate little discussion, but denials and "no comments" do. The offender may offer mitigating circumstances—why, for example, it was impossible to make contact with the parole officer, or the conditions surrounding being fired from employment.

Sometimes discussion becomes heated as members of the board confront the inmate concerning failure to comply with the parole agreement. If the individual is viewed by the board as being combative, resistant to cooperation, refusing to accept responsibility for behavior, unable to stay away from drugs, and in general not making a genuine effort to be a law-abiding responsible citizen, the individual's parole will be revoked and good time lost. The board does not tolerate excuses. For example, if an inmate admits to a drinking charge, he may be confronted: "Who took you out and caused you to drink?" If the offender tries to pass the buck and make their behavior someone else's responsibility, a board member may state: "*You* took yourself away from your family, *not us*. If your family is in a difficult position, it is *you* who has placed them there—not us. You are playing games, and you are not going to win because we make the rules! I am listening to you and wondering how come you feel it is OK to violate the rules, and then *you* are the one who feels his rights have been violated!"

While such statements may upset offenders, they are intended to let the inmates know that the board has heard all the excuses and is not easily deceived, that they respect inmates' efforts that are sincere and genuine but simply lack sympathy for those who are not making the attempt to comply. An inmate who is up front with the board and makes no excuses for bad behavior is likely to fare better than one who denies complicity in any wrongdoing.

If, on the other hand, the board determines that the individual *has* been making a genuine effort, has *not* engaged in very serious infractions, has admitted to having problems and appears sincere in his or her effort to resolve them, they are likely to continue the inmate on parole with admonitions that any further negative interaction with parole officers will result in parole revocation. Such threats may be enough to keep the offender out of prison—the parolee has had a very close call.

When the discussion is completed, the inmate's responses are read aloud and the parole administrator is asked to present a recommendation (either to revoke or to continue parole). A majority vote of the parole board completes the decision-making process unless a board member requests that they go into executive session.

Native Americans and the parole process

While most Indian inmates face the parole board when the day of their hearing is scheduled, there are certain Indian prisoners who decide not to consider parole as an option for their release. Rather, they wish to "jam" out and do all the time imposed by the courts. To an outsider, this would appear to be a rather self-destructive decision, as foregoing parole opportunities certainly lengthens a sentence. However, a number of issues have contributed to this attitude among Indian prisoners, and they may change only with efforts on the part of the board, the correctional authorities, and the inmates themselves.

First, some Indian inmates believe that the parole board discriminates against them. While there is no evidence to support this, Indians are aware that other minorities have been represented on the board—there have been blacks and Hispanics, and female members as well. Lacking such representation, Indian inmates do not feel there is a member who understands and can take into consideration their culture. Consequently, Indian prisoners believe, the board will be less sympathetic to them and their needs.

Like most Native Americans who are not incarcerated, Indian inmates are extremely wary of paternalistic control, a condition suffered because of historic Bureau of Indian Affairs domination over their decision-making and economic welfare. The fear of control and paternalism follows them into the prison system, where they can deal with surrendering their freedom *while incarcerated* but are not willing to subject themselves to "domination" during their freedom. Of course, parole is not the same as freedom; it is still punishment, only with opportunities to reside and work in the community. But it is naturally regarded as "getting out" and would be considered better if it were totally free of domination. Indian prisoners resent the considerable number of restrictions imposed on their freedom during parole, which may be one of the reasons for their relatively high recidivism rates. And so, for some, it is better to do the time, to complete the entire sentence, than to subject themselves to the trials of parole.

Probably the most notable problem Indian prisoners have with the parole process is their belief that the board does not understand either their rejection of the prison's mental health programs or their preference to address the nature of their offenses in the Indian style—via the Sacred Pipe, sweat lodge, other Indian ceremonies, and through participation in NASCA. To some extent, these concerns are well-founded. Although an individual from the Indian Center was once appointed to serve as liaison between Indian inmates and the Nebraska Board of Parole, this relationship was ineffective and was subsequently discontinued. Indian inmates have had no formal channel to communicate their preferences for methods of rehabilitating themselves to the board, and have done so only sporadically and individually in their parole hearings. But Indian inmates—like most others—are intimidated by the parole process and are disinclined to be verbose or very explanatory about their beliefs to the board. Consequently, an inmate may be denied parole or furlough because the board had indicated in his review that he needed to avail himself of mental health programming and he preferred to address his crime (and the causes of it) in non-mainstream prison programs (like the Indian Center anger group) or through participation in the sweat lodge. The board has been likely to regard that as not participating in recommended mental health programs.

Today, such situations are slowly giving way, as the board gains more knowledge of and sensitivity to Indian spiritual issues. However, with particularly violent offenders or those convicted of sex offenses, the board generally does not believe that involvement in the sweat lodge is adequate to address the issues that underlie such offenses and members "generally refuse parole to Native American inmates who have failed to avail themselves of prison mental health programs" (Grobsmith and

Dam 1990:12). Even where parole board consciousness has been raised concerning Indian rehabilitation, parole officers are seldom so enlightened and may fail to implement the more culturally specific and sensitive recommendations of the board.

Indian offenders have been agitated for years by the board's lack of understanding of and appreciation for their cultural precepts and beliefs. But Indian inmates have not taken the time or initiative to systematically educate the board. In my observation of the parole process, it became more and more apparent that Indian inmates singularly were not reaching the board but collectively might have some impact. As a volunteer and sponsor for NASCA, I brought one member of the board to a NASCA club meeting at the Pen, where inmates could express, on their own turf and in the context of their normal regular Indian activities, their concerns about the board's not understanding offenders' rejection of mental health approaches to recovery and their desire to substitute the sweat lodge and prayer with the Sacred Pipe. Indian inmates expressed their wish that *their* activities be acknowledged by the board as being as effective for them as mainstream mental health programs might be for non-Indians. The dialogue between the board and the Indian inmates had begun, and word got out to other institutions that the board was being receptive to learning of the Indian inmates' preferences.

A second meeting was arranged, between the same parole board member and the NASCA group at the Lincoln Correctional Center, where similar discussions and exchanges took place. Finally, two board members traveled to the Omaha Correctional Center to initiate an exchange with Indian prisoners there. Once again, the board demonstrated their willingness not only to listen to Indian inmates' concerns but also to try to incorporate what they learned into their decision-making during hearings. Then the members of the board requested that Indian inmates put together a presentation about the programs they participated in, showing the ways in which they were more effective in addressing Indian rehabilitative issues, and enumerating the concerns they wanted the board to consider. While this has not yet taken place in writing, the amount of communication between Indian inmates and the board has increased so dramatically that there is no question that the board has begun to act on their newfound understanding.

This is not to say that the board of parole will not continue to require involvement in mental health programming for Indians. But there is now some flexibility in determining what kinds of rehabilitative programming are considered acceptable. The board may parole an Indian inmate if they have evidence that the inmate has attended sweat lodge ceremonies regularly, has kept away from alcohol and drugs despite easy access, has refrained from getting into trouble that might result in misconduct reports—in other words, if the entire picture is one of sincerity in straightening out a life in prison—the board *will* grant parole based on Indian rehabilitative activities. It would be inaccurate, however, to suggest that involvement in Indian spiritual activities is a definite key to parole board approval; it certainly is not. Much depends on the inmate, the crime, behavior in prison, the psychological evaluation, and the reports of the supervisors. And even where the parole board is being more culturally accommodating, this does not necessarily imply that the Department of Correctional Services is.

Problems arising from types of rehabilitation that are of interest to Indian inmates but are not necessarily acceptable to boards of parole are not unique to Nebraska. A Native American inmate in an Ohio correctional facility challenged the Ohio parole board's refusal to accept involvement in Native American spiritual activities as evidence of his attempts to rehabilitate himself. The board's insistence that the inmate participate in Alcoholics Anonymous or Narcotics Anonymous behind the walls, despite the fact that there was a two- to three-year waiting list to enter such programs; and their refusal to accept participation in Indian spiritual activities as an alternative, led to the inmate's denial of parole (Little Rock Reed 1990, personal communication).

Nebraska Indian parolees

Despite the problems that Indian prisoners believe they have with obtaining parole, and despite the preference of many to jam their time instead, statistics from the corrections department show that the majority of Indian inmates in Nebraska do seek early release through parole. Unfortunately, their success rates are low and recidivism rates high. In a follow-up study three years after my original 1986–87 research (Grobsmith 1989a), I tracked inmates after they left prison, using Department of Correctional Services computer data. Of the forty-two original subjects who were released from prison, twenty-six (62 percent) chose parole, while only sixteen (38 percent) chose to jam their sentences (Grobsmith and Dam 1990:409). Of the forty-two who were released, either unconditionally or with parole, seventeen individuals (40 percent) had new contact with the law enforcement system resulting in revocation of their parole status or new charges being filed against them after they had been discharged from parole. Twelve of these individuals (46 percent) failed to comply with the provisions set forth in their parole agreements or absconded from parole supervision entirely (Grobsmith and Dam 1990:5); the other five who were returned to custody had new contact with the criminal justice system after their release. The seventeen individuals altogether comprise nearly two-thirds of the twenty-six who were released with parole; the sixteen who jammed out could not be tracked (see Figure 1 for an overview of the parole status of the forty-two offenders).

When a parolee leaves the county of parole without permission from his or her parole officer, a charge of "absconding parole supervision" is filed against the inmate, which may or may not result in revocation of parole status (if the parolee is returned to custody, he or she must bear the cost of the return). However, if an inmate leaves the state without written permission from the Nebraska Board of Parole, it is considered a felony charge of "escape," and the parolee is likely not only to be returned to custody and have parole revoked, but also to be convicted of the escape charge, which carries a one- to five-year sentence in Nebraska. Normally, inmates who have left the state and are sentenced for escaping serve approximately six months' additional time.

Recidivism rates are calculated by the Department of Correctional Services by determining the number of inmates who have come back to prison after having been released for three years and the number charged with a felony escape for violating their parole agreements. A DCS 1988 recidivism study indicates that the institutional recidivism rate for all inmates is 23.6 percent, but the report notes that this is a conservative estimate since inmates committed to institutions in other states are not tracked by this system. Additionally, inmates having other contact with the criminal justice system, such as being confined only in county jails, are not included in these rates either. The study found that inmates who discharge their sentences "have the same likelihood of recidivism as those who go on parole" (Nebraska Department of Correctional Services 1988:7).

Indian recidivism rates appear unrealistically low in correctional statistics. According to the 1988 DCS study, blacks and Hispanics have recidivism rates that are higher than the overall institutional average (38 percent and 32 percent respectively), while American Indians have a

Figure 1. Status of Offenders in Three-year Follow-up Study

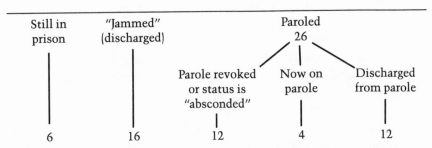

*Because of inmates' discharge and return to prison, and because of continual change in status, numbers in different columns may contain the same individual (e.g. if one was "revoked" and sent back to prison, but has since "jammed" or discharged his sentence), so columns do not necessarily add up to the total.

SOURCE: Elizabeth S. Grobsmith and Jennifer Dam, The Revolving Door: Substance Abuse Treatment and Criminal Sanctions for Native American Offenders, *Journal of Substance Abuse* 2, no. 4 (1990):409. Reprinted with the permission of Ablex Publish Corporation.

slightly lower rate (23 percent) and whites have the lowest recidivism rate (18 percent). Indian inmates may appear in the statistics less often as recidivists by the DCS definition—that is, those discharging their sentences and returning to prison three years or more after their release from the institution—but they experience high rates of parole failure and revocation, figures which are not calculated in recidivism rates. Return to prison following parole revocation occurs more often for Indian prisoners than successful completion of parole. According to corrections statistics for fiscal year 1988, Native Americans comprised 4.2 percent of the releases to parole, but for the same period they comprised 6.2 percent of the parole revocations (Nebraska Department of Correctional Services 1988). Native Americans are returning to prison through parole revocation at faster rates than they are being released.

There is little question that parole failures can largely be attributed to loss of sobriety; according to the established pattern, a parolee's intoxication leads to a single violation, which sets off a chain reaction. For example, a parolee may drink to excess at a party. That could go undetected by the parole officer, except that the inmate might not return to his place of residence or show up for work the next day. Now, two or three parole violations have occurred, not just one. An employer might then fire the employee, resulting in a fourth parole violation. By the time the inmate is tracked, he may have five or six violations charged to him. Parolees break the law by driving while intoxicated, getting into fights, which results in an assault charge, or simply not paying a ticket or having a vehicle properly insured or registered. They then face greater discipline for having broken an important provision of their parole agreements—obeying the law. Parolees who abscond from supervision but remain within the state boundaries face discipline, but sometimes no new felony charges are filed.

The serious roller-coaster effect that results in parole failure and revocation appears to be a progression from less serious offenses to more serious ones. An inmate who falls off the wagon and fails to return home or to work fears that he has blown it and decides to take off since he knows he is in trouble anyway. A decision to leave the state without permission leads to an encounter with the parole board and revocation as well as going to court to face the charge of felony escape. By the time a parolee has had his parole revoked, is returned to custody, loses good time, and perhaps serves an additional sentence for a felony escape, it is likely that the individual will end up doing more time than if he had simply jammed out to begin with. Here the real problem lies. Why should an Indian inmate take parole and risk violation and return to custody when he can just "lay down" (serve his full time), be released from the institutions without any conditions of parole placed on him, and be totally free of what he perceives as meddlesome, controlling interference by parole officers? Evidently, this is the thought process expressed by many Indian offenders.

Parole failure not only affects the offender who returns to prison, it affects all the Indian inmates in the system. Many become angry when they see a brother come back to prison. They fear that reinforcement of the stereotype that Indians, especially those returning to the reservation, cannot stay away from alcohol and will eventually drink and re-offend harms other Indian offenders' chances for success. An image of Indian failure and instability cannot help but jeopardize another Indian inmate's prospective release or parole. Indian inmates are deeply critical of each other in such instances, and the sincerity of the parole violator's spiritual values is often brought into question. This, in turn, may affect the welfare of the inmate once he is re-integrated into daily prison activities. Inmates also fear that such failures will reflect poorly on their religious commitments and may result in curtailment of prison religious activities.

Returned inmates experience a good deal of embarrassment and guilt.

They not only have to face their families and friends, who may be unable to understand why they took such risks while on parole, but they have to face inmates who might have heard them promise that they would *never* return to custody. In a letter to me one inmate wrote: "I don't quite know how to begin this letter because of the guilt and shame that I have caused on my family and friends. I was sentenced yesterday to another term in the Nebraska Correctional and Penal Complex. . . . I have accepted these consequences and I have made up my mind to do something for myself." Another inmate wrote: "It's really amazing how it seems we just don't learn! Sometimes I think one gets twisted up so much while being locked down it's impossible to get untwisted."

Inmates who believe their recovery from alcoholism during their incarceration is complete find themselves without the necessary tools for remaining sober on the outside. Because many do not drink in prison (despite the availability of alcohol), inmates may equate not drinking with sobriety. Upon their release, they find out that not drinking is *not* the same as having made a commitment to sobriety. Many are unable to resist the temptation, and inevitably drinking brings them back to a social situation in which responsibilities are not met, steady work habits they may have established in prison are discontinued, and they fall back into a destructive pattern that ultimately ends in their arrest—generally for a minor infraction involving alcohol—and revocation of parole. Many are in a state of disbelief when this happens.

Inmates want the freedom to make their own decisions about whether or not they wish to take a drink while on parole. The freedom to decide for themselves frequently costs them their freedom in the community. Some delude themselves that taking a personal risk a few times need not cost them parole. Unfortunately, for the majority of inmates this self-delusion ends in over-consumption and eventual contact with the criminal justice system: parole revocation and, again, incarceration.

7

Indian Prisoners
Nationwide

Nebraska Indian prisoners have served as a model for Indian inmates nationwide since they began the process of asserting their rights to religious freedom. The dissemination of information concerning Indian prisoners has now become widespread, and two major channels of communication have served to inform both correctional administrators and inmates of what practices are commonly accepted in prisons across the country: Native American travel in and out of the state of Nebraska, and legal decisions handed down by the U.S. District Court in Nebraska, Eighth Circuit, which have guided correctional policy as it pertains to Indian prisoners. Correctional authorities in other states have contacted the Nebraska Department of Correctional Services for information on ways in which they have addressed Indian inmates' concerns, and firms such as the Native American Rights Fund in Boulder, Colorado, have provided information to prisons on issues they have litigated. Native American prisoners also have strong communication links with brothers in other penal institutions, supported by regular publication of newsletters such as the *Iron House Drum* and *Journal of Prisoners on Prisons* and national conferences sponsored by the Native American Prisoners Rehabilitation Research Project. Reprints of scholarly publications on issues of incarceration are requested by Indian inmates in a number of states, resulting in an increase in interprison communication and plans for initiating new litigation. Within a decade, it is likely that prison policy concerning Native American cultural and spiritual practices will be significantly more uniform and culturally tolerant.

Because there is a paucity of published information concerning Native American prisoners nationwide, I designed a survey and sent it to all state and federal correctional facilities in the United States during 1988 and 1989. All six federal facilities and all but three states responded. Presenting data on each question from every institution responding to the survey would be unwieldy and sometimes confusing, so the replies from penal institutions within each state correctional system have been collapsed into one response per state. Federal responses are presented separately.

Survey response from state penal institutions

Since states were inconsistent in the manner in which they responded to the survey, the numbers of Indian prisoners may be greatly underrepresented. For example, in one state only one correctional facility may have responded to the survey, while another state system duplicated the survey and sent in responses from five or six different facilities. Some states, such as Oklahoma, collated responses from all their institutions and provided a single summary for the entire state. In the interest of consistency, Indian prison population figures from *The Corrections Yearbook 1992* are presented in Table 5, Indian Prison Population by State. In most instances, those figures were very close to the survey figures.

The identification of tribal affiliations in prisons was also problematic. During intake, administrators usually ask for an inmate's racial or ethnic identity, but the intake officer may record this information based solely on appearance. The tribes represented in Table 5 reflect only those *known* by the prison administration. The race/ethnic affiliation on intake forms is "Native American," not a specific tribe; further, if an inmate is Native American but doesn't necessarily conform to the stereotype of what Indians look like, he or she is likely to be classified by intake officers as black, Hispanic, or "other."

In twenty-one states the Indian inmates make up 1 percent or more of the state prison population. Approximately half the states in this grouping are located in the plains. In South Dakota, Indians comprise 7 percent of the state population but represent approximately 26 percent of all inmates in the State Penitentiary in Sioux Falls (Grobsmith 1989a:286). Other states with relatively large Indian populations also have disproportionately large Indian prison populations, notably Idaho, Minnesota, Montana, North Dakota, Oklahoma, Oregon, Washington, Wyoming, and Alaska. Alaska has the highest population of incarcerated Indians

Table 5
Indian Prison Population by State

State	Number of Native Americans	% of Prison Population†	Tribes Represented
Alabama	*	0.0	
Alaska	800	31.9	Tlingit, Haida, Inuit
Arizona	* *	3.1	* *
Arkansas	*		*
California	362	0.5	Pomo, Sioux, Pit River
Colorado	47	1.3	*
Connecticut	12	0.1	Cherokee, Maliseet, Passama-quoddy, Choctaw, Penobscot, Aleut, Shawnee
Delaware	2	0.1	Nanticoke
District of Columbia	*	0.0	*
Florida	16	*	*
Georgia	*	0.0	*
Hawaii	12	0.9	*
Idaho	42	4.3	Shoshone, Nez Perce
Illinois	27	0.2	*
Indiana	15–20	0.2	*
Iowa	43	1.6	Sioux (and others unknown)
Kansas	50	1.4	Kickapoo, Yakima, Potawatomi, Navajo
Kentucky	1	0.4	*
Louisiana	2	*	*
Maine	19	1.0	Penobscot
Maryland	7	<1	*
Massachusetts	12	0.2	*
Michigan	108	0.4	Ojibway, Chippewa
Minnesota	207	8.3	Sioux, Chippewa
Mississippi	8	0.1	Choctaw
Missouri	18	0.2	*
Montana	234	18.3	Kootenai, Salish, Cree, Chip-pewa, Crow, Blackfeet, Sioux
Nebraska	100	3.9	Omaha, Winnebago, Sioux, Chip-pewa, Cherokee, Ponca
Nevada	56	1.4	Washoe, Paiute, Shawnee
New Hampshire	*	0.3	
New Jersey	4	*	*

continued on next page

Table 5 (cont.)

State	Number of Native Americans	% of Prison Population†	Tribes Represented
New Mexico	* *	3.0	
New York	25	0.2	Mohawk, Onondaga, Seneca, Cayuga
North Carolina	360	2.2	Lumbee, Cherokee, Tuscarora, Haliwa
North Dakota	106	22.2	Sioux, Chippewa
Ohio	* *	0.0	
Oklahoma	360	5.7	Cherokee, Creek, Choctaw, Seminole, Chickasaw, Ponca, Arapaho, Kansa, Osage, Caddo, Comanche, Otoe, Cheyenne, Apache, Sioux, Chippewa, Shawnee, Kiowa, Potawatomi
Oregon	107	2.2	Klamath, Modoc, Siletz, Sioux, Eskimo, Shoshone, Umatilla, Warm Springs, Paiute, Tlingit, Cherokee, Comanche, Blackfoot, Grand Ronde
Pennsylvania	8	0.1	*
Rhode Island	3	0.2	Narragansett
South Carolina	13	0.1	*
South Dakota	262	25.4	Sioux, Winnebago, Omaha
Tennessee	* *	0.0	* *
Texas	4	0.01	*
Utah	42	3.4	*
Vermont	0	0.0	*
Virginia	*	0.0	*
Washington	258	3.7	Yakima
West Virginia	*	0.1	*
Wisconsin	148	2.2	Chippewa, Oneida, Winnebago, Menominee
Wyoming	43	5.4	Sioux, Shoshone, Crow, Arapahoe, Cheyenne

† Figures from Camp and Camp 1992:4–5, except where no data are available; in these instances, percentages reflect survey data.
* Too few to count or unknown.
* * No survey response (data may be available elsewhere).

and Alaska Natives, but this is not surprising since they represent proportionately such a large percentage of the general population. In Nebraska, the Indian prison population has ranged in the last several years between 3.1 percent and 4.4 percent, approximately triple the percentage of Indians residing in the state.

The more specific issues addressed by the survey are discussed individually.

Indian clubs and access to religious activities

The survey requested information about Native American religious and culture clubs formed in each institution, and specifically about the use of the sweat lodge, the Native American Church, powwows, access to ceremonies such as the Vision Quest and/or Sun Dance, or other religious activities. Too few Native American programs exist nationwide to be put in tabular form, but regional trends are evident in the practices of particular tribes in particular regions of the country (e.g. the plains, Northwest Coast).

Alaska prisons have a Native American culture club and several sweat lodges throughout their facilities as well. The Arizona corrections system did not respond to the survey, but documents indicate the state has permitted access to the sweat lodge since about 1984 (*Roybal v. Deland*, Utah Civil No. C 87-0208A, Findings of Fact and Conclusions of Law on Plaintiffs' Motion for Summary Judgment, p. 5). California prisons have Indian self-help groups and sweat lodges, and inmates are permitted to have an average of two powwows per year at the majority of their facilities. California has a large urban Native American population. Because it was a major Indian relocation center during the 1950s, it is likely that the inmate population has far larger numbers of non-California tribes represented than other states.

Colorado is reputed to have a sweat lodge, but they did not so indicate on the survey. Despite the relatively small Indian population in Connecticut prisons (0.1 percent), inmates there have Sacred Pipe ceremonies and access to the sweat lodge and are permitted to burn sage and sweet grass ceremonially. The administration also permits prisoners to have medicine bags in their possession and hold annual Green Corn festivals, prayer groups, and singing circles. Idaho has an Indian prison group called the Medicine Sun's Society of the North American Indian League. Sweat lodge and Pipe ceremonies are permitted, and powwows are held annually. Iowa's prisons—despite the relatively small number of Indian inmates—permit Native Americans to have an Indian culture club, with sweat lodge and Native American Church ceremonies (without peyote). Kansas has a United Native American Indian Culture group and United Tribes organization; access to the sweat lodge is permitted at some facilities but not others. Travel from the prison into the community is permitted for powwows in one facility and for one sweat lodge a month in another.

Michigan's Indian inmates have a cultural club, but no ceremonial privileges. Minnesota, a state with a large Native American prison population, has an Indian culture club and access to both sweat lodge ceremonies and powwows in prison. Montana's Indian population has a culture group called Prayer Warriors and is permitted weekly sweat lodge ceremonies and a drum group as well. (Nebraska's access to religious activities is not discussed here since it is presented in detail throughout the book).

Nevada prisons permit sweat lodge services and Native American Church services (without peyote). Although no survey data are available for New Mexico, prisoners do have access to the sweat lodge. New York inmates have a Native American cultural group, but no ceremonies are permitted. In North Dakota, Indian inmates have a Native American Ancestral Group, which has both sweat lodge ceremonies and powwows throughout the year and has access to traditional religious materials. Oklahoma has Indian clubs at ten of its twelve penal facilities. Although Native American Church ceremonies (without peyote) are permitted, no facility has a sweat lodge. Inmates are permitted to possess eagle feathers and wear long hair, and to burn cedar, sage, and sweet grass.

Oregon prisons have an Indian group called Lakhota Oyate-ki Culture Club, which is permitted sweat lodge and pipe ceremonies. South Dakota Indian inmates have an active organization, the Native American Council of Tribes, which is permitted to have sweat lodge ceremonies and powwows; members have special permission to wear long hair and retain religious paraphernalia. Texas does not permit the sweat lodge, according to my survey, but it is listed in legal briefs as one of the institutions that does allow it. Indian prisoners in Utah facilities have been denied access to the sweat lodge, but their Many Feathers club has been permitted to have powwows. In the state of Washington, three tribal organizations exist; all are permitted routine access to the sweat lodge and have powwows. Wisconsin's Indian population has the Waupon Indian

Council. They are allowed access to the sweat lodge and Native American Church ceremonies without peyote. Finally, Wyoming inmates have a White Cloud group, which has access to both sweat lodge services and Native American Church ceremonies without peyote. At times Wyoming prisoners have been allowed both powwows and attendance at the Vision Quest or Sun Dance.

In all, a total of twenty states permit routine access to Native American religious services, in particular the sweat lodge: Alaska, Arizona (no survey response), California, Colorado, Connecticut, Idaho, Iowa, Kansas, Minnesota, Montana, Nebraska, New Mexico (no survey response), Nevada, North Dakota, Oregon, South Dakota, Texas, Washington, Wisconsin, and Wyoming. A legal brief by the Navajo Nation submitted as Amicus Curiae in Utah Civil No. C 87-0208A cites Oklahoma as a state where Indian inmates have access to the sweat lodge, but survey data indicate that this is not so; if it is available, this raises the number of states where prisoners use the sweat lodge to twenty-one.

Use of a religious coordinator

Survey respondents were asked whether Native American prisoners have the services of a correctional employee whose job it is specifically to assist in accommodating Native American spiritual beliefs, i.e., a religious coordinator or someone serving as a link between the inmates, the correctional system, and Indian spiritual leaders. In Nebraska, after the Consent Decree was awarded, the Department of Correctional Services employed a religious coordinator to serve as sponsor for the Native American Spiritual and Cultural Awareness group (NASCA) and as liaison with Indian medicine men who might be willing to come into the prisons and offer their services as spiritual counselors and/or conduct ceremonies. In 1990, the job description of the Nebraska religious coordinator was revised. The inmates retained their liaison with Indian spiritual advisors, but they no longer had a club sponsor. The consequence was different for each institution—in some the lack of a club sponsor meant the NASCA group could not meet regularly because an outside sponsor had to come in. The lack of predictability of sponsors coming in has been destructive at some institutions, and even where temporary sponsors have been provided by the correctional system, those not specifically familiar with the special needs of Native Americans (for tobacco, sage, sweet grass, or cedar for prayer and/or the sweat lodge, for use of the kitchen and ceremonial foods for Indian celebrations) are not able to provide all the services to which Indian prisoners believe they are entitled. Unhappiness with this system resulted in new attempts to initiate litigation in Nebraska, but because the Indian club has not technically been discriminated against (they do have a club sponsor, albeit not a Native American one), efforts have not been successful. Without a Native American liaison, Indian prisoners find it exceedingly difficult to get the services they believe are guaranteed by the 1974 Consent Decree, consequently they believe their religious freedom rights continue to be violated.

The majority of correctional institutions in the United States do not specifically employ a Native American religious coordinator as does Nebraska; however, prisons with relatively large numbers of Indian inmates do hire Indian employees or use the services of Indian community members to assist in meeting inmates' religious needs. Many prisons—Alaska, Colorado, Kansas, Kentucky, Michigan, Mississippi, New York, North Carolina, North Dakota, Oklahoma, some Oregon facilities, Wisconsin, and one of the Nebraska institutions—utilize the services of the prison chaplain to accommodate Native American spiritual requests, but may also occasionally bring in medicine men when available. In California, Montana, and Oregon, Indian community members and spiritual leaders are permitted entry to the prison to conduct sweat lodge and other ceremonies. Connecticut specifically employs a Native American religious coordinator, as do Oklahoma (which also has an Indian minister at one of its institutions), Oregon, South Dakota, and Washington (an Indian chaplain). Wisconsin has a Native American staff advisor. Wyoming has at times had a Native American counselor.

Some institutions have a volunteer services manager who arranges for Indian spiritual consultants to come in, and Iowa employs a Native American consultant to serve the needs of the Indian population. Still other states (notably Massachusetts) have made efforts to locate Indian religious coordinators but have not been able to do so. In Maryland, a religious services coordinator handles all religious requests, including those of Native Americans. Some states, including Minnesota, have an Indian medicine man on contract to the correctional system. The trend toward using one medicine man in Nebraska repeatedly has resulted in court action. Because of the variety of Indian religions within any single institution, using one particular medicine man to serve the needs of all Indian inmates, regardless of differences in their languages and cultures, presents difficulties.

Some prisons, including some of the Oregon facilities, utilize either a recreational therapist or staff to supervise and coordinate all club activities, including those of the Native Americans.

Guard sensitization

Cultural sensitization of correctional officers toward Indian religious and spiritual affairs continues to be an area that Native American inmates in Nebraska believe gets far less attention than is warranted. The Consent Decree addresses the necessity for Indian employees to be sought and others sensitized to the concerns of the Indian population: "The defendant and plaintiffs' counsel shall formulate an affirmative action hiring plan designed to locate job applicants and to secure employment and training by the defendant of qualified Indian personnel, recognizing the unique cultural needs of Indian inmates" (CV 72-L-156, 1974, no page no.). All new correctional officers in Nebraska participate in an in-service training program that has a section on Native American religious practices, but once it has been completed no further discussion or training is conducted. Hence, complaints about guards' insensitivity persist.

A number of institutions indicated in the survey that their staff does not understand Indian affairs and that training or sensitization of staff is critical in relations with Indian prisoners, but few have any ongoing or even occasional training programs. An Indian Affairs coordinator in the California system provides some information to staff on the premises of Indian thought and religion, and a similar procedure is found in Iowa and Kansas. Prisoners in Michigan, Minnesota, Oregon, Utah, Washington, and Wisconsin conduct racial/ethnic sensitivity discussions, but not specifically directed at Native American culture. In Montana's new staff training, correctional employees learn about Native American values and culture in a class. Nevada has developed written materials that describe Indian religious articles and activities, and specifically discuss materials used in sweat lodge services (as well as who is permitted to attend). Prisons in the process of setting up correctional officer training programs include North Carolina and North Dakota (in consultation with tribes). States such as Oklahoma, with large Indian prison populations, claim to have sufficient familiarity with Native American culture to serve the Indian population adequately. Some offer occasional intensive seminars on Indian culture sponsored by one particular tribe, for example, the Kiowa. South Dakota conducts an employee orientation on

Native American culture and makes use of video tapes on Indian culture and traditions, while Wyoming's training programs emphasize specific aspects of Native American religious traditions.

Litigation

Few prisons nationwide have had litigation brought against them resulting in directives from the courts that correctional facilities ensure religious freedom among Native American prisoners. A California suit compelled institutions to permit inmates to practice certain religious rites such as the sweat lodge and also specified that a spiritual coordinator be employed to provide such services to Indian prisoners. Connecticut inmates have litigated for use of sacred paraphernalia such as eagle feathers and more frequent access to sweat lodge ceremonies. In Idaho, while inmates had access to pipe and sweat lodge ceremonies, further litigation in state court resulted in a consent decree that assured their rights to other practices and religious apparel, including possession of medicine bags, wearing of headbands, and the use of eagle feathers. In their case, litigation resulted in a formal recognition of their religion and the acknowledgment that certain religious items were a necessary part of those practices. In Indiana, Indian prisoners brought litigation against the correctional authorities with regard to their right to wear their hair long, one of the original issues in the Nebraska Consent Decree. Iowa inmates litigated (*Reinert v. Scurr, Walker v. Scurr*) for the right to practice the sweat lodge, as did Indian prisoners incarcerated in Kansas facilities. For Kansas, this suit set a precedent for the practice of American Indian religions within the institutions.

Montana inmates were not successful in litigating their concerns about rights to wear their hair long, but when the prison was approached by inmates requesting accommodation of Native American religious and cultural preferences for long hair, this practice was permitted. Pressure by Indian inmates in Nevada resulted in the development of an institutional procedure to describe permissible religious articles, activities, and materials needed for the sweat lodge ceremony, as well as prison directives on who should be allowed to attend such activities. New York State, in 1972, entered into a consent agreement whose purpose it was to accommodate Native Americans' religious and cultural preferences. North Carolina has been in the process of developing a policy with regard to Native American spiritual practices. In North Dakota, Indian inmates litigated for religious freedom rights, but the court determined that the institution was fulfilling its requirement of guaranteeing religious freedom to Native Americans and that no discrimination against Indian inmates was occurring. Oklahoma Indian inmates brought suit against correctional authorities for denying them the right to wear their hair long. The inmates won this case, and the prison policy concerning hair cutting is waived for Native Americans. Because of the suit, there has developed a greater awareness and appreciation of Indian religious expression within the Oklahoma system; inmates are bolder in their requests for religious ceremonies, and traditional ways of worship preferred by Native Americans have now been clarified for the administration.

In Oregon, three Indian inmates requested use of the Sacred Pipe and access to the sweat lodge in 1978. Denial of access was the basis of a lawsuit, which was settled out of court. In 1984, Oregon inmates filed suit concerning inmates in segregation (protective custody) being denied access to religious services. The court's determination in Oregon echoed the Nebraska decision—inmates in protective custody were not permitted access to the sweat lodge—and the reason was probably the same: segregation status is intended to keep dangerous or undisciplined inmates from interacting with the general population for their protection or the protection of other inmates, so association with others at the sweat lodge could not be permitted. In Oregon, unlike Nebraska, spiritual leaders are permitted to come to segregated areas (which they also call "the hole") to provide religious services once a month. Oregon correctional authorities state that they make every attempt to accommodate religious concerns as long as they do not pose security conflicts.

Oregon inmates participated in a film venture that had tremendous impact on awareness of Indian spiritual concerns by correctional authorities and brought national attention to issues of religious freedom. The film *The Great Spirit Within the Hole*, produced in 1983 by KTCA Public Television in Minneapolis-St. Paul, Minnesota, depicted inmates within various Oregon prison facilities practicing their religious activities. In interviews men and women prisoners discussed the tremendous beneficial effect that participation had on their rehabilitation, both for those whose traditional practices included ceremonial use of the pipe and sweat lodge, and for those who knew little of their history, culture, and traditions prior to their incarceration. The growth of pride in heritage and self-respect as a result of revitalization of Indian spiritual practices in prison has had a strong impact on Native American prisoners by validating their right to religious freedom and communicating solidarity with Indian prisoners in parts of the country far from their own.

Clark v. Peterson (Civil No. 85-6559-PA), a lawsuit brought by Oregon Indian inmates in 1985, claimed that requirements and restrictions imposed by prison officials on the possession of medicine bags, on participation in ceremonies held at times when movement by inmates is otherwise restricted, and on the availability of an outside religious volunteer to lead ceremonies unconstitutionally limited the exercise of their religion. The lawsuit was dismissed on the grounds of prison security concerns.

In 1983, on behalf of Indian prisoners in Utah, the Navajo Nation established the Navajo Inmate Spiritual and Social Development Program. It was later described as an effort "to assist state and federal prisons in meeting the spiritual and cultural needs of Navajo inmates . . . to encourage . . . spiritual development through the practice of traditional Navajo religion" (Utah Civil No. C-87-0208A, Motion for Leave to File Brief Amicus Curiae, Jan. 31, 1989, pp. 1–2). The program had largely been devised because Anglo-American methods of alcohol rehabilitation were considered failures with Indian prisoners. Navajo religious practices had been cited as being instrumental in enhancing the rehabilitation of Navajo inmates and assisting with their readjustment to Navajo life. The brief pointed out that nineteen state prison systems and the federal prison system permitted Indian religious practices and the building of Indian religious structures such as the sweat lodge, and that the program had as its goal not only to enhance Indian religious activities in prison, but to educate and sensitize prison authorities about them. The program was instrumental in promoting sweat lodge ceremonies in Southwest prisons.

In 1985, six Utah inmates filed a class action lawsuit against the Utah Department of Corrections (*Roybal et al. v. Deland*), claiming that "they couldn't practice an integral part of their religion—the sweat lodge ceremony—without such a structure." The federal magistrate "urged Utah and its Indian inmates to settle their dispute and avoid trial over whether a ceremonial sweat lodge" was to be built for Utah prisoners, but the state was opposed to having the sweat lodge for "safety, security, management and control reasons and the added burden to the state because of the costs" (*Omaha World-Herald*, Oct. 6, 1988, p. 54). Upon the recommendation of the court, authorities from Utah were urged to contact Nebraska correctional authorities for information on Nebraska's policies. Joseph Vitek, former director of the Nebraska Department of Correctional Services and defendant in Nebraska's lawsuit, testified as to the remarkable results produced through use of the sweat lodge: "But what I did see specifically . . . (was) that a lot of Indians, not all of them, developed a great deal of self-esteem and pride in themselves. There was an apparent increase in what I call good grooming, the clothing, . . . there seemed to be a prideful thing that was kind of fun to watch. Sense of identity, if you will" (Vitek, in Utah Civil No. C-87-0208A, Motion for Leave to File Brief Amicus Curiae, Jan. 31, 1989).

Vitek's deposition included testimony as to how the Nebraska prison had feared security problems with a sweat lodge in the Nebraska prisons, fears which didn't materialize. Both Arizona and New Mexico correctional authorities testified, as did Vitek, that permitting sweat lodge practices did not impose additional costs or concerns beyond those normally associated with prison activities. Navajo attorneys stated:"The State of Utah's prison policy banning the sweat lodge threatens to impair the ability of the Navajo Nation to participate materially in the rehabilitation of its members. The Navajo Nation seeks to protect the religious rights of its members. The Navajo Nation therefore seeks to inform the Court of its viewpoint and law in support thereof, which advocates a ruling in favor of the plaintiffs" (Utah Civil No. C-87-0208A, Motion for Leave to File Brief Amicus Curiae, Jan. 31, 1989).

The court ruled in 1989 that there were no legitimate reasons to prohibit the construction and use of the sweat lodge among Utah inmates and that the prison must not only permit such construction but bear associated costs for its maintenance, as with any other chapel. While Utah inmates are now permitted to wear their hair long, possess religious articles such as medicine bags, and smoke the pipe, sweat lodge ceremonies were still not being conducted among Utah prisoners, according to the survey respondents.

In the state of Washington, a federal court ruling in 1983 resulted in a mandate that the state correctional authorities could not cut the hair of Native American offenders in the reception units. In the state of Wisconsin, *Sturdevant v. Sondalle* addressed the alleged infringement of Native American rights, but the court found no evidence that such allegations were valid.

The influence of cultural activities on rehabilitation

Correctional institutions were asked to indicate in the survey whether it was their perception that participation in Native American spiritual and cultural activities had a notable effect on Indian inmate rehabilitation. Those institutions who were able to respond to this question were certain that the effect such activities had was positive. California authorities claimed that appreciation of Indian heritage reduced violence and afforded inmates a sense of pride in brotherhood, and that this cooperative attitude carried over into their social reintegration into society. In Connecticut, officials believed that Indian activities in prison helped the Native Americans to get in touch with themselves and increase awareness and consciousness of issues of cultural pride. For Idaho inmates, Native American practices in prison enabled inmates to come together in mutual self-help; according to the survey, "All the Indian activities and ceremonies bring Native Americans together, helping each other to see what they are about. It is definitely rehabilitative for those individuals that have no direction in life or no concern or understanding for self or others." Iowa correctional authorities believe such activities also have some benefit to Indian inmates.

Montana prisons indicate that Native American cultural and religious practices have helped encourage a law-abiding lifestyle, prohibiting the use of alcohol and drugs among inmates. Those Nevada Indian inmates who participate in Indian-oriented activities demonstrate a more positive attitude and take more pride in their culture than those not participating, say administrators. Similar claims are heard for New York inmates: appreciation of history is greater, fraternalism and peer support develop, and community outreach for re-entry into society has a greater rehabilitative value. For Oklahoma inmates, the survey indicates, participation in Indian cultural affairs has a positive effect on discipline, helping inmates to overcome loneliness, improving their sense of self-worth, enhancing resocialization back to home and assisting in communication with Indian groups in the community, and developing a more positive Indian identity.

In Oregon facilities, Indian activities are said to promote a sense of self-worth, well-being, and peer acceptance, and to assist in the maintenance of ties with the outside community. These in turn provide a sense of stability to Indian inmates and motivation to return to a more productive lifestyle upon release. For both Wyoming and Washington state prisons, participation in Indian activities was said to have a positive impact on inmates' sense of identity. There seems little question that for prisons with relatively large numbers of Indian inmates, participation in Indian cultural and spiritual activities has a definitive and positive impact on the personality characteristics essential to recovery—personal dignity, self-actualization, and peer support in affirming positive rather than negative behaviors.

Alcohol or drug programs for Indian prisoners

The high recidivism rates for drinking and incarceration among Nebraska Indian inmates presented in chapter 6 and the failure of the alcohol treatment programs that serve them led to my request for information from prisons nationwide concerning their efforts at treating alcoholism and drug abuse in Native American offenders. Since all prisons have some kind of alcohol/drug mental health program (such as Alcoholics Anonymous), only information on programs specifically oriented to the Native American population was sought.

Alaska prisons have counseling groups for Eskimos and Alaska Natives. In one of Idaho's facilities, the North American Indian League has been trying to arrange for a tribal council member from a nearby reservation to establish regular counseling sessions with a tribal professional counselor, who could travel to the prison specifically to hold sessions with Indian prisoners with substance abuse problems. In a Kansas facility, the National American Indian Alcoholic Association provides counseling services to Kansas Indian inmates. Minnesota inmates similarly can attend an American Indian chemical dependency program operated out of St. Cloud.

North Dakota inmates have an alcohol/drug group which utilizes the Red Road approach, a philosophy developed by Medicine Wheel, Inc., utilizing combined western therapeutic approaches (confrontation, role playing) and native ("natural") styles of addressing personal crises that have contributed to alcoholism and drug abuse (see chapter 5 on approaches to alcohol recovery for a more detailed discussion of this approach, specifically the section on the Native American Alcohol Treatment Program in Sergeant Bluffs, Iowa). Oklahoma institutions do not have Native American-oriented programs per se, but at one facility, an Indian employee assists with a drug abuse program called "Life Steps."

Oregon facilities appear to have an exemplary program. "The Corrections Department Treatment Services holds a two-week seminar yearly that specifically caters to substance abuse problems in Native Americans. The Sweat Lodge, Pipe, and Talking Circle Ceremonies are all incorporated as therapy in this seminar. The Corrections Department contracts with an outside Spiritual Leader to conduct this program . . . (and) offers an AIDS seminar targeted at Native Americans as well. Many Native American inmates participate in the alcohol and drug seminars offered for the general population. . . . Many of the instructors are Native American." Individual and group therapy with a Native American therapist on contract with the treatment division of the Oregon prisons is available. Red Willow, an outpatient Native American substance abuse program, also serves Oregon Indian ex-offenders, and drug and alcohol services for Klamath Falls tribes are available to tribal members upon release into the community.

South Dakota has some limited drug and alcohol programs oriented specifically to Native Americans. Washington State has Indian Alcoholics Anonymous programs available to offenders. While no prison drug/alcohol programs are available to Wisconsin offenders, there are two halfway houses contracted for Native American parolees.

The presence of Alcoholics Anonymous groups in prison is quite common in correctional facilities: thirty-five states had AA groups available in at least some of their institutions. Of these, Native Americans are participants at twenty prisons. This is clear indication of a national rejection of Alcoholics Anonymous programs by Native American prisoners, consistent with the perspectives of the Nebraska Indian population. In the twenty prisons where they do participate, Indians usually represent a minority of those attending, although in Connecticut, Minnesota, and some Kansas and Oregon institutions, Indian prisoners who participate in AA make up a majority. Other states indicate that there is variability across their institutions as to whether Indian offenders constitute a majority or minority or simply reflect a percentage proportional to the total population. The existence of exclusively Indian-oriented AA groups in the nation's prisons is rare: Minnesota and Washington appear to be the only states possessing them (in Washington, Native Americans are regular AA participants only when it is a Native American AA program).

Other special programs for Native Americans

Survey respondents were asked to provide information on activities that focus specifically on Indian prison issues—political, religious, cultural, or educational. Few institutions had such programs. Alaska prisons offer life skills training, financial aid guidance, discussion of the Alaska Native Claims Settlement Act, opportunities for the expression of Alaska Native art and dance, and services from the local Totem Heritage Center. Kansas and South Dakota have some special Indian-oriented activities, but were not specific as to their nature. The Minnesota correctional authorities operate a halfway house for Indian prisoners who are released to the community. Oklahoma inmates enjoy a wide variety of Indian-oriented cultural activities sponsored by the Indian Keepers of the Land organization; programs are broadcast on inmate television with information about varying tribes. North Dakota inmates' cultural group brings in speakers and guests to talk on specific topics.

Oregon, despite its relatively low Indian prison population, has a wide variety of Indian-oriented activities, including a Lakhota club, celebration of Native American week, projects to promote Indian art, a yearly spiritual run, and a weekly Indian culture class. At one Oregon facility, an Indian drug and alcohol class that deals with culture, religion, and alcohol issues is held for three weeks twice a year and holds graduation ceremonies to honor those completing the recovery program. Other Oregon facilities have regularly scheduled religious services and regular alcohol and drug treatment for Native Americans. In Washington State, a chaplain conducts classes on Native American issues, and in Wyoming the Indian prison population has organized cultural and religious activities subject to the availability of tribal resources in the community.

Involvement in political activity

As is evident from the discussion on Nebraska inmate litigation, Nebraska Indian inmates have been quite active in seeking relief with respect to religious freedom in the courts. My survey attempted to discover the extent to which Indian inmates in other states' penal institutions were considered by those administrations to be litigious, especially compared to other ethnic groups. The first question in this area asked whether Indian inmates were less or more vocal about their concerns than other inmates. Seventeen of the fifty-one responding institutions (33.3 percent) indicated that Native Americans were less vocal than others, while only three institutions—Oregon, Montana, and North Dakota—believed their Native American population to be more vocal than other groups (these are prisons with relatively large Indian populations). Oregon's Indian population, while not very large overall, appears very active in Indian activities, according to other survey questions. Five institutions (9.8 percent) indicated that Indians were about as vocal as other groups in prison, while sixteen (31.3 percent) indicated that this question was not applicable to them. When asked whether Indian inmates filed more or fewer grievances than other inmates, nearly all institutions indicated that Native Americans filed fewer grievances or said this information was unknown; only two prisons indicated that the amount of litigation filed by Native Americans was equal to other incarcerated groups. When asked whether they would characterize the Indian population as "very litigious" or "not deeply involved in litigation," nearly all institutions responded they were not deeply involved or that the question was not applicable. Iowa characterized their Indian inmate population as "very litigious," and Oregon suggested that when cultural and religious issues were at stake, the Indian population was *very* active in legal inquiry, making heavy use of the legal library.

Respondents were asked whether Indian inmates had high or low visibility within the prison. While the majority of institutions indicated that their Indian populations kept a low profile, four indicated that it was about the same for Native Americans as for others and five prisons—interestingly enough, all in the plains and all with relatively high percentages of Indian inmates (Wyoming, Montana, North Dakota, and South Dakota as well as Nebraska)—indicated that Indians were very visible. This finding probably can be attributed to the high level of political activism among Plains Indians (especially Sioux) during the 1970s and the relatively large number of Sioux among Indian inmate populations in these states.

"Problematic" behavior

Prisons were asked to describe the Indian population with respect to misconduct reports/violations or write-ups, and whether this group differed significantly from others in prison. All respondents indicated that Indian inmates received fewer or about the same number of misconduct reports.

Ways in which Native Americans differ from other populations

Institutions were invited to indicate other ways in which Native Americans compared with or differed from other groups of inmates. Several institutions mentioned that Indian inmates were more active in their religion than other prisoners, and one mentioned that Indian prisoners had a strong identification with and loyalty to other Indian inmates (this was considered to have both positive and negative effects). One institution noted that they were different in their drinking-related activities and the fact that they stood out as different in *not* seeking help with drinking problems through prison AA programs. At one institution, inmates were seen as "clannish" and keeping to themselves, and as very suspicious of authority, perceiving a wrong to one Indian as an affront to all Indians. This response is certainly consistent with the notion of close family-like ties among Native American prisoners, as evidenced by their reference to each other in Nebraska as "brothers." Finally, one institution pointed out that Indian inmates were very artistic, creative, and sensitive.

Services of medicine men

Correctional authorities were asked to indicate whether spiritual leaders or medicine men were permitted to come in to visit or conduct services with Native American inmates. States that provide access to Native American religious leaders include Alaska, California, Connecticut, Idaho, Indiana, Iowa, Kansas, Louisiana (when there is a request), Minnesota, Montana, Nebraska, Nevada, New York, North Dakota, Oklahoma, Oregon, South Dakota, Utah, Washington, Wisconsin, and Wyoming. Often religious leaders are brought in for initial dedication and blessing of sweat lodge facilities. Their functions, besides counseling Indian inmates, are to conduct sweat lodge, *yuwípi,* or Sacred Pipe ceremonies, and to provide information on tribal cultural heritage. Seven prisons mentioned that at least some of the medicine men were Sioux, which is not surprising since the Sioux are so populous and frequently reside in urban areas as a result of the 1950s government relocation program.

Involvement of activist organizations

Correctional authorities were asked whether Indian rights organizations (such as the National Congress of American Indians, Native American

Rights Fund, American Indian Movement) were active or vocal within their communities regarding the rights of Native American prisoners. Idaho officials indicated that the Native American Rights Fund had been actively involved in the evolution of prisoner religious freedom rights; Nevada, Minnesota, Hawaii, and Utah also indicated such activity, but were not specific as to which organization was involved. Numerous Oregon organizations assist with Indian prison rights issues, including the Native American Rights Fund, the Oregon Commission on Indian Services, the Urban Indian Council of Portland, the Native American Rights Association, the Tahana Whitecrow Foundation, and the Organization of Forgotten Americans. The American Indian Movement was involved with Indian religious freedom rights in the state of Washington.

It is likely that correctional authorities responding to this survey may not be aware of which, if any, organizations were involved with efforts by Indian prisoners to seek protection of religious freedoms in the courts. The Native American Rights Fund, which worked with Nebraska Indian prisoners in the development of their Consent Decree, has consulted and corresponded with Indian prisoners in many states, but prison officials may not be aware of it unless the grievances reach the stage of litigation.

Perceptions of needs

Finally, prison authorities were asked what they perceived were the greatest needs of their Indian prison populations, and whether the correctional authorities' perspectives on these needs were consistent with the Native American view. Mentioned repeatedly were the need for support of prisoners from their families, particularly getting Native Americans in the community to become involved with Indian prisoners, training in life skills (preparation for employment), improved education (resulting in increased literacy rates), and leadership training. Professional Indian counseling was also mentioned as a high priority, particularly in the context of strong support for religious approaches to rehabilitation.

Native American prisoners were seen as potentially profiting from alcohol treatment that specifically addressed addiction and therapy that focused on family issues. Particularly noted was the desire for inmates to have more contact with spiritual leaders. "Recapturing their heritage" emerged repeatedly as a goal correctional authorities saw as worthwhile and likely to have positive effects on rehabilitation and sobriety. Several institutions mentioned that their Indian populations required more access to their religious leaders and development of Indian-oriented education programs and more cultural programming.

Survey response from federal penal institutions

Federal penal facilities also participated in this research. The U.S. penitentiaries are located in Atlanta, Georgia; Leavenworth, Kansas; Marion, Illinois; Lewisburg, Pennsylvania; Lompoc, California; and Terre Haute, Indiana. Native Americans comprise approximately 1.6 percent of the populations of the six federal penal facilities (66,472 total prisoners, according to Camp and Camp 1992:3,5). According to my survey data, California has the largest Native American federal prison population (approximately 4 percent of all federal prisoners in California are Indian), followed by Illinois (2.3 percent) and Indiana (2 percent), with Indian populations in Georgia, Kansas, and Pennsylvania federal institutions all under .05 percent. Sioux inmates make up the largest tribal group represented in California, Illinois, and Kansas; Cherokee is the dominant tribal affiliation in Georgia. Four of the six federal institutions have Native American culture clubs, and all but one permit Indian inmates to participate in sweat lodge ceremonies. As with all the state penal institutions, federal prisons disallow use of peyote in Native American Church ceremonies. Because peyote is perceived by correctional authorities as a potentially dangerous, hallucinogenic drug, it is unlikely that its use will ever be permitted within a penal institution. Illegal trafficking as well as security concerns are likely to result in a permanent prohibition against its use "behind the walls."

Three of the federal facilities permit Native American inmates to have powwows at their institutions; only one institution permits Native American prisoners to have access to the Vision Quest or Sun Dance. Other cultural activities are routinely allowed at all but one facility, including drumming and singing, Indian video programs, spiritual and education seminars, taping of tribal singing and ceremonies, and use of the pipe and its associated herbs and tobaccos (two institutions specifically mentioned use of the Sacred Pipe). While medicine men or spiritual advisers are on contract at some federal penitentiaries, the majority have a chaplain whose responsibility it is to serve American Indian prisoner needs. Only one facility provides a chaplain exclusively to serve the needs of its Indian prisoners. The chaplains appear to play significant roles in sensitizing correctional employees about Native American cultural beliefs, in part by conducting training and orientation sessions where staff are familiarized with materials Native Americans are allowed to have in their possession for ceremonial purposes.

There appears to be less Native American litigation in federal prisons than in state correctional facilities. In *Standing Deer v. Carlson*, California federal inmates sued for the right to wear headbands. The court ruled that the prison's ban on headbands or religious headgear was not a violation of their Constitutional rights, but they were permitted to wear such articles on ceremonial occasions. In Pennsylvania, a lawsuit was brought by a community member who sought the right to participate in a volunteer program in prison. The plaintiff was successful and was permitted such participation. Five of the six federal penal facilities indicated that Indian religious freedom laws had affected their American Indian populations by making it possible for them to participate in sweat lodge ceremonies, to purchase religious paraphernalia for ceremonies to be conducted in prison, and to contract with spiritual leaders and community volunteers to come into the institutions. All such activities were viewed positively by prison authorities in that religious activities were seen as improving self-respect and promoting a strong self-image and sense of identity, all leading to positive behavior and encouraging participation in education and vocational training.

Unlike many of the state penal institutions surveyed, *no* federal institutions have special alcohol or drug treatment programs specifically geared for the Native American population. While all but one have some form of drug or alcohol treatment available, no special Indian-oriented programs exist. Five of the institutions have Alcoholics Anonymous groups; the other indicated that it does not because creating of such a group poses security risks. Native Americans appear to attend AA groups where they are available, although their participation was noted as "irregular." Four institutions noted that where Indians do attend AA, they are definitely a minority.

No federal facility indicated, as did several states, that their Indian populations are more vocal or have more grievances or legal concerns than other prison ethnic groups. Indian prisoners are viewed in all six institutions as not being very active in prison litigation and keeping quite a low profile. Four institutions indicated that Indian prisoners appear to receive misconduct reports at rates comparable to other ethnic groups;

one prison reported they have more than other inmates, one prison pointed out that the infractions that do occur tend to be alcohol-related. A different facility stated that their Indian population suffers from drinking problems—that they "do drink and get drunk more frequently" but utilize the sick call less.

Further perceived differences between Indian prisoners and others included the characterization of Indians as being more group-conscious and placing greater emphasis on socialization of incoming inmates. Only one prison indicated that organizations are active in Indian prison reform, and that organization is the American Indian Movement (AIM). Finally, prison authorities believed that their services for Native Americans would be improved if they could offer them better education, regular access to medicine men, and greater opportunity to have religious ceremonies, and one institution mentioned the importance of creating a post-release program.

The obvious differences between state and federal prison services for Native Americans appears to be attributable to two major factors. One is the much smaller percentage of Native Americans who appear in federal facilities (large numbers of Indian prisoners certainly appear to have an impact on the degree of cultural activity and profile), and the other is custody. While confinement for Native Americans in a federal facility is sometimes seen as a result of where the offense was committed—on the reservation (trust land) or off the reservation—rather than the type of crime committed, it is nevertheless true that Native Americans are not assigned to a federal penal facility unless their offense is defined by law as one of the major crimes over which the federal government has jurisdiction. Consequently, it is only to be expected that greater security constraints will be operative in a federal facility, where all inmates are serving sentences for very serious offenses.

8

The Future
for Native American
Prisoners

Trying to reorient the direction of Native American incarceration is akin to reversing the course of Indian history and all its consequences. Economic, cultural, and social oppression have contributed not only to a culture of poverty but to the emergence of a particular subculture within that, reflecting both urban and reservation styles. Indian urban ghettos, well known in large metropolitan cities, have been the subject of numerous books and films (*The Exiles* was a particularly poignant film about the San Francisco urban Indian population following the period of government relocation). This subculture has been dominated by disproportionately high rates of alcohol addiction and has accordingly suffered its devastating effects.

Changing this course is a monumental and daunting prospect, given the host of factors that have contributed to the problems—economic poverty, high unemployment, inadequate health care, lack of access to social welfare programs, and so on. Nor can one alter the historic vacillation in federal policy, or modify the principles that underlie funding patterns to tribal peoples. It is unrealistic to expect a total redirection in American Indian health care priorities, community alcoholism education, employment profiles, and juvenile delinquency. One can, however, work at the micro level, to provide analysis, evaluation, perspectives, and observations to inform future policy recommendations. Setting realistic goals is crucial, and the most basic and central one is to provide a path to sobriety. Positive change *is* occurring, and although it is hampered by national economic recession and the accompanying cuts to social welfare programs, results are beginning to be tangible. The important documentation of the Canadian band of Shuswap at Alkali Lake, which achieved nearly 100 percent sobriety, demonstrates the potential for community action. Representatives of this model group have visited tribes throughout the nation—including some in Nebraska—to share their message of hope in reversing the course of reservation alcoholism.

In the area of Native American incarceration, approaches to relief involve a clear set of objectives that must be embraced by all participants before any measurable effects can be achieved. Strategy must be proactive rather than circumstantial and must involve the united efforts of all involved parties: the inmates, who want to reverse the increasing trend toward alcoholism, criminal involvement, and incarceration; the states, represented by correctional authorities, who direct the use of public funds toward societal benefits; parole authorities, who bear responsibility for bringing offenders into rehabilitative opportunities; and the courts, which are ultimately responsible for interpreting how constitutional rights must be interpreted within state penal institutions. Getting all parties to agree on the problem—much less the solution—may seem unlikely, but on a state-by-state basis negotiations can be developed. The issues, as I see them, are: (1) the political relationship between correctional authorities and Indian inmates, (2) federal support for Indian relief through prison litigation, (3) the state's commitment to alcohol treatment and rehabilitation in prison for offenders with serious alcohol and drug dependency problems, and (4) articulation of such programs with parole policies and procedures as inmates prepare to resume their participation in the greater society. Each of these issues will be discussed in turn.

The political relationship between correctional authorities and Indian inmates

It would be a fair characterization to say that for Nebraska inmates, every single cultural or religious freedom gained for prisoners represents an outcome of a battle. Indian people have become accustomed to having to draw major attention to their concerns before they are able to obtain relief; it will be no different for Indian prisoners. The history of Indian militancy reflects the frustration Native American people have experienced in having their needs addressed, and Indians have periodically had to resort to drastic measures to bring national attention to a crisis situation. Like the leaders of such organizations as the National Congress of American Indians and the American Indian Movement, Indian prisoners

(many of whom were active AIM members or "militants") have cam-
paigned first within the penal institutions and ultimately in the courts
to make Indian religious freedom an accepted tradition in prison. Long
before the passage of the American Indian Religious Freedom Act in
1978, a strong commitment to activism was reflected within the Nebraska penal system.

Inmates in Nebraska have certainly taken the lead nationwide, and
now in approximately twenty states, prisons have sweat lodge facilities
and permit some form of Indian religious and cultural activity. But there
is little long-term understanding and acceptance of such practices, and
the hold on them seems tentative, fragile, and perhaps endangered. Ongoing battles between correctional authorities and Indian prisoners
seem to indicate that the authorities comply with Native American requests only when forced to do so by the courts. Conversely, letting up on
litigious behavior appears to result in a loss of privileges previously
allowed.

"Irreconcilable differences" pose obstacles to peaceful relations between Indians and the prison system. Twenty years have passed since
Nebraska Indian inmates first pursued litigation to protect religious
freedom, but the Nebraska penal system still provides no in-depth cultural training of guards or correctional officers. Although some generic
ethnic sensitivity training is offered, there is not sufficient focus on particular cultural groups' needs, nor is there regular enough incorporation
of such elements in training to resolve the problems. As a result, daily
conflicts between prisoners and guards continue to occur with regard to
religious practices and paraphernalia. For example, sweat lodge services
are officially approved at Hastings, yet during one period inmates were
not permitted to use their towels at the sweat lodge. The prison authorities know that the men sweat with no clothes on and use towels when
they emerge from the ceremony. Provision of blankets for use as tarps
over the sweat lodge structure was also prohibited, so the Indians took
the blankets off their bunks. The sweat lodge was shut down for lack of
"supplies." Eventually the prisoners requested my intervention. In my
negotiation with the administration, I urged them to comply with the
Consent Decree's mandate of "access to the sweat lodge" by permitting
the use of the prison's towels and providing the inmates with some tarps
or blankets, explaining that cooperation would be much more productive than more litigation—and the prisoners' requests were *not* unreasonable. Correctional intervention—discussion between inmates and

prison administrators—yielded a mutually satisfactory outcome. Such conflicts need not occur if administrators remain sufficiently informed about the protections of the decree and *comply with them.*

Another continuing conflict is caused by the relegation of the Native American cultural group to the status of a "self-betterment" club. While the purpose of such clubs is for inmates to expand their connections in the business community, such categorization by definition conflicts with the goals of NASCA, the Indian organization. Inmates see it as a religious, cultural, *and* spiritual group (hence its name: Native American Spiritual and Cultural Awareness group); however, according to prison regulations, it must be classified as either a club or a religious group (not both), because each category is entitled to different privileges within the institution. This conflict has fostered endless disagreements and has been the source of ongoing conflict for at least seven years. Requests for approval of Indian activities such as powwows, Hand Games, Native American Church services, *yuwípi* meetings, and the like all come back to the issue of whether NASCA is a club or a religious group; requests by inmates are denied on the grounds that NASCA is, according to prisoners, a club, and so cannot sponsor activities that require longer periods of time (as religious events may). The prison's explanation for denials of requests is that approval would mean treating one self-betterment club different from another. Not infrequently, the result is cancellation and rescheduling of an activity because of a lack of agreement on its time or length, the type of food served (and whether Native Americans may have access to the kitchen to prepare traditional foods), the guest lists, or other policy measures. In the absence of a clear guideline for Indian activities, every request on the part of the Native Americans is met with resistance and a long series of "kites" (official memos of correspondence). The resulting grievances and the responses they engender become the exhibits offered into evidence in the many trials arising from inmates' accusations of non-compliance with the Consent Decree. While it might seem that classifying NASCA as a religious group rather than a club would resolve these conflicts, that would result in a loss of privileges for weekly meetings, symposia, and banquets.

One issue that is likely to continue to be a thorn in prisoners' sides for decades to come is the issue of family members no longer being admitted to NASCA activities. Because NASCA is classified as a club and no self-betterment clubs are permitted to have family members participate in their activities, Indian prisoners find themselves not being able to invite family members—or anyone on their visiting lists, for that matter—to their special cultural or religious events. From the Native American perspective, no celebration or ceremony is proper without family members present.

The irreconcilable conflict between prison and prisoner ultimately lies in the fact that the prison believes it must treat all inmates in the same way, and perhaps in the view of the courts they must. But the Indian inmates perceive themselves as a special class, and according to federal law, they are. No group in the United States has an entire branch of the federal government devoted exclusively to it except for Native Americans. No other group in the United States has free health care nationwide simply as a result of treaty negotiations. No group but Native Americans has access to controlled substances such as peyote, or religious articles from endangered species such as eagle feathers. So to make the argument that Native Americans in prison ought to be treated the same as other inmates is one that is inconsistent with federally recognized modes of accommodation. Nevertheless, prisons are state institutions and in their funding, policy, and procedures, they insist that they apply regulations uniformly to all inmates. In obtaining the support from prisoners to write my book, several admonished me to be sure and focus on this very important issue.

Another indicator of irreconcilable differences is the continual disagreement about the use of religious articles in prison and the access to sites of religious worship. The use of plants in Indian ceremonies is something that does distinguish Native Americans from other religious groups in prison, and the burning of plant substances has caused grief and will probably continue to do so. The burning of sage, cedar, or sweet grass in Indian prayer is tolerated at the sweat lodge but prohibited in the cells because of fire hazards and the confusion caused by their aromas. So the inability of an inmate to burn sage or sweet grass in personal prayer continues to be regarded by inmates as a denial of a basic personal freedom and a violation of constitutional guarantees of freedom of religion.

Use of ceremonial foods, while not posing the same risks to security as the use of plants, also raises conflict. Indian culture demands that ceremonies be accompanied by native foods and traditional ways of serving them, from offerings made to the spirits before food is consumed to offering relatives leftovers to feed their families at home. The Nebraska penal system has barred such activities. It is not that the prison cannot accommodate these wishes; they can and historically have. The conflict arises when inmates who have enjoyed these privileges for years are suddenly denied such requests with no explanation except "equal treatment" arguments as they pertain to other self-betterment clubs. The inmates see this sudden inflexibility as arbitrary and capricious.

Conflict appears to be increasing over the desire of other cultural groups to have access to a sweat lodge. Because of the Nebraska prison's requirement to allow equal access to religion for all groups, they cannot prevent the Odinists or other non-Native Americans from worshiping in a manner acceptable to them. But the proximity of these "other" sweat lodges to the Indians' sweat lodges poses perceived threats, not only to the uniqueness of their activities but to the isolation and solemnity of the site set aside for spiritual activity.

All of these issues have one thing in common: rather than taking a proactive role in establishing a policy that regulates all Indian cultural activity, the prison *reacts* to every proposal and grievance and has to negotiate anew each privilege every time. Postponement or cancellation of banquets, celebrations, powwows, ceremonies, and Hand Games due to breakdown in the negotiation process is routine, a fact that builds anger and defensiveness among the inmates. Such breakdown further alienates them from the prison administration, resulting in more litigation. And so the cycle continues in Nebraska.

The lack of guidelines, the lack of proactive policy, the lack of guard training, the disproportionately low number of Indian correctional employees, and the irregularity in the services of a religious coordinator to assist Indian inmates leave the relationship between administrator and inmate ambivalent at best, and hostile and resentful at worst. The result is more and more litigation, more use of attorneys and time in the courts, and endless negotiations that result in recommendations that either fail to be implemented or are not followed until litigation forces the prison administration to comply.

An informed, ongoing consultative relationship between Native American inmates and the prison administrations could result in positive planning and produce negotiations that clarify policy and privileges. Many of the confrontations cited above might have been resolved with some dialogue. But prisoners are not normally entitled to sit down and discuss their views. They correspond with the administration via one-way directives and receive only formal written responses. A positive, interactive negotiation process would yield significant benefits for both parties: it would reduce the barrage of grievances thus reducing paperwork for the prison, and simultaneously provide the inmates with a clear framework for their religious and cultural practices.

Federal support for Indian relief through prison litigation

Without the decisions that have been made in federal court, there would be no special provisions for accommodating Indian religious needs in prison. Fortunately, the court has upheld Native Americans' rights of access to their religious practices, and has recognized the uniqueness of their religious requirements. It has at the same time drawn a clear line with regard to the use of normally illegal substances in prison, such as peyote. The issue of prison security has colored every decision, for whether an inmate has the right to sweat alone, to drink peyote tea, burn sage in his cell, or carry wrapped-up articles with the sacred pipe, all depend on what protections the court can provide without jeopardizing state concerns for prison security. Without court protections, the principles of religious freedom cannot be upheld, and whatever privileges are gained could be easily lost.

The original Consent Decree set the stage for the interpretation of all religious privileges, and while that document has been extremely important, its limitations nevertheless exist. Whatever was not specifically addressed in that decree in 1974 or 1976 simply has no chance of being considered. Peyote is an example of this. While it has been demonstrated that the Native American Church necessarily includes the use of peyote, the lack of specific reference to peyote in the decree, whether inadvertent or intentional, has permanently precluded its consideration. It is unlikely that peyote would be allowed in any prison under any circumstances, but its omission from the decree renders it *not negotiable* in court. The entire issue could be considered under new litigation, but not as part of the original Consent Decree.

The assignment of the Lincoln law firm Cline, Williams, Johnson, Wright and Oldfather to screen Indian prison grievances for their applicability to the Consent Decree was one of the most important support mechanisms Indian prisoners enjoyed. Such review permitted inmates access to attorneys who assisted with preparation of their materials for filing and, more importantly, aided inmates in understanding the legal mechanisms under which their concerns could be addressed in court. The termination of this law firm's unique role in 1990 may have a tremendous negative impact on the Indian prison population in three major ways. The inmates no longer have access to an attorney free of charge to consider the applicability of their grievances. Over the years many Indian inmates filed grievances knowing very little of the history of Indian prison activity or of the ways in which their concerns resembled those that had previously been filed or litigated by other inmates. The law firm served as a clearinghouse, and this service will be sorely missed. Second, inmates will no longer have a liaison with the prison's attorneys to discuss problems that might be resolved informally through negotiation and not require litigation. And finally, prisoners will no longer have the benefit of legal review of their documents for proper form for submission to the court. This last issue may seem minor, but lawsuits have been rejected for their lack of proper form. Whether the court decides to appoint another firm to take the place of Cline, Williams, Johnson, Wright and Oldfather will remain to be seen. It seems likely to me that the court will determine that whatever issues were going to be litigated from the original Consent Decree have been litigated, and if few issues remain to be evaluated, a new appointment is unnecessary. I hope this is an incorrect presumption.

The consequences of having no law firm to screen grievances is compounded by the court's simultaneous decision that only inmates at the Penitentiary and Lincoln Correctional Center have the protections of the original decree. Other inmates (e.g., women prisoners at York or minimum-custody inmates from Hastings or Omaha Correctional Centers), who were not originally named in the class action suit do not fall under the group entitled to its protections. This ruling seems to me to be fraught with difficulty. The "class" of inmates who filed the original suit reflected "any Native American who has ever been in prison or will ever be in prison" and refereed to "all Indian inmates presently incarcerated at the Nebraska Penal and Correctional Complex and those Indians who may be incarcerated there in the future" (CV 72-L-156, Order Designating Class Action, Nov. 21, 1973). The penal facilities may initially have consisted only of the Penitentiary and the Men's Reformatory, which later became the Lincoln Correctional Center, but surely the "penal complex" as alluded to in the Consent Decree was not intended to include only certain facilities and not others. All adult incarceration facilities in Nebraska are part of the penal complex, are state-funded, and fall under the present direction of the Director of the State of Nebraska Department of Correctional Services. It is therefore difficult to see how or why the privileges afforded in the decree would not apply equally to all members of this class as previously defined. Ultimately litigation will (once again) need to take place to redefine who the recipients of the class are, and to determine whether or not the class extends to inmates in state penal facilities that did not exist at the time the decree was awarded. My assumption in this case is that it will ultimately happen. Once again, however, it will take a major battle—and many tax dollars—to effect it.

The state's commitment to alcohol rehabilitation in prison

This is a complex and extremely serious issue. The first aspect of the problem is that inmate intake procedures, including assessments of the extent of alcohol and drug addiction, are inadequate and unable to discover the true extent of addiction in this population. In an era of economic recession and state budget reductions, it may be impossible to correct the situation. Such underestimates effectively limit the dimensions of alcohol treatment programs that can be considered for a prison population, both quantitatively and qualitatively. First, the number of inmates requiring intervention and the appropriate degree of intervention are not really known. Perhaps more importantly, the quality or nature of the interventions cannot be anticipated without more accurate assessments of the ways in which alcoholism plagues this population. Without more sensitive instruments and procedures, the endemic nature of substance abuse, addiction, and the deep social pathologies will never be fully discovered, much less addressed.

Even if processing corrections could be made, actually providing improved therapeutic rehabilitation would involve monumental problems, not the least of which is funding. Prisons may not be prepared in the coming decades to meaningfully address inmate psychological problems; realistically they may only provide protection to the public as well as security and isolation for social offenders. But the costs of recidivism must be factored into the decision as to what rehabilitation can be afforded—surely when two out of three offenders return to incarceration, the cost of *not* rehabilitating inmates is even more unacceptable.

Recovery and rehabilitation are clearly not services that prisons can offer to Native Americans without the help of those trained specifically in native-oriented treatment. This is not, however, an attitude that correctional authorities share. They may recognize their lack of success with Native American clients, but they fail to see that their inability to attract Indians into therapy or deeply involve them once they get there is not a matter of plain stubbornness or resistance on the part of the Indian prisoners—it is a matter of perceived irrelevance to their lives. Indian inmates are seen by most mental health personnel as being like other minorities, suffering the same consequences of poor socioeconomic backgrounds experienced by other impoverished ethnic groups. While these similarities are certainly valid, the need to tailor intervention programs to make them culturally acceptable remains legitimate. As has been pointed out by every Indian-oriented treatment program, treating Native Americans requires intimate familiarity with the uniquely Indian cultural milieu—their family life, culture, kinship, religion, and tradition. Coupling Western approaches to psychotherapy with applicability to Indian culture may be the only acceptable approach for Native Americans.

Alcoholics Anonymous has had a demonstrable lack of success among Indian prisoners, so continuing to direct inmates to its meetings will continue to be fruitless. Indian inmates may attend AA to earn good time or to appear cooperative for the sake of their jackets or prospects of parole, but unless they relate to it, invest in it, and find it psychologically meaningful, such attendance will serve no useful purpose. Despite the overwhelming national success of AA, Nebraska Indian prisoners' rejection of it is not unique to them. Indians in others prisons throughout the nation share the same concerns and have the same hesitancies about its usefulness. The possibility of Indian-oriented AA programs is a very appealing option, and the dependence on them in urban Indian communities continues to grow, but restricting any therapy group to one particular ethnic type is incompatible with the objectives and approaches of prison rehabilitation. Be that as it may, unless there is an all-Indian group in which therapy can take place, it is simply not realistic to expect any genuine recovery in prison.

Prison mental health programs are defensive about their lack of success with Indian inmates in both the sex offender and the alcohol/drug programs. But when the suggestion is made that culturally relative programs may be a more feasible avenue, arguments are presented that such programs are neither philosophically desirable nor financially feasible. So we are back to square one.

This situation is not unlike the others faced by Native Americans and could be dealt with by correctional authorities in the same way: by being

proactive, by designing a culturally acceptable program staffed by qualified Native Americans (even paraprofessionals), by inviting an Indian
AA group into prison, and by incorporating the Native American inmates into the decision-making process. With culturally appropriate
treatment, perhaps some hope of alcohol recovery exists. Of course, such
a program represents an increased cost to the taxpayer. But the alternative—the cycle of release, reoffending, and reincarceration—is ultimately more expensive, both socially and economically.

Articulation of treatment programs with parole policies

If treatment avenues are perceived as closed by Indian prisoners, release
from prison holds little hope for maintenance of sobriety. In fact, sobriety in prison is more often by default than by conscious intent. Release
from prison may be accompanied by a parole agreement that requires abstinence from alcohol, disassociation with ex-offenders, and attendance
at AA meetings, but without a prior psychological commitment to recovery and sobriety, such agreements are fraudulent. Coordination between prison mental health programs and parole planning does occur to
an extent, but with such low success in the parolee treatment programs,
parole plans can hardly be developed that reflect meaningful choices.

The obvious beginning point for parole development is communication between Native Americans and parole authorities. Organization of
Native American efforts in prison could yield significant guidance and
guidelines for the parole board, parole administrators, and officers in implementing culturally acceptable recommendations. This enlightened
approach must occur on all fronts, however, for while the parole board
makes the ultimate determinations, it is the parole officers who must
enforce it and the parole administrators who must take action if plans
are violated—and both of these groups are correctional employees, not
parole board employees.

The greatest paradox is how any inmate can survive and actually remain free of the criminal justice system. In our parole and recidivism
study, Jennifer Dam and I concluded:

> With a population of ex-offenders who have had little or no oppor-
> tunity for therapy in prison, the risk of failure at treatment is
> greater. It is possible, then, that an Indian inmate who has been in

prison for a decade will leave on parole or "jam" out . . . having had little or no therapy and no opportunity for working with a qualified therapist, and may not even have addressed the real nature of his or her offense or the social/environmental factors which contributed to it. It is not unlikely that an inmate will approach his or her final parole hearing at which he is being set for release without ever having worked through the offense he or she committed, its impact on society, and an understanding of how not to repeat history. (Grobsmith and Dam 1990:423–24)

Another creative possibility is having a person—perhaps the religious coordinator—serve also in the capacity of a liaison with the board. This had in fact occurred, upon occasion, but had not been formalized or made permanent. No infrastructure supported the maintenance of such a liaison. Inmates who find difficulty in addressing the board (many find the experience overwhelmingly intimidating) could benefit from having a "cultural broker," advocate, or intermediary who understood their cultural and rehabilitative needs and could present them to the board. This strategy could only be effective, however, if the basic precepts about rehabilitative avenues were altered among all parole employees. With continuing turnover of parole board members, they too—like correctional employees—could profit from an ongoing training program.

All the parties involved in these issues—the Indian inmates, the parole board, the mental health staff, and the correctional authorities—have one thing in common: frustration. We know that whatever programs and provisions exist for Native American offenders are not being successful, yet state dollars continue to be expended. The Native Americans turn inward to look for solutions, but have not developed effective strategies for positive outcomes. The correctional authorities acknowledge that it is their responsibility to devise successful rehabilitative strategies, but they know too they have not been effective. Michael Kenney, superintendent of the Hastings Correctional Center, eloquently summarized the impasse: "I agree . . . it's not working—but what does? Faced with overcrowding, escapes, and violent disruptions, I *really believe* prison administrators are desperately seeking the 'key' that will change this self-destructive pattern in which literally everyone loses" (Kenney 1990, personal communication).

Responsibility for change falls not only to inmates and their jailers, but to the academic scientific disciplines that study such phenomena.

Criminal justice, sociology, counseling, anthropology, psychology—all have responsibility to bring scientific knowledge to bear on alleviation of society's concerns. Correctional authorities may argue that in fact it is their domain to inform correctional policy. "We need some very specific guidance, instruction, revelation," said Michael Kenney. "Interestingly, it seems to fall upon prison officials to 'correct' these human deficiencies—but why not the police or the judges? Wardens are no more responsible for antisocial behavior than police or judges, but it falls on us to 'fix' this problem, I suppose because we're the most recent custodians of their persons. Ironically, we look to the sciences—criminology, anthropology, sociology, psychology—to provide *us* with the 'key' to understanding, no, *changing* human behavior" (Kenney 1990, personal communication).

The last century has seen the emergence of a new phenomenon: the disruption of American Indian families, the economically depressed conditions of indigenous peoples, complete with disproportionately high rates of alcohol and drug addiction, delinquency, crime, and incarceration. Clearly an unacceptable situation such as this can be confronted only in one manner: on all fronts. Perhaps with all parties assuming responsibility for change, the next century may see a return of Native American youth to their communities, which drastically require their services, and to the greater society, which so greatly stands to profit from the contribution Native Americans make.

Appendix A:
Consent Decree

IN THE UNITED STATES DISTRICT COURT
FOR THE DISTRICT OF NEBRASKA

INDIAN INMATES OF THE)   Civil No. 72-L-156
NEBRASKA PENITENTIARY,)
)
          Plaintiffs,)
)
       vs.)
)
JOSEPH VITEK,)
)   ORDER - JUDGMENT
          Defendant.)   AND DECREE

Plaintiffs who comprise the class of Indian inmates incarcerated in the Nebraska Penal and Correctional Complex sued defendant Charles L. Wolff, Jr.,[1] claiming certain deprivations of rights secured to them under the First and Fourteenth Amendments, by filing a pro se complaint. Counsel was then obtained for plaintiffs. Specifically, plaintiffs claimed that officials refused to permit an Indian Culture Club; that access to Indian religion, including the Native American Church was denied them; and that they were discriminated against in various ways in the rehabilitation process including work release, work assignments and the failure to provide Indian counselors and instructors.

Upon the pleadings all proceedings heretofore had herein, and upon agreement of the parties represented by counsel and upon the Court's finding that the interests of the class have been fairly represented here, it is:

ORDERED, ADJUDGED AND DECREED that the defen-

---

1. Joseph Vitek, Director of Correctional Services is
substituted as defendant under Rule 25, F.R.C.P.

dants, their agents, servants, employees and their successors in office are hereby permanently enjoined and ordered to:

    1. Permit the wearing of traditional Indian hairstyles, provided such
hairstyles are kept clean at all times.[2]

    2. In order to meet the religious and spiritual needs of the plaintiff
class, defendants shall allow inmates access to Indian medicine men and spiritual leaders
and provide facilities for spiritual and religious services, including but not limited to the
Native American Church. Further, defendants will set aside a percent of its budget [that reflects the percent of the Indian inmates in the Penal Complex] which at any given time is
allocated for other clergy salaries and expenses attendant to providing services to members
of other religious faiths, to payment of fees and expenses attendant to providing Indian religious services or ceremonies.

    3. To take the necessary steps to instruct all employees that all bene-
fits presently given to inmates for "religious participation" be extended to those members
of the plaintiff class who participate in the aforementioned Indian religious services, ceremonies, or culture group meetings.

    4. Extend official recognition to an Indian inmate spiritual culture
club composed of members of the plaintiff class and take the necessary steps to ensure that:

        (a) The same privileges presently extended to other inmate clubs,
            such as the Gavel Club and the Junior Chamber of Commerce, are
            extended to the Indian Culture Club; and that
        (b) Active membership in the Indian Culture Club be given the same
            recognition in terms of inmate pay raise points or other benefits
            presently given for active membership in other inmate self-better-
            ment or religious groups.

    5. The defendant and plaintiff's counsel shall formulate an affirmative
action hiring plan designed to locate job applicants and to secure employment and training
by the defendant of qualified Indian personnel, recognizing the unique culture needs of Indian inmates. Said plan will be submitted to the Court for its approval by the parties within
thirty days after the effective date of this Consent Judgment.

    6. The Indian club will designate certain representatives to participate
in advising the Athletic and Recreation Committee concerning the type of movies to be
shown at the Complex.

    7. The defendants will offer accredited courses in Indian studies at the
Nebraska Penal and Correctional Complex within a reasonable time after the effective date
of this Order. The plaintiffs[3] will aid the defendant in obtaining personnel, materials, and
financial resources, as well as aiding in the formulation of the course subject matter.

---

    2. On July 29, 1974, Defendants rescinded the penitentiary's
       hair length regulation which Plaintiffs challenge, and
       promulgated the following rule which reads in part:
       "In conjunction with this, the following grooming guide-
       lines are delineated:
          Length of Hair: Hair may grow over the ears to any
          length desired by the inmate. The hair must be neatly
          groomed and kept clean at all times."
    3. The parties will utilize Indian educational resources
       agreed to by the parties in developing the Indian Studies
       course, such as the Institute of American Indian Studies
       of the Bureau of Indian Affairs, United States Department
       of the Interior.

8. Plaintiffs waive counsel fees.

Warren K. Urbom
District Judge

Consented To:

Roy S. Haber
Walter Echo Hawk
Native American Rights Fund
1506 Broadway
Boulder, Colorado 80302

Attorneys for Plaintiffs

Mel Kammerlohr
Assistant Attorney General
2119 State Capitol Building
Lincoln, Nebraska 68509

Attorneys for Defendants

Appendix B:
Supplemental Consent Decree

IN THE UNITED STATES DISTRICT COURT
FOR THE DISTRICT OF NEBRASKA

INDIAN INMATES OF THE NEBRASKA PENITENTIARY,	)	Civil No. 72-L-156

INDIAN INMATES OF THE)   Civil No. 72-L-156
NEBRASKA PENITENTIARY,)

            Plaintiffs,   )

        vs.   )

JOSEPH VITEK,   )

)   SUPPLEMENTAL
            Defendant.   )   CONSENT DECREE

          The parties to this action entered into an ORDER-JUDG-
MENT AND DECREE which was signed by the Court and filed on October 31,
1974. Since the date of the signing of the ORDER-JUDGMENT AND DECREE a
dispute has arisen regarding the meaning of Paragraph 2 which states in part as
follows:

          2. In order to meet the religious and spiritual needs of
the plaintiff class, defendants shall allow inmates access to Indian medicine men and spiritual leaders and provide facilities
for spiritual and religious services, including but not limited to
the Native American Church. . . .

          Upon agreement of the parties that a sweat lodge is a "facility"
for the worship of Indian religion, and

          Upon the pleadings, depositions and all proceedings heretofore
had herein, and upon agreement of the parties represented by counsel and upon
the Court's findings that the interests of the class have been fairly represented, it is:

          ORDERED, ADJUDGED AND DECREED that the defendants, their agents, servants, employees and their successors in office are hereby permanently enjoined and ordered to:

1. Permit the construction of a sweat lodge, within a reasonable time, at the Medium Security Unit of the Nebraska Penal and Correctional Complex, by an Indian medicine man to be agreed upon by the parties. The plaintiffs will bear all costs and expenses of building the sweat lodge, which will be a dome-like structure, approximately six feet in circumference, constructed with a sapling frame and covered by blankets; the interior will contain a small pit for the sacred rocks, along with a water bucket; the floor of said sweat lodge will be covered with pine or cedar branches, or other material as designated by the parties' medicine man.

2. The defendants will permit routine access to this sweat lodge at reasonable times to be agreed upon by the parties. The use of the sweat lodge will be available to all inmates subject to the same rules and regulations as govern other religious services, recreational clubs and similar facilities at the Nebraska Penal and Correctional Complex.

3. Within one month of the date that the sweat lodge at the Medium Security Facility is built, or as soon thereafter as may be practical, plaintiffs will be permitted to build an identical sweat lodge at the Penitentiary, unless defendants determine that there are security problems attendant to the use of the sweat lodge at the Medium Security Unit. In the event defendants determine that security problems have arisen, they will submit a report to plaintiffs outlining the exact nature of the problem or problems that have come up, setting forth names of inmates involved, dates of occurances and what action was taken against the inmates involved.

After receipt of the report from defendants, plaintiffs will issue within 15 days a response. The parties will then meet and attempt to resolve the security problem so that a sweat lodge may safely be built at the Penitentiary.

In the event that the parties fail to agree on a solution, they will have recourse to petition the Court for further relief.

Warren K. Urbom
District Judge

Consented To:

Walter Echo Hawk   Mel Kammerlohr
Roy S. Haber   Assistant Attorney General
Native American Rights Fund   2119 State Capitol Building
1506 Broadway   Lincoln, Nebraska 68509
Boulder, Colorado 80302

                                      Attorneys for Defendants

Attorneys for Plaintiffs

Glossary of
Lakhóta Terms

čhąnúpa: the Pipe, or Sacred Pipe. The term refers both to the actual Sacred Pipe and, more generically, to a set of religious beliefs and activities based on Lakhóta ideology and cosmology.

hąbléčheya: "They cry for a vision." Also known as the Vision Quest, this undertaking is one of the Seven Sacred Rites of the Sioux.

heyóka: "a clown" or Dakota god, called by some the antinatural god. *Heyóka* refers to an individual who is considered contrary or opposite in behavior. Usually this is a sacred individual who performs acts opposite of conventional behavior.

Lakhóta: the division of Western or Teton Sioux. Lakhóta is both a cultural/political and a linguistic division of the Sioux. Lakhóta speakers comprise seven subtribes of the Teton Sioux within the Sioux Nation or Seven Council Fires. The term is written in English without the diacritical mark.

lowápi: a healing ceremony; hymns or singing.

mitákuye oyásʔį: literally, "all my relatives." This phrase is spoken at the end of Lakhóta ceremonies and as an ending to all prayers.

pheží: "grass, herbs, hay"; used to designate marijuana.

Thųkášila: a Lakhóta kinship term meaning "grandfather." This term is used to address God, the Great Spirit, and is a more personal term used in prayer.

Wakhą́ Thą́ka: the Great Spirit, Great Mystery, God. The deity in Lakhóta cosmology who embraces sixteen different spirits or forces.

wathéča: a bucket of food or leftovers taken home by guests, similar to a doggie bag. The taking home of leftover food is an important event, symbolically, for in traditional times this food was used to feed families and represented a way of distributing goods and wealth.

wóžapi: a berry pudding that is still enjoyed by Native Americans. It continues to be a part of traditional meals, even in prison.

yuwípi: literally, "They wrap him up" or "They roll it up" (Kemnitzer 1970). The term refers to a healing ceremony in which the medicine man is wrapped and bound in a quilt. Prayer with supernatural spirits allows the medicine man to break free of his bonds.

NOTE: The orthography used throughout this book is that of Taylor and Rood (1976). In some cases, exact definitions of terms were taken from Buechel and Manhart (1970).

References

Beauvais, Fred, E. R. Oetting, and R. W. Edwards
    1985   Trends in the Use of Inhalants Among American Indian Adolescents. *White Cloud Journal* 3:3–11.

Brown, Joseph E.
    1971   *The Sacred Pipe, Black Elk's Account of the Seven Sacred Rites of the Oglala Sioux*. Penguin Books, Baltimore, Md.

Buechel, Rev. Eugene, SJ, and Rev. Paul Manhart, SJ
    1970   *Lakota-English Dictionary*. Institute of Indian Studies, University of South Dakota, Vermillion, S.D.

Camp, George, and Camille Camp
    1992   *The Corrections Yearbook*. Criminal Justice Institute, South Salem, N.Y.
    1990   *The Corrections Yearbook*. Criminal Justice Institute, South Salem, N.Y.
    1989   *The Corrections Yearbook*. Criminal Justice Institute, South Salem, N.Y.

Carroll, Eleanor
    1977   Notes on the Epidemiology of Inhalants. In *Review of Inhalants: Euphoria to Dysfunction*, Charles W. Sharp and Mary Lee Brehm, eds., 14–24. National Institute on Drug Abuse, Research Monograph 15, Rockville, Md.

Carter, Richard T.
    1966   Contemporary Shamanism Among the Teton Dakota: A Plains Manifestation of the Conjuring Complex. Master's Thesis, University of Nebraska, Lincoln.

Cohen, Sidney
    1977   Inhalants Abuse: An Overview of the Problem. In *Review of Inhalants: Euphoria to Dysfunction*, Charles W. Sharp and Mary Lee Brehm, eds., 2–11. NIDA Research Monograph 15, Rockville, Md.

Cross, John
    1982   The Economics of Indian Crime. In *Indians and Criminal Justice*,

Laurence French, ed., 53–63. Allanheld, Osmun Publishers, Totowa, N.J.

Deloria, Vine, Jr., and Clifford M. Lytle
1983   *American Indians, American Justice.* University of Texas Press, Austin, Texas.

Dozier, Edward
1966   Problem Drinking Among American Indians: The Role of Socio-cultural Deprivation. *Quarterly Journal of Studies on Alcohol* 27:72–87.

Fenna, D., L. Mix, O. Schaefer, and J. A. L. Gilbert
1971   Ethanol Metabolism in Various Racial Groups. *Canadian Medical Association Journal* 105:472–75.

Field, Peter
1962   A New Cross-Cultural Study of Drunkenness. In *Society, Culture and Drinking Patterns*, David J. Pittman and Charles R. Snyder, eds., 48–74. John Wiley and Sons, New York.

Flute, Jerry, Elizabeth Grobsmith, and Mickey Revenaugh
1985   A Generation at Risk, American Indian Youth in the Great Plains: A Report from 15 Reservations. Association on American Indian Affairs, New York.

French, Laurence, ed.
1979   *Indians and Criminal Justice.* Allanheld, Osmun Publishers, Totowa, N.J.

Goldstein, G.
1976   Inhalant Abuse Among the Pueblo Tribes of New Mexico. Unpublished paper.

Graves, Theodore
1967   Acculturation, Access and Alcohol in a Tri-Ethnic Community. *American Anthropologist* 69:306–21.

Great Spirit Within the Hole
1983   Film. KTCA Public Television, Minneapolis/St. Paul, Minnesota.

Greenberg, Stephanie W.
1981   Alcohol and Crime: A Methodological Critique of the Literature. In *Drinking and Crime: Perspectives on the Relationships between Alcohol Consumption and Criminal Behavior*, James J. Collins, Jr., ed., 70–109. Guilford Press, New York.

Grobsmith, Elizabeth S.
1992   Applying Anthropology to American Indian Correctional Concerns. *Practicing Anthropology* 14, no. 3:5–8.

1991–92 Inmates and Anthropologists: The Impact of Advocacy on the Expression of American Indian Culture in Prison. *High Plains Applied Anthropologist* 11/12:84–98.

1989a   The Relationship Between Substance Abuse and Crime Among Native American Inmates in the Nebraska Department of Corrections. *Human Organization* 48, no. 4 (Winter):285–98.

1989b   The Impact of Litigation on the Religious Revitalization of Native

American Inmates in the Nebraska Department of Corrections. *Plains Anthropologist* 34, no. 134:135–47.

1981 *Lakota of the Rosebud, A Contemporary Ethnography.* Holt, Rinehart and Winston, New York.

Grobsmith, Elizabeth S., and Jennifer Dam
1990 The Revolving Door: Substance Abuse Treatment and Criminal Sanctions for Native American Offenders. *Journal of Substance Abuse* 2, no. 4:405–25.

Grobsmith, Elizabeth, and Jerry Flute
1985 Juvenile Justice Concerns of the Fifteen Tribes of the Aberdeen Area. Association on American Indian Affairs, New York.

Grobsmith, Elizabeth S., and Beth R. Ritter
1992 The Ponca Tribe of Nebraska: The Process of Restoration of a Federally Terminated Tribe. *Human Organization* 51, no. 1:1–16.

Hall, Roberta
1986 Alcohol Treatment in American Indian Populations: An Indigenous Treatment Modality Compared with Traditional Approaches. *Annals of the New York Academy of Sciences* 472:168–78.

Harring, Sidney
1982 Native American Crime in the United States. In *Indians and Criminal Justice,* Laurence French, ed., 93–108. Allanheld, Osmun Publishers, Totowa, N.J.

Horton, Donald
1943 The Functions of Alcohol in Primitive Societies: A Cross-Cultural Study. *Quarterly Journal of Studies on Alcohol* 4:199–320.

Jensen, Gary F., Joseph Stauss, and V. William Harris
1977 Crime, Delinquency, and the American Indian. *Human Organization* 36:252–257.

Jorgenson, J. G.
1972 *The Sun Dance Religion: Powers to the Powerless.* University of Chicago Press, Chicago.

Kemnitzer, L. A.
1972 The Structure of Country Drinking Parties on the Pine Ridge Reservation, South Dakota. *Plains Anthropologist* 17:134–42.

1970 The Cultural Provenience of Objects Used in Yuwipi: A Modern Teton Dakota Healing Ritual. *Ethnos* 1–4:40–75. National Museum of Ethnography, Stockholm.

Korman, Maurice
1977 Clinical Evaluation of Psychological Factors. In *Review of Inhalants: Euphoria to Dysfunction.* Charles W. Sharp and Mary L. Brehm, eds., 30–53. NIDA Research Monograph 15, Rockville, Md.

Kuttner, Robert E., and Albert B. Lorincz
1967 Alcoholism and Addiction in Urbanized Sioux Indians. *Mental Hygiene* 51:530–42.

Lane, E. B., H. W. Daniels, J. D. Byland, and R. Royer
1977 The Incarcerated Native. *Canadian Journal of Criminology and Corrections* 20, no. 3:308–16.

Leland, Joy
    1976   *Firewater Myths: North American Indian Drinking and Alcohol Addiction.* Rutgers Center of Alcohol Studies, New Brunswick, N.J.
Levy, Jerrold E., and Stephen J. Kunitz
    1974   *Indian Drinking, Navajo Practices and Anglo-American Theories.* John Wiley & Sons, New York.
Lewis, Thomas H.
    1990   *The Medicine Men: Oglala Sioux Ceremony and Healing.* University of Nebraska Press, Lincoln.
Lex, Barbara
    1985   Alcohol Problems in Special Populations. In *The Diagnosis and Treatment of Alcoholism,* 2nd ed., J. H. Mendelson and N. K. Mello, eds., 89–186. McGraw-Hill, New York.
Lurie, Nancy O.
    1974   The World's Oldest On-Going Protest Demonstration: North American Indian Drinking Patterns. In *The American Indian: Essays from Pacific Historical Review,* Norris Hundley, ed., 55–76. Clio Books, Santa Barbara, Calif.
Mail, Patricia D., and David R. McDonald, eds.
    1980   *Tulapai to Tokay: A Bibliography of Alcohol Use and Abuse Among Native Americans of North America.* HRAF Press, New Haven.
May, Philip A.
    1986   Alcohol and Drug Misuse Prevention Programs for American Indians: Needs and Opportunities. *Journal of Studies on Alcohol* 47:187–95.
Mohatt, Gerald
    1972   The Sacred Water: The Quest for Personal Power Through Drinking Among the Teton Sioux. In *The Drinking Man,* D. McClelland, W. Davis, R. Kalin, and E. Wanner, eds., 261–75. Free Press, New York.
National Clearinghouse for Alcohol and Drug Information
    n.d.   *Alcohol and Ethnic Minorities.* Reprints from *Research World,* Rockville, Md.
National Indian Health Board Reporter
    1986   NIHB Reporter 4, no. 4 (June).
Nebraska Board of Parole
    1984–8Sixteenth Annual Report.
Nebraska Department of Correctional Services
    1992   Monthly Statistical Reports, Lincoln, Nebraska.
    1991   Monthly Statistical Reports, Lincoln, Nebraska.
    1990   Monthly Statistical Reports, Lincoln, Nebraska.
    1989   Monthly Statistical Reports, Lincoln, Nebraska.
    1988   Recidivism among Fiscal Year 1985 Adult Releases. Lincoln, Nebraska.
Parker, Linda
    1988   The Missing Component in Native American Substance Abuse Prevention. Paper presented to 87th Annual Meeting of the American Anthropological Association, Phoenix, Az.

Powers, William K.
   1982   *Yuwipi: Vision and Experience in Oglala Ritual*. University of Nebraska Press, Lincoln.
Prucha, Francis Paul
   1984   *The Great Father*. University of Nebraska Press, Lincoln.
Reed, Little Rock
   1989   The American Indian in the White Man's Prisons: A Story of Genocide. Unpublished manuscript.
Schneider, Mary Jane
   1984   Religious Diversification Among Contemporary Northern Plains Indians. Paper presented to Annual Meeting of Plains Anthropological Society, Lincoln, Nebraska.
Stewart, Omer C.
   1964   Questions Regarding American Indian Criminality. *Human Organization* 34:61–66.
Taylor, Allan, and David S. Rood
   1976   *Beginning Lakhóta*, Vols. I and II. University of Colorado Lakhóta Project, Department of Linguistics, University of Colorado, Boulder.
U.S. Department of Health and Human Services
   1987   Sixth Special Report to the U.S. Congress on Alcohol and Health, Public Health Service, National Institute on Alcohol Abuse and Alcoholism, Rockville, Md.
Weibel-Orlando, Joan
   1989a Treatment and Prevention of Native American Alcoholism. In *Alcoholism in Minority Populations*, Thomas D. Watts and Roosevelt Wright, Jr., eds., 121–39. Charles Thomas, Publishers, Springfield, Il.
   1989b Hooked on Healing: Anthropologists, Alcohol, and Intervention. *Human Organization* 48, no. 2:148–55.
   1987   Culture-Specific Treatment Modalities: Assessing Client-to-Client Treatment Fit in Indian Alcoholism Programs. In *Treatment and Prevention of Alcohol Problems: A Resource Manual*, M. Cox, ed., 261–83. Academic Press, New York.
   1985   Indians, Ethnicity, and Alcohol: Contrasting Perceptions of the Ethnic Self and Alcohol Use. In *The American Experience with Alcohol: Contrasting Cultural Perspectives*, L. Bennett and G. Ames, eds., 201–16. Plenum Press, New York.
Westermeyer, Joseph
   1986   *A Clinical Guide to Alcohol and Drug Problems*. Praeger Publishers, New York.
Whittaker, James O.
   1963   Alcohol and the Standing Rock Sioux Tribe, II: Psychodynamic and Cultural Factors in Drinking. *Quarterly Journal of Studies on Alcohol* 24:81–90.

Index